THE TEEN LIBRARY
INTERNSHIP HANDBOOK

THE TEEN LIBRARIAN BOOKSHELF

About the Series

The Teen Librarian Bookshelf is designed to be a comprehensive resource for young adult librarians. The series provides the breadth and depth of information that teen librarians need to serve the teen audience in school and public libraries. With their experience and expertise, authors in the series are mentors for librarians serving tweens and teens.

About the Series Editor

RoseMary Ludt has written and edited for the young adult librarian audience for nearly twenty years, working for Neal-Schuman Publishers, Kurdyla Publishing LLC, and American Library Association. She was the editor in chief of *VOYA Magazine* for ten years and is a former editor for VOYA Press and *YALS Journal*. Among her books are *101+ Teen Programs That Work* and *More Teen Programs That Work*.

Before her writing and editing career, Ludt worked for twenty-five years in the Coshocton Public Library. While there, she created the position of young adult services coordinator and served eleven years in the position. Some of her original programs are still enjoyed by teens at the library.

Ludt has presented over seventy workshops, keynotes, and audio and video presentations for librarians serving teen and senior adults in the United States and Canada, encouraging librarians to connect with their audiences by working and creating with them.

Coming full circle, Ludt has returned to libraries, working in the circulation department of Muskingum County Library System in Ohio.

Books in the Series

Totally Tweens & Teens: Youth-Created and Youth-Led Library Programs by Diane P. Tuccillo
Think Big!: A Resource Manual for Teen Library Programs That Attract Large Audiences edited by RoseMary Ludt
Connecting Teens with Technology at the Library by Kelly Czarnecki and Marie Harris
The Teen Library Internship Handbook by Diane P. Tuccillo

THE TEEN LIBRARY INTERNSHIP HANDBOOK

Diane P. Tuccillo

ROWMAN & LITTLEFIELD
Lanham • Boulder • New York • London

Published by Rowman & Littlefield
An imprint of The Rowman & Littlefield Publishing Group, Inc.
4501 Forbes Boulevard, Suite 200, Lanham, Maryland 20706
www.rowman.com

6 Tinworth Street, London SE11 5AL, United Kingdom

Copyright © 2021 by The Rowman & Littlefield Publishing Group, Inc.

All rights reserved. No part of this book may be reproduced in any form or by any electronic or mechanical means, including information storage and retrieval systems, without written permission from the publisher, except by a reviewer who may quote passages in a review.

British Library Cataloguing in Publication Information Available

Library of Congress Cataloging-in-Publication Data

Names: Tuccillo, Diane P., 1952- author.
Title: The teen library internship handbook / Diane P. Tuccillo.
Description: Lanham : Rowman & Littlefield, [2021] | Series: Teen librarian bookshelf | Includes bibliographical references and index.
Identifiers: LCCN 2021020515 (print) | LCCN 2021020516 (ebook) | ISBN 9781538148921 (cloth) | ISBN 9781538148938 (paperback) | ISBN 9781538148945 (ebook)
Subjects: LCSH: Interns (Library science)—Handbooks, manuals, etc. | Teenage volunteer workers in libraries—Handbooks, manuals, etc. | Libraries and teenagers. | Libraries and teenagers—United States—Case studies.
Classification: LCC Z682.4.I58 T83 2021 (print) | LCC Z682.4.I58 (ebook) | DDC 023/.9—dc23
LC record available at https://lccn.loc.gov/2021020515
LC ebook record available at https://lccn.loc.gov/2021020516

*To all the tweens and teens in school and public libraries everywhere
who have participated in volunteering, working in, promoting, supporting,
using, enjoying, learning, and becoming through, in, and with their libraries.*

*To all the youth and teen services librarians, teachers, library administrators,
library staff, adult volunteers, parents, and others who have encouraged, supported,
advocated for, and positively developed tweens and teens through, with, and in libraries
so that they may become the readers, leaders, supporters, and library users of the
future, where they then can pass the torch to others.*

Contents

List of Figures	ix
Series Foreword	xiii
Foreword	xv
Acknowledgments	xix
Introduction	1
1 Teaching Teens about Real-World Job Skills through Internships	5
2 Why Have Teen Library Internship Opportunities?	29
3 Developing Teen Library Internships	53
4 A Close Look at Public Library Teen Internships	83
5 Unique Internship Experiences at Schools, Universities, Public and Special Libraries, and through Partnerships	115
6 The Importance of Feedback, Evaluations, and a Positive Internship Conclusion Process	139
7 Dealing with Teen Library Internships When the Library Must Be Closed	155
Appendix A: Rancho Cucamonga Public Library—Summer Teen Volunteer Internship Application	167
Appendix B: Sonoma County Library PLA Inclusive Internship Initiative Application	171
Appendix C: Template—Teen Library Intern Feedback Form	173
Appendix D: Template—Teen Library Intern Time Sheet and Task Record	177

Appendix E: West Custer County Library Teen Summer Internship
Job Description   179

Selected Bibliography and Webliography   181

Index   183

About the Author   191

List of Figures

Figure 1.1.	During the Adult 101 Life Skills for Teens Time and Stress Management program at the Rancho Cucamonga Public Library in California, teen interns Nayana Thompson and Morea Lee explain to the participating teen attendees how to make and decorate woodblock desk calendars. Credit: Janet Monterrosa.	12
Figure 1.2.	A solid relationship between teen interns and their mentors makes all the difference to a successful experience for everyone. Here, teen intern Sade Wilkens El and her mentor, Cody Brownson-Katz of the Baltimore County Public Library, smile as Wilkens El receives her certificate for the completion of the Public Library Association's internship grant requirements. Credit: Zach Miller.	13
Figure 1.3.	Cheyenne Jones enthusiastically describes her accomplishments as a teen intern at the Auburn Public Library in Georgia. Jones was hired by the library through a grant from the Public Library Association. Credit: Zach Miller.	24
Figure 2.1.	Sade Wilkens El shares her thoughts at the Public Library Association's Inclusive Internship Initiative wrap-up meeting in 2019. Wilkens El was hired for a permanent position after her internship. Credit: Zach Miller.	33
Figure 2.2.	At the September PLA wrap-up event in Washington, D.C., for the 2019 Inclusive Internship Initiative, Yasmeen Chavez from the Alameda County Library is shown speaking about her internship project. She was hired as a permanent library employee following the internship. Credit: Zach Miller.	34
Figure 2.3.	Aaron Vivanco speaks about his teen internship experience at the Laredo Public Libraries in Texas during the PLA Inclusive Internship Initiative wrap-up event in the fall of 2019. Credit: Zach Miller.	41

List of Figures

Figure 2.4.	Mary Hirsh presents teen intern Yasmeen Chavez from the Alameda County Library with a certificate of recognition at the fall 2019 PLA Inclusive Internship Initiative event. Credit: Zach Miller.	45
Figure 2.5.	Teen interns Nayana Thompson (left) and Morea Lee (right) help measure, pour, and make glitter calming jars during the Adult 101 Life Skills for Teens Mental Health program. Their internships were funded by a YALSA/Dollar General grant. Credit: Janet Monterrosa.	46
Figure 3.1.	The Sonoma County Library's promotional publicity for its teen library internship posting. Credit: Sonoma County Library.	60
Figure 3.2.	The flyer for the Sidney Johnson Summer Internship at the St. Louis County Library is appealing and clearly states the essential details for interested teens. Credit: St. Louis County Library.	64
Figure 3.3.	Interns Marcus Bennett (right) and Zach Rude (center) direct incoming Teen Council member Emma Weisler to her station as the group begins to set up for a life-size Candyland game. Bennett and Rude used a detailed list with instructions and a timeline while empowered to be in charge of training the council members as they arrived and monitored quality control. Credit: Patricia VanArsdale.	73
Figure 4.1.	The outline of the project plan created by Yasmeen Chavez at the Alameda County Library's Newark Public Library Branch. Credit: Yasmeen Chavez.	84
Figure 4.2.	Emily Brooks celebrates her eighteenth birthday during her internship at the Auburn Public Library in Georgia. Credit: Bel Outwater.	86
Figure 4.3.	Teen interns Cheyenne Jones and Christina Miller pose with mascot Scout from the Auburn Public Library in Georgia. Credit: Bel Outwater.	87
Figure 4.4.	Sade Wilkens El shows the products that were donated to battle period poverty for her internship project at the Baltimore County Library. She organized a PAD Packing Party for teens as a key part of the project using the donations. Credit: Cody Brownson-Katz.	91
Figure 4.5.	As one of her duties, a library teen intern trains Teen Volunteer Corps members about a portion of the Teen Summer Reading Program. Interns and volunteers were placed into small groups and rotated stations, providing intimate and in-depth training for each specific part of the program. Credit: Hussey-Mayfield Memorial Public Library.	97
Figure 4.6.	Intern Aaron Vivanco and librarian mentor Analiza Perez-Gomez from the Laredo Public Libraries in Texas attended the September wrap-up event for the 2019 Inclusive Internship Initiative in Washington, D.C. Credit: Zach Miller.	102
Figure 4.7.	Nayana Thompson (left) and Morea Lee (right) show their big smiles as they end one of their final shifts as teen interns at the Rancho Cucamonga Public Library. Credit: Brittany Garcia.	105
Figure 4.8.	A catchy and informative flyer promotes the Rancho Cucamonga Public Library's teen internship. Credit: Rancho Cucamonga Public Library.	109

List of Figures

Figure 5.1.	Haitian immigrant and Waltham High School graduate, Annie Jean-Baptiste, now attending Brandeis University, leads the discussion about immigration that she had developed as a paid teen Real Talk leader. Credit: Luke Kirkland.	129
Figure 5.2.	Real Talk teen leaders Stevenson Youyoute, Alia Touadjine, and Rachel Cosgrove went to Washington, D.C., where they presented about Real Talk at the American Library Association annual conference in 2019. Credit: Luke Kirkland.	134
Figure 6.1.	Mentor Holly Burrell and teen intern Cheyenne Jones from the Auburn Public Library in Georgia are shown attending the Public Library Association wrap-up meeting in Washington, D.C. The mentor-intern relationship and the final evaluation process they go through together are essential parts of any internship. Credit: Zach Miller.	144
Figure 6.2.	Interns can showcase their work in their community or library, at state events, and sometimes even nationally. The Public Library Association holds its closing event each year in the fall, where teen interns from around the country present their internship projects to a gathering of interns and mentors from around the United States. Credit: Zach Miller.	147
Figure 6.3.	Teen Leaders Stevenson Youyoute, Alia Touadjine, and Rachel Cosgrove from the Waltham Public Library presented their Real Talk paid teen leaders' programs at the Massachusetts Library Association Conference in 2019. Credit: Luke Kirkland.	148

Series Foreword

TEENS ARE GETTING A HEAD START ENTERING the adult working world through internships in libraries. Actual work experience builds confidence, college applications, and resumes for the teens, while offering insight into life working in libraries through real work accomplishments that benefit the library and its customers.

Through many years of experience and a love of teen library services, Diane P. Tuccillo keeps a clear eye on current trends and teen services topics. Teen library internships are an avenue some libraries offer to teens serious about pursuing library careers or who want real-life work experience. Tuccillo pens an indispensable guide for the Teen Librarian Bookshelf series with *The Teen Library Internship Handbook*. The reader will learn what constitutes an internship, how to organize one to fit the teen applicant and the library, and what other libraries and organizations do to make the experience a success. Tuccillo covers multiple types of libraries, how to evaluate the teen intern and the mentor librarian, and how to manage an internship program when the library must be closed. This book will open your eyes to new opportunities for teens in your library.

RoseMary Ludt
Teen Library Bookshelf, series editor

Foreword

I HAVE KNOWN AND ADMIRED Diane Tuccillo for many years through my association with her, as I have served for nearly twenty years on American Library Association, Young Adult Library Services Association (YALSA), and Association of Library Service to Children award and selection committees. Her mission has always been to advocate for teens and their interests and the staff in libraries who work with them.

So much has changed in what libraries offer in resources and programs in the over thirty-five years since I began working in public libraries. The shushing librarian is still often portrayed in television ads. Yet, community organizations and stakeholders have realized the vital role librarians and libraries play in offering a wide array of programs for their communities. Still, I don't think even the most faithful library users, like the teens and tweens who show up at the library daily after school (pre- and post-pandemic) and attend library programs, are aware of all that's involved in working there. Additionally, although much has changed in library programming and design, libraries still struggle to attract staff who reflect the diversity of the communities they serve.

This is why Tuccillo's book on teen internships at the library is such an invaluable and necessary resource. If we want to make significant inroads into broadening the diversity of staffing in public libraries, we need to provide teens with more opportunities to gain experience working in a library as an intern (paid or unpaid). They need to experience what it's like firsthand. We want to give them more agency to create and carry out programming that appeals to them and their teen and tween peers. They might become more interested in pursuing a library career if they are more aware of what working there entails. This book makes a point of illustrating the importance of diversity in teen internships.

I know from personal experience working with teens as an adult/young adult librarian in a public library that teens excel when given the freedom to initiate their own programs and follow through in carrying them out. I've seen firsthand the impact on teens in libraries that have makerspaces run by the teens themselves—teens who are passionate about what they are creating. They feel a sense of ownership, and it empowers them to think of inventive ways to meet their own and their community's needs.

Tuccillo's book succinctly describes examples of teen internships. It explains in detail what teens will get from library internships, including the benefit of having the opportunity to work on library projects they're interested in pursuing (also known as connected learning) that might lead to a career in the field. She discusses some of the developmental concepts concerning teens engaging in internships that educators feel are important to their growth, such as social and emotional learning. The cognitive changes that teens experience during these years mean that positive and productive experiences they have in their internships can lead to future success beyond high school.

In my current job as the youth services specialist for lifelong learning at the New Jersey State Library, two frontline library staff from public libraries and I are participating in the YALSA/Chief Officers of State Library Agencies initiative, funded by a grant from the Institute of Museum and Library Services, called Transforming Teen Services: A Train the Trainer Approach. Through this project, library staff members working with youth receive training about connected learning and computational thinking. Being familiar with both concepts and incorporating them into library internships helps the teens gain valuable life skills and will help the library staff advocate for the youth they serve in the library.

As someone who has worked with teen volunteers in public libraries in the past and more recently as a mentor for a young adult who interned at the New Jersey State Library, I understand how vital internships and mentorship are. I provided this intern with firsthand access to resources and editors working in the field that helped her pursue her dream of becoming an editor of young adult books.

Due to limited school time, high schools may not be offering as many career days as in years past for teens to have the opportunity to really see what some occupations entail. My state's labor and workforce development department provides resources and services for employers and employees in the state. They are actively working with libraries and other organizations that work with young people to make sure they know about possible employment opportunities. They want to educate and employ young people in jobs that will enable them to be productive and gain job skills that will help them, and ultimately, benefit the state's economy.

Diane Tuccillo's thoroughly researched book serves as a vital tool to assist libraries and other organizations and agencies in doing that. Chapter 2 of her book discusses specific internship grants available to public libraries, such as the Public Library Association's Inclusive Internship Initiative and YALSA's Summer Teen Internship Program Grant, which the Dollar General Literacy Foundation had provided. I am familiar with them because several New Jersey public libraries have received them. They have provided teens with internships to assist during the summer months with summer reading programming, but I didn't know the criteria involved in receiving one. Tuccillo's book provides that information in her in-depth look at both initiatives, plus at other sources of support. Her book is invaluable to help those libraries that have contemplated offering internships but need guidance on the ins and outs of doing so.

As this is being written, the COVID-19 pandemic is still raging, and libraries remain unsure when they might be able to offer in-person programming. Teens who rely on part-time jobs in fast food and retail stores may not be able to get them during the pandemic. During this time, public library internships are even more valuable for teens than they have ever been. This makes the chapter that Tuccillo has provided on resources to assist in providing virtual internships especially useful.

Offering teenagers internship opportunities in libraries ensures that libraries will continue to provide programming and other interest and value opportunities to young people. These youth-driven connected learning experiences allow the young people to gain valuable life skills in the process, enabling them to become more confident and competent to participate in and contribute to their communities.

Sharon Rawlins, MLS
Youth Services Specialist for Lifelong Learning
New Jersey State Library

Acknowledgments

A BOOK LIKE THIS THAT GIVES practical guidelines and uses real-life experiences and testimonials to illustrate them can only come about through the kind input from those librarians, other library staff members, and teen interns who were willing to share their information and stories. I received many generous responses from those who had something to share from around the country, and to those people, I am sincerely grateful.

Adults who supervised, mentored, advised, led, or otherwise were instrumental in arranging or approving teen internships that came about and sent me details of, documents from, and photos of their experiences are: Scott Bahlmann; Cody Brownson-Katz; Holly Burrell; Hayley Burson; Eric Button; David Clark; Zayda Delgado; Kathy DeWeese; Brittany Garcia; Mary Hirsh; Luke Kirkland; Joanna Kolosov; Christie Lassen; Angela McCaffery; Zach Miller; Janet Monterrosa; Bel Outwater; Sierra Pandy; Analiza Perez-Gomez; Lindsey Tomsu; Patricia VanArsdale; Anna White; Natalie Williams; and Joe Wisniewski.

Likewise, the teenagers who were chosen as teen library interns and shared their thoughts, ideas, advice, and images with me are: Ty Allen; Iris Alvarenga; Marcus Bennett; Yasmeen Chavez; Kathleen C.; Rachel Cosgrove; Emily Brooks Friel; Matthew Heath; Annie Jean-Baptiste; Cheyenne Jones; Madelyn Lakeman; Morea Lee; Christine Miller; Makynna Reiff; Jaishna Sivakumar; Sam Stucky; Nayana Thompson; Alia Touadjine; Aaron Vivanco, Jr.; Emma Weisler; Sade Wilkens El; Bethany Worrell; and Stevenson Youyoute.

Thanks also to my astute and encouraging editor, RoseMary Ludt, who has helped me make my book the best it can be, and to Sharon Rawlins for writing a foreword that is a perfect fit.

Finally, I have a great appreciation for my readers. Those of you who have read my books and put the information to practical use have helped lead our teenagers into the future and are essential to a book like this. For me, my books are a labor of love that allows me to share knowledge and wisdom with you so that you can pass it on in various ways with our next generation. Thanks for keeping the light shining brightly for our teenage library leaders!

Introduction

FOR THE MANY YEARS I WORKED as a librarian who specialized in serving teenagers, I mentored and supervised several library interns. These were adult students aspiring to focus their upcoming library careers on teens and tweens in public libraries. Some hoped to become school librarians, and a few were even prospective teachers who had a special interest in libraries and their importance to young people. Some of these adult intern opportunities were paid, and others were unpaid, as they were requirements for college graduation credits. However, as noted, these interns were all *adults* from library-oriented graduate school programs, school library media specialist programs, and undergraduate teaching programs. Each intern received intensive experience in our library teen services areas, and each one went on to become a librarian or teacher working with adolescents. None of the interns were teenagers themselves.

At the same time, the libraries where I worked that were approving and hosting these interns, with me usually advising and supervising them as part of my assigned duties, were also extremely amenable to encouraging middle- and high-school-age youth to volunteer in the libraries. In those roles, teens did everything from participating in library teen advisory groups, book discussions, designing and running library programs or activities for peers, and assisting with various other library events as needed. Occasionally, teens seeking specific high school credentials or satisfying class requirements were assigned to shadow an adult in a position to which they aspired one day. For this shadowing, several teens who were considering library careers interviewed me or other teen or youth services library staff members. They accompanied other library staff members and me for varying lengths of time both in the library and when doing outreach, and they completed reports on their public library experiences. In addition, teen services staff members were occasionally represented at career fairs held at local high schools to encourage teens to explore a myriad of future employment options, including as librarians or other library workers.

In recent years, I began to wonder about combining or adapting these initiatives so that teenagers could also participate through their libraries in doing actual internships, like college and university students had been doing, while still practicing lively youth participation. While researching for two of my previous books, *Library Teen Advisory Groups* (second edition) and *Totally Tweens & Teens: Youth-Created and Youth-Led Library Programs*, I discovered that some libraries were already doing just that. I also became attuned to the notion of teen library internships being enthusiastically promoted by the Young Adult Library Services Association of the American Library Association. Although I found more and more wonderful examples of these kinds of teen library internships and support for funding them, I realized there was not yet a guidebook or handbook that thoroughly addressed how libraries could offer them. I decided to make the teen library internship concept my latest book's focus.

I have learned from investigating teen internships that opportunities like them help young people feel valued and successful, in addition to allowing them to survey potential career choices. Teen internships can go beyond helping with library teen spaces and providing librarians with advice about and assistance with teen services programs. Further, I realized that there is no reason why internships cannot be offered for teens in library areas serving children and adults; in school, public, special, and university libraries; in areas of libraries beyond public service areas; and as partnerships between outside agencies and libraries. A bonus is that such experiences give teens the chance to include their internship stories and mentors' references for them on college, scholarship, and employment applications.

The concept of dynamic teen library participation in school and public libraries has been a catalyst throughout my forty-year library career working with teenagers. I have highly touted the benefits of not only permitting but encouraging tweens and teens to be leaders in their libraries and to have active involvement in all sorts of interesting and effective ways. My other four books cover these aspects of teen participation extensively. Now, I am promoting a new library trend that is intrinsically connected.

As some in the business and organization worlds outside of schools and libraries have already discovered, internships are valuable and useful to help teens learn and grow productively into adulthood. In this book, you, too, will learn the essentials to point teens in this same direction. Although the predominant examples given in this book are from libraries or with libraries as partners, I have also described internships and similar opportunities that have been offered in other businesses, service agencies, and organizations. Essentially, these could be adapted to a library setting. For example, a youth-oriented internship with an environmental focus through a parks department could be adapted to a library that wants to create a community garden on its campus grounds with teenagers in charge during an internship. Keep this in mind as you are reading.

In the first chapter, you will find a wide-ranging discussion of what teen internships are—and are not—in general. You might be surprised to discover the many facets you need to consider to get teen internships off the ground and what teen internships entail, including such elements as legal issues and focusing on several layers of learning concepts.

The second chapter discusses why teen *library* internships are a valuable function of youth services. It explains the difference between these kinds of experiences and traditional teen volunteering opportunities and how such internships promote library professions. There are even illustrations of teen interns who have gone on to get regular paying jobs in libraries after their internships.

Foundational information in this chapter will help you get your teen library internship started, including seeking approval and funding. It will help you configure any teen library internships you would like to offer. But first, you will need to create a proposal, consider funding, and get the go-ahead from your administrators and others who may be in charge. Once approval is in hand, you can proceed using the advice given.

Chapter 3 addresses designing an application, promoting open teen library internship positions, interviewing teen job candidates, and helpfully encouraging teens who do not make the cut after the interviews. There are then details on devising and creating a teen library internship handbook based on the specific internship(s) you wish to offer. The handbook can be a step-by-step guide to putting all the details and documents you need into a centralized location or locations that you can share with teen interns, library staff, supervisors, and mentors to use for orientations, guidelines, and reference as the internship(s) get underway and progress.

Next, in two chapters, you will find an assortment of teen library internship examples that have taken place in recent years. These examples are from public libraries and school, special, and university libraries, and some are from behind-the-scenes settings. You will notice that several opportunities related to and serving as "internships" of sorts are also included, such as working partnerships with other community agencies; library leadership programs for which teens get paid; and unpaid internship positions that allow teens to earn school credit. Essentially, an "internship" can fall under many guises, but all of them give teens valuable teamwork and leadership experiences plus chances to investigate a prospective career area up close and personal.

After you explore the varieties of internship examples, a chapter covers vital progressive and culminating steps. Those steps allow teens to evaluate themselves on their internship experiences, which gives them important insights into what they may have gained, where they might need to improve and learn more, and how they now feel about a possible library career. However, evaluation does not stop there. Reactions and input from internship mentors or supervisors are also parts of the evaluation picture, including having those taking on these roles appraise themselves. Finally, there is counsel on dealing with intern resignations and the need to let an intern go due to performance issues.

As I began my work on this book, the global pandemic was about to reach the United States. Like everyone else, I never anticipated its intense effects on our society as a whole, especially the closures of businesses, organizations, agencies, and libraries everywhere. Of course, most teen library internships arranged for the summer of 2020 were suddenly called off or postponed. Many teens who had been or had hoped to be hired were left in the lurch. I learned that while many internships hoped to be offered again in 2021 and beyond, there are no guarantees. Meanwhile, teens' developmental needs continue, and in some places, attempts have been made to rearrange internships to fit a virtual or another long-distance format to accommodate those needs. I decided to add a closing chapter that offers some reasoning and suggestions for building advance plans to provide alternative internships, volunteering, and other leadership roles for teens in libraries when health or other emergencies strike.

Lastly, there are appendices with forms and information that can be adapted to library teen internship settings, plus a selected bibliography and webliography that offer additional useful resources.

For the most part, I will refer to teens, teenagers, and young adults as those for whom the library internships are designed. However, in some circumstances, there might be a desire and option to create internships for younger recipients—those we call "tweens," or young people in approximately fifth through eighth grades. If developing an internship or similar kind of experience for a preadolescent or young adolescent age group is something you would like to pursue, the ideas and information presented in this book can be adapted for your needs.

As already mentioned, I have always strived to incorporate the philosophy that lively and positive youth participation is essential in school and public libraries, and that philosophy has been the basis of this and my other four books. Giving teens ways to have an active voice and to take action in their libraries makes them feel a connection that usually remains with them throughout their lives. Teen library internships can fill a niche for teens who are anxious to have opportunities to investigate libraries behind the scenes, to see firsthand how libraries tick, and to make decisions about pursuing library work as a future career. Because of these internships, teens are often likely to study about and populate a variety of positions in many aspects of the library world. However, as important as that fact may be, they will doubtless learn workforce, communication, and other necessary skills; become library users and supporters through adulthood; and share a passion for libraries with other people, young and old, as they move forward in their lives—even if they do not end up employed in a library.

Results like these can likewise occur when libraries provide teen councils, teen focus groups, teen volunteer programs, teen peer homework help, teen-created and -led programs, or any number of other opportunities. Nevertheless, it is important to touch all bases. Adding teen library internship options to the mix can go a long way in establishing the knowledge, ability, and enthusiasm bases so vital in fostering a strong outlook for our overall library community.

Most upcoming teen internships that I had hoped to feature in this book were either canceled or postponed due to the pandemic. However, I had already gathered a good selection of inspiring examples of relatively recently completed internships that I could include. I think you will find them inspirational and beneficial as you create or improve teen library internships in your community.

In this handbook, I have presented rationales, tools, guidelines, advice, and examples that will assist you in making teen library internship goals a reality. My sincere desire is for you to discover meaning, value, food for thought, and helpful direction in its pages.

1

Teaching Teens about Real-World Job Skills through Internships

For many years until the present time, internships were adult-only territory provided in various businesses, organizations, agencies, medical facilities, and community services. True, many of those adults who have been and are interns were and are college students and very new adults, but not all. Some older adults who changed careers or only just embarked on one after raising a family have been and are interns.

In the last decade or so, internships have altered to include younger people still in high school. This is a positive change because it affords teenagers a chance to test the waters before deciding upon and heading off to a college or university; to pursue other higher education; to get worksite training through an employment area of interest; and, overall, to learn numerous real-world job skills.

In this chapter, we will examine the concept of internships for teens in general and three in-depth reasons why they are a beneficial experiential model for the young adult age group and their adult sponsors.

The Value of Teen Internships as Experiential Learning

Teenagers can be given opportunities to participate in many forms of experiential learning. These include volunteerism, service-learning or community service, civic engagement in any number of ways that enhance and advocate for vital issues in a community, project-based learning, job shadowing, student employment, and internships. For this book, internships will be the primary consideration, although the information you will find can be adapted and applied to other kinds of teen experiential learning.

On that note, let us begin with a detailed look at internships and what they encompass. Reflecting upon a definition and general description is a good start:

> Internships are work-based learning activities in which teenagers engage in learning through practical and relevant experiences at various internship sites. They are targeted to career goals and allow teens to explore careers that require additional degrees, certification, or on-the-job training following high school.[1]

This basic definition fits teen internships of any kind and those taking place in any field. However, meaningful internships go well beyond the definition. The specifics that accompany the definition are complex and require attention to several aspects:

Dynamic internships provide students with opportunities to develop an understanding of career area duties and responsibilities, terminology, company culture, protocol, and other information that will enable them to analyze and evaluate their career goals. There must be agreements, understandings, instructions, and orientations for all participants; coordination between the teens and the adults providing the opportunity; evaluation of each intern's experience; and program analysis for future internship improvement.[2]

As all of these elements come together, the advantages unfold. Teens who participate in internships are one step ahead of the game as they enter the higher education and adult work realm because they gain several essential benefits:

- Internships allow teenagers to combine and apply their high school coursework into meaningful and relevant outside-the-classroom experiences. Teens can connect with the world at large and gain information and skills to pursue further education to be better prepared to enter the adult workforce later.
- Through internships, teenagers can better see the value of their high school education and experiences. Instead of questioning why what they learn in school is important, teens can apply many things they have learned in real-life settings. They can envision the relationships between academics and actively contribute in a multifaceted workplace.
- As they work with adult mentors during their internships, teens can experience modeling of and develop a foundation of general workplace skills needed for their anticipated career path.
- Internships provide students with focused, structured, active, and meaningful knowledge, through which they find out about targeting timelines, meeting deadlines, making decisions, and working with others.[3]

There are documentation and research to back all this up, which will be shared periodically throughout this book. High school students might think that an internship is something you pursue as a college junior and senior in preparation for your career after college. As mentioned earlier, for many years, that was the common expectation, and in many circles, it still is. However, according to a study conducted by Millennial Branding, a research and consulting firm, and Internships.com, an online resource for student work experience, gaining new skills and professional connections as early as high school can help position students for future success.

Although the study is from 2014, it reveals and confidently supports teen internships through the last several years to the present day and beyond. Data was gleaned from 4,769 high school and college students and 326 employers from all over the United States. Half of the employers polled said they plan on or are currently accepting internship applications from high school students. Most employers, or 90 percent, agreed that early internship experiences could enhance students' chances of acceptance when applying to colleges and universities. Additionally, they noted that the experience would add to students' marketability when looking for a college internship or job, and the internships give them a better chance of securing a higher-paying job after graduation.

One high school intern described it like this: "I think it's important to hire student interns like me because they gain experience, develop skills, make connections, and strengthen their resumes. Students learn about the company and their field and figure out if what they are currently doing is the best option for them. It's a great way to assess their career interests and abilities. Companies also gain something from hiring student interns. They find future employees. If they see that the intern is going beyond what they expect, the company may want to hire them in the future. These companies that hire student interns help make positive futures a more reachable goal for the students involved."[4]

As we delve deeper into the exploration of teen internships throughout this book, specifically in library or associated settings in subsequent chapters, you will see the substance of the comments made by this student unfolding and being brought center stage.

Before we move on to those, and despite the positive elements of internships, there are important additional points to remember. Though teen internships are, for the most part, encouraged and desirable, experts give supplementary advice that teens must be sure to take care as they apply for and embark on internships during high school. They need to build a realistic schedule that balances schoolwork, extracurricular activities, and an accepted internship. Getting experience and making connections is important, but overloading the activities in which they are engaged can be counterproductive and cause stress. No one can put their best foot forward when juggling too many priorities.[5]

Adult mentors for teen internships would be wise to be aware of these warnings and assure that arranging balanced teen schedules is always a priority. One way adults can alleviate this challenge is to offer internships in the summer, during other breaks from school, or by encouraging job shadowing as an alternative—more about that last option later in this chapter.

TEXTBOX 1.1 RESOURCES FOR TEENS TO LEARN ABOUT INTERNSHIPS, HOW TO GET THEM, AND HOW TO SUCCEED

When offering a teen internship, you might consider making the following online resources available to teens who would like to apply and who need guidance:

Find the Right Internship for You

All the details about internships can be found on this interactive website where teens can get career advice, discover how to find and keep an internship position, and even get advice for coping with an internship during a pandemic.[1]

Exploring U.S. Department of Education Career Clusters

This is an online library of information and activities that teens can use to research the various career clusters and sub-clusters for exploring various field choices.[2]

The Essential Benefits of Internships

For high school teens who want general information about internships, but especially if they are also interested in pursuing them in college, this self-navigating website is a useful, in-depth tool.[3]

> **Notes**
>
> 1. "Find the Internship That's Right for You." 2020. Chegg Internships, https://www.internships.com/.
> 2. "US Department of Education Career Clusters." 2019. Exploring.org, https://www.exploring.org/activity-library-category/us-department-of-education-career-clusters/.
> 3. Loretto, Penny. July 17, 2019. "The Essential Benefits of Internships," The Balance Careers, https://www.thebalancecareers.com/what-is-an-internship-1986729.

Hardwiring the Teen Brain in a Positive Direction

One of the most effective things adults who work with teenagers can do is to provide ways for teens to participate in positive and enlightening experiences that hardwire their brains for a secure future as an adult. Offering teen internships is a significant way to accomplish this goal.

Thomas Armstrong, a psychologist and educator who is also the American Institute for Learning and Human Development director, says that adolescent experiences hold enormous consequences for their future adult lives. Because the teenage brain is still in a state of neuroplasticity, the things that occur in teens' lives significantly impact the wiring, structure, and overall development of their brains. Early childhood development is crucial, but likewise so is teen brain development, the timing of which offers a last chance to affect impacts on adulthood. Because of this factor, Armstrong encourages methods that enhance brain development while considering the changes teenagers are going through.

One of the changes that preteens and teens experience is a different perspective on education. For youngsters in the primary grades, school is, in general, much more engaging and fun. As young people reach and enter adolescence, schoolwork becomes increasingly rigorous and academically oriented. To channel teens' evolving emotions, school often includes more discipline and homework—at a time when self-expression and social interaction in all their forms become essential. Armstrong suggests that activities that incorporate teen emotions, such as musical and other creative events, are beneficial. In addition, he says:

> Why don't we have students engaging in more apprenticeships and more internships, which can be wonderful ways to help them build decision-making skills and work through emotions in a real-world but controlled setting? Teens want to be out in the world—in fact, that's what evolution has prepared them for. We can't fight a million years of evolution with a role-play in the classroom.[6]

Armstrong further argues that students need to learn the hard skills and build the soft skills that support them. Teens need positive environmental factors and risks to counteract the negatives ones that they will find in the present and the world beyond school. Offering meaningful internships can boost these positive effects and seal them into teen thinking for the future.[7]

Not only can internships and similar opportunities advance positivity in the teens who are partaking in the actual experiences themselves, but they can model the effects and the results of these experiences for younger people who may observe them and decide to follow in their footsteps. For example, in Pittsburgh, leaders partnered with the Student Conservation Association and the city/county workforce investment board, Partner4Work. They created an internship corps through which local teenagers were offered six weeks of paid employment on local conservation projects. Participants who joined the program and lacked exposure to conservation values, outdoor recreation, and environmental education came away demonstrating strong skills in all three. One young man continued as a member of the corps for two summers, plus a year in high school, which led him to attend community college and take on further internships. He has become an inspiration to other young people as one of the first African American park rangers in Pittsburgh.[8]

Another great example comes from New York City's Metropolitan Museum of Art teen internship program. The Met has provided internships both during the school year and in the summer, which has given participants a chance to connect with professionals in the arts and develop their own professional skills in creating art or in many areas that support art, such as administration. Teens from across New York City have been participants in the internships.

Experiences teens have encountered in the program include step teams, singing, spoken word, tattooing, bookmaking, creating a silent disco party, gardening, and much more through New York City organizations such as The Studio Museum in Harlem[9] and the Wave Hill Cultural and Garden Center in Riverdale.[10] All of the teen interns have been given a chance to shine during their Teens Take the Met night, funded by the Gray Foundation,[11] at the esteemed museum's sprawling two-million-square-foot space during which teen attendees celebrate youth voice.[12]

As these locations contributing to the Met program do, libraries that offer tween and teen participatory activities can also make a difference. Considering what internships can provide, making them available can allow teens to delve more deeply than they could through volunteer activities and become immersed in a taste of the skills and responsibilities required for work in a library setting. Complete details about how libraries can tailor teens internships in this manner will be addressed in upcoming chapters.

Internships hold an important place in offering the many kinds of opportunities communities can provide to help teens grow in ways that will make them productive future adults in society.

Further Benefits of Internships to Teenagers

By now, you may be wondering exactly how internships can develop teens into industrious adult workers. Internships can accomplish this goal by paying attention to the concepts of *social-emotional learning* and *connected learning* in planning and monitoring teen internships. Let us examine the relevance of these concepts.

A prime aspiration in today's educational world has become incorporating social-emotional learning and connected learning within teens' experiences. These are directly related to positive youth development and hardwiring the teen brain for good, and they can be addressed in the classroom, in other areas of schools, and through learning partnerships with businesses, organizations, and agencies in communities. When teens are given a chance to practice hands-on learning in an enriching environment to which they are drawn from personal interest, social, emotional, and connected learning can occur.

Social-emotional learning and connected learning are essential facets of teens' opportunities to steer them in constructive directions. This applies to any enriching and encouraging activities through which teens can meet these ends, including internships. Thinking about and reinforcing Thomas Armstrong's message, the National Parks and Recreation Association explains:

> Teens are among those most vulnerable to at-risk behaviors and violence. Nearly seventy percent of urban youth have experienced some form of direct or witnessed violence in their neighborhood. Teens of color are disproportionately more likely to be exposed to violence and less likely to receive

services for their mental health needs. The ongoing insistence that public schools prioritize academics has refocused attention on park afterschool programming as a practical venue for teaching social-emotional skills to teens. Park afterschool programs are uniquely positioned to teach and reinforce the resiliency skills necessary for teens to develop as healthy and productive citizens.[13]

When teenagers are led to opportunities through such programs as these from which they can grow and learn because they *want to*, not because they are told they must, it makes all the difference. Internships can fill a vital role in social-emotional learning and connected learning. They can help foster teen resiliency, positive self-esteem, collaboration, and leadership abilities.

There is recent evidence to back up the importance of this kind of learning, and more studies are underway. The Search Institute, which is one agency at the forefront of this current research, aims to show that their definition of "developmental relationships as close connections through which young people discover who they are, gain abilities to shape their own lives, and learn how to interact with and contribute to the world around them" holds true.

For one study, students in grades six through twelve who were participating in out-of-school time programs were surveyed. Overall, when they reported stronger developmental relationships and more diverse, equitable, and inclusive environments through their experiences, results showed a higher level of social-emotional competence.[14] These results demonstrate that assuring teen internships meet this positive description is vital to a meaningful work atmosphere.

At this point, you might be wondering—what exactly are the concepts of social-emotional and connected learning? Even if you are already familiar with these terms and have put them into practice in your teen programming and activities, it can be a good idea to refresh your thoughts about these concepts. We will start by taking a closer look at the former.

SIDEBAR 1.1 TEEN VANTAGE POINT

The focus of our library's teen internships is prepping teens for future jobs through interview skills, customer service, establishing work ethics, and following instructions. The interns are there to be a go-between between the summer Teen Volunteer Corps members and the librarians. The volunteers run the summer reading program, and the interns assist them while also working on special projects for the librarians. The internships allow teens to grow in leadership skills while assisting the public.[1]

Bethany Worrell
Hussey-Mayfield Memorial Public Library, Zionsville, Indiana

Note
 1. Worrell, Bethany. July 2020. Email message to author.

Social-Emotional Learning

Social-emotional learning, also known as SEL, comprises a broad spectrum of skills, attitudes, and values that promote success both in school and in the outside world. It includes life skills such as managing emotions, setting and reaching goals, persevering through adversity, and working in a team. SEL meets teens at their individual points of ability and curiosity and allows those with learning differences, growing up in poverty, or facing other kinds of challenges to level out the playing field. It permits teens to develop "soft skills," which include, for instance, solving unfamiliar problems, setting goals, dealing with feelings, or working effectively with colleagues from diverse walks of life, all of which will be assets in teens' futures in addition to the academic knowledge they have gained. Incorporating SEL helps the whole teenager learn and succeed while teen brains are still elastic.[15]

Research indicates that attention to and incorporation of SEL is the foundation of thriving in life. Young people with strong social and emotional skills get along better with their peers. They are also more likely to graduate from high school and get a full-time job.[16] This is not just an observation. A twenty-year study by the Robert Wood Johnson Foundation tracked youth's development until adulthood. The study determined that when SEL is addressed:

- 54 percent of youth were more likely to get a high school diploma
- Youth were twice as likely to get a college degree in early adulthood
- 46 percent of the youths were more likely to have a full-time job at twenty-five.[17]

These findings are significant because they tell us that paying attention to SEL in school and other learning environments works. When going hand-in-hand with the concept of connected learning, SEL is strengthened.

Connected Learning

Connected learning, or CL, is a combination of supportive relationships, opportunities, and personal interests. It encompasses learning in an age of abundant access to information and social connection that embraces all young people's varied interests and backgrounds.[18] Similar to the research supporting SEL, CL provides a foundation for documentation through the Connected Learning Research Network, which keeps records of applicable projects and the positive effects of the concept demonstrated through them.[19]

As you will find out later in this book, if you are not already familiar, CL is such an essential element to teen success in an internship environment that the Public Library Association requires all teen library interns who are hired through its grants program to complete connected learning projects reflecting their personal interests and creativity.[20]

Internships and Supportive Relationships

Learners thrive when peers and mentors work well together. In certain circumstances, even working with public members will foster supportive relationships. All of these relationships can help teens to persevere when they face setbacks and challenges. They also contribute greatly to positive outcomes.

The peers that teens may encounter in internship settings can cheer each other and teach each other new things. At the same time, an appreciative clientele can heighten teen interns' self-esteem. Similarly, adults who effectively supervise, advise, guide, and mentor teens during internships can make all the difference in the experience's final results. To achieve constructive results, it is important to assure that those working with and supporting teen interns are compatible, encouraging, caring, knowledgeable, and value and respect one another. A wide range of positive human interactions can boost the desire to partake in and learn from meaningful connected learning opportunities.

FIGURE 1.1
During the Adult 101 Life Skills for Teens Time and Stress Management program at the Rancho Cucamonga Public Library in California, teen interns Nayana Thompson and Morea Lee explain to the participating teen attendees how to make and decorate woodblock desk calendars. Credit: Janet Monterrosa.

When there are two or several teen interns at once, it helps give them a chance to get to know and interact with each other and work on assignments together when possible. Doing this allows teen interns to teach each other new things, share ideas and advice, enjoy working together, and give each other confidence. Encouraging teamwork among interns who are peers can be a significant way to help them progress and grow.

Likewise, when teens have occasions to work with and guide peers and others representing various ages from the community, they practice leadership, put their interests and knowledge to good use, and hone self-reliance skills. Providing ways for teens to become successful leaders through internships can be a huge plus. Perhaps they plan and run a gardening program for young children or create and implement a class to teach elders in their neighborhood how to navigate computers. While building their knowledge and skills in these subject areas, they are also building their leadership and interpersonal skills. The realization that they have taught someone else a valuable lesson through their growing interests and abilities goes a long way in reinforcing connected learning—and social-emotional learning as well.

Qualities of Mentors and Other Adults Working with Interns

Above all, effective mentors can be the most influential component to meaningful connected learning and social-emotional learning experiences. Whoever is chosen needs to have the background, enthusiasm, and skills to successfully take on managing and supervising teen interns. Sometimes this is one individual, and sometimes it is a small group working together, perhaps as mentor, supervisor, and assistant.

For the most part, upper-level managers and administrators are typically not placed in these roles. They are tasked with approving the establishment of internship programs, and although they are usually very supportive, they only take on such supervision if the internship is taking place in a small setting. Most human resource specialists ensure that proper documentation and procedures are in place for internships. They, too, would most likely not serve as mentors, unless, of course, a teen was doing an internship in their area of expertise. However, they and top managers and administrators frequently assign just the right person or persons to serve as mentors and supervisors of interns. They can and often do express

FIGURE 1.2
A solid relationship between teen interns and their mentors makes all the difference to a successful experience for everyone. Here, teen intern Sade Wilkens El and her mentor, Cody Brownson-Katz of the Baltimore County Public Library, smile as Wilkens El receives her certificate for the completion of the Public Library Association's internship grant requirements. Credit: Zach Miller.

their appreciation and support for interns as they progress. In cases where they do happen to be serving as mentors themselves, they need to have the same qualities and skills as anyone they might appoint.

No matter the circumstances, there are a number of qualities and skills to consider for each role. A capable supervisor can do such things as answer questions, manage schedules, supportively enforce goals and deadlines, and share knowledge. A good mentor is there to share expertise, serve as a sounding board, and encourage growth. As noted, sometimes there is one person who acts in both capacities, and sometimes two people work as a team to fill these roles. In some instances, there might be one or more additional people involved in facilitating the internships. Whether one or more people are involved, any or all of them need to possess the following skills to plan and manage teen internships effectively:

- Strong interpersonal skills
- Credibility, expertise, and knowledge of their field
- Genuine enjoyment and appreciation of teenagers
- Desire to be a role model
- Teaching or training experience
- Patience
- Flexibility
- Sensitivity
- Respectfulness, trustworthiness, and the ability to trust
- Concern for the progress and development of teen interns
- Ability to communicate and offer constructive feedback
- Strong organizational and planning skills
- Belief in inclusivity
- Good listening skills[21]

Internships and Opportunities

Going hand-in-hand with positive relationships, learning success during internships depends on tangible connections to real-world career and civic opportunities. Several conditional aspects encompass the system of opportunities that benefit teen interns:

- Flexible sponsorship of youth interests means recognizing the diverse curiosity of youth and providing mentorship, space, and other resources to address a wide array of variances. Interns need to have the chance to express themselves and work on projects and tasks that suit their individual needs.
- Shared practices, which point to ongoing, shared activities that allow for collaborative production, friendly competition, joint research, and civic action in an enjoyable setting with peers and adults involved together, tying in the supportive relationships.
- Shared purpose, which signifies that learners have a sense of belonging and can contribute to a community as members encounter connected learning. Groups fostering connected learning share culture and values, welcome newcomers, and encourage sharing and feedback among participants—again, this opportunistic element bonding with supportive relationships.

- Building connections across various settings allows learners to access various programs, surroundings, and opportunities through internship-oriented partnerships and openly share ideas via networked platforms and portfolios.[22]

Internships and Teen Interest

The last key point in CL is personal teen *interest*. Interest is an essential element in any successful learning plan. Without interest, supportive relationships and opportunities can fall flat. A teen who is not drawn to gardening will probably not be excited about an internship that requires learning about this skill and offering programs to teach others about it. But that same teen might greatly enjoy working with computers and be champing at the bit to engage others with lessons on a new computer technology they have encountered and are mastering.

Teen interest is the essential element that helps to hardwire the teen brain with the skills, knowledge, and determination for pursuing their next phases of life. It is also a fundamental feature of any programs or activities in which teens *want to* be involved. If teens are not interested in something, they might do and learn the minimum to get by when needed, but if they find something appealing, they will *want to* take part and keep finding out more actively. During the latter, learning and growing come naturally.

Internships hold an especially strong association with teen interests. Teens apply for internships and take them on because they are drawn to certain subject areas and opportunities. They can see their potential career or educational outlook reflected in what an internship might impart. Matched with supportive relationships and relevant opportunities, interest is the final key to a fruitful and memorable—and maybe even life-changing—internship experience.

The Science of Teen Interest

In recent years, the study of "interest" has become a science. Interest is an excellent element to reflect upon when designing an internship. We talk about having "interest" in things all the time, but what precisely does this mean? What exactly is *interest*?

According to scientists, "Interest is a psychological state of engagement, experienced in the moment, and also a predisposition to engage repeatedly with particular ideas, events, or objects over time. Interest also *focuses* experience. In a world too full of information, interests usefully narrow our choices: they lead us to pay attention to *this* and not to *that*."[23] Interest in a particular career field can lead teenagers to be enthusiastic about a related internship opportunity they encounter. By participating in it, they might then be instilled later with a desire to pursue studies on topics they are drawn to through it.

Another way interest has been defined is that it is a "knowledge emotion." Feelings that accompany interest are senses of being "energized, invigorated, captivated, and enthralled." Interest, in effect, turbocharges thinking. Teens interested in something pay closer attention; process information and use strategies such as critical thinking effectively; connect old and new knowledge; and work harder and persist longer. Science has shown that even academic difficulties and perceptual difficulties can be overcome by interest.[24]

Promoting interest is crucial whenever adults join together with teens to create learning and growing environments. This is key when internships are involved because teens will be working in areas they are drawn to and usually do not know a great deal about. They will be expected to work independently and in teams during these experiences. To get as much out of internships as they can and contribute as much as they can, *they must be interested*.

How do adults planning and promoting internships incorporate this element of interest? Here is how it works:

- Interest operates through a "catch" and "hold" process. Interest must be captured, and then it must be maintained. Internship planners can accomplish this by making the publicity, job descriptions, and formats for the opportunities clear, attractive, and engaging. What the job entails and options within it need to be carefully addressed as part of the interview process to assure teens get a true sense of their relative personal interest.
- Interest is drawn when the internship opportunities are *novel, complex*, and *comprehensible*. This means that through the internships, teens are aiming to find out about unfamiliar things that are *novel* to them. While doing that, internships need to balance complexity to include both elements that are not too difficult to deal with nor too easy. Most of all, understanding the scope and purpose of internships will allow teens to appreciate them, stick with them, and absorb what they learn. Careful planning and guidance by adult mentors are a big part of this picture.
- Successful internships need to encourage curiosity. Curiosity is raised when teens become focused on gaps in knowledge they want to fill with answers. They need to feel free to ask questions, make suggestions, and work out problems to come up with solutions that might lead to planning an activity that fills a need, having an aha moment about how things might be best done, and getting the satisfaction of offering assistance with new knowledge gained.
- Mentors need to develop an awareness of individual teen strengths and weaknesses to steer internships through a course that allows competence, self-efficacy, and taking risks. Good planning and guidance come into play through all the aspects of promoting interest.[25] In chapters 4 and 5, you will discover many excellent examples of actual internships that have encompassed teen interest.

Exploring Career Clusters through Internships Promotes Interest

Teens who are unsure of what they want to do in the future—most of them—and in what fields they might be interested can find direction by exploring career clusters before embarking on an internship. It is a helpful idea for adults who are creating and conducting internships for and with teens to be familiar with the career clusters, too.

Career clusters give teens an overview of how they might proceed to focus their interests so that an internship will be as rich an experience as possible. The best internships allow teens to have a tailor-made experience that gives them the ability to work within their interests and within the parameters of the internship job description to investigate related issues, areas, and ideas.

The career clusters are updated as needed as work environments evolve. Here is the most recent list of career clusters:

- Agriculture, Foods, and Natural Resources
- Architecture and Construction
- Arts, A/V Technology, and Communications

- Business Management and Administration
- Education and Training
- Finance
- Government and Public Administration
- Health Sciences
- Hospitality and Tourism
- Human Services
- Information Technology
- Law, Public Safety, Corrections, and Security
- Manufacturing
- Marketing, Sales, and Service
- Science, Technology, Engineering, and Math (STEM)
- Transportation, Distribution, and Logistics[26]

Apprenticeships, Cooperative Education, and Diversified Education

Other kinds of teen preparatory employment experiences are apprenticeships, cooperative education (co-ops), and diversified education through high schools. Although this book's scope does not target these particular options, they are associated with and closely related to the overall topic of internships and so are explained. It is good to know they are available for young people and in what circumstances teens might wish to apply for one of them. Under the right conditions, libraries could entertain the idea of incorporating these other kinds of work experiences for young adults, perhaps when partnering with high schools. Some have begun to offer apprenticeships in addition to internships.

Here is some background about apprenticeships for comparison with internships, already defined. Registered Apprenticeships are special kinds of learn-and-earn programs that the Department of Labor officially regulates, and some are specifically for youth. They are usually unaligned with any high school program and are run through employers. Since 1937, these programs have met many of America's skilled workforce needs, providing training for lifelong careers to millions of qualified individuals. Apprenticeships offer structured, on-the-job learning in traditional industries such as construction and manufacturing, plus emerging industries such as health care, information technology, energy, telecommunications, and more. These opportunities connect job seekers looking to learn new skills with employers looking for qualified workers, benefiting both.[27]

There are several differences between internships and apprenticeships. Although the United States Department of Labor does not have official definitions, in general, the differences are the length of time they take place, with internships usually a short term of one to three months, and apprenticeships being longer at one to three years. The other differences may involve how they are structured:

- Apprenticeships include an in-depth training plan, focusing on mastering specific skills an employer needs to fill an occupation within their organization. Internships are not as structured and usually focus on entry-level general work experience.
- Apprentices receive individualized training with an experienced mentor who walks them through their entire process. Internships do not always include mentorship (but will have a supervisor or advisor of some kind).

- Apprenticeships are paid experiences that often lead to full-time employment. Internships are sometimes unpaid and, in most cases, do not lead to a full-time job.
- Apprenticeships can lead to an industry-recognized credential of some sort. Internships typically do not lead to a credential.
- Internship and apprenticeship experiences may be accepted for school credit, and some apprenticeship programs can lead to a college degree.[28]

Co-ops and diversified education are specifically run through high schools and usually vocational and technical high schools. Co-ops integrate classroom-based education with structured, practical, real-life work experience in traditional business and industry. Students earn high school credit while getting on-the-job training in their chosen career field. They learn in school part of the time and work in paid or unpaid positions. Diversified education is similar. It is a high school program through which a student opts for employment in a nontraditional work area while still attending school. A student is paired with an expert in the chosen field, receives both individualized and classroom instruction, and masters essential attitude and habit standards particular to the career field in which they are hired.[29]

Externships, or "Job Shadowing," as "Mini Internships"

Sometimes, teens want to know about a career, but they are not able to get an internship because of their schedules, lack of a local internship for which to apply, or not becoming a successful candidate after interviewing for a competitive internship opportunity. Despite such obstacles, they may still be able to explore a career of interest if businesses and organizations encourage and are open to requests for an externship or "job shadowing." Other situations that would warrant this aspect of career exploration could be a requirement to do a job shadow as a middle school or high school class assignment or accommodating a request from a junior or senior in high school who is wondering about what to pursue as a career and where to apply to college.

Through the years of working with tweens and teens in libraries, I have had many chances to provide these kinds of job shadowing experiences to young adults who requested them. Some simply ended up with a student turning in a career investigation report to a teacher afterward. Others resulted in a teen's decision to apply for a job in our or another library or to study to become a school or public librarian at a university. Still others gained insights into and appreciation for libraries as they navigated higher education and entered adulthood, even if a library career was not their ultimate choice.

Some job shadowing situations are set for a period of time on one day, while for others, teens may return to shadow at additional times and on various occasions. For a job shadow, a teen is paired with a mentor who will answer questions and serve as a guide, and the mentor may coordinate times for the job shadower to meet with others on staff.

Most job shadows permit a teen to listen and observe as an employee or employees go about their day, but sometimes a teen gets a chance to do a simple task or two. During the school year, a job shadow would most likely be scheduled after school, in the evening, or on a weekend if that timing synchronizes with the employee or employees being observed. Occasionally, a student may get permission to miss a day or part of a day of school to go to a scheduled job shadow. In the summer, teens can usually be more flexible with scheduling.

In essence, job shadowing is on-the-job learning without the pressure, commitment, or expectations of an internship. Because teens "shadow" a professional in their intended field of study or one that they want to know more about before deciding, it is a great way to get some in-person, and possibly hands-on, experience in that career. Even if an internship is not available, job shadowing is a worthwhile endeavor to make time away from school in the summer productive. The time spent can be added to teens' college applications, resumes, and future job applications. Doing so shows that a teen took the initiative to explore their interest further, and potential employers and college admissions boards will be impressed with their ambition and resourcefulness.[30]

TEXTBOX 1.2 TIPS FOR TEENS ON JOB SHADOWING

If you encourage job shadowing at your library, if local businesses offer job shadowing opportunities, if you conduct programs focusing on college and career preparation information, or if you post a section about it on your teen web page, you may desire advice to share with teens about job shadowing. Here are some tips you may consider sharing:

Prepare for the job shadowing by:

- Learning about the company or organization ahead of time by reading up on it on their website
- Researching the job title(s) of the person or persons who will be shadowed
- Creating some questions about the job(s), the career field, or advice needed and bringing them along, such as
  - Why did you choose this job?
  - What do you like and dislike about this job?
  - How does a person become successful at this job?
  - What classes are needed for this career field?
  - What skills are helpful to have to do this job well?
- Double-checking in advance on the scheduled time and place for the job shadow.

Prior to and during the job shadow:

- Personally confirm the job shadow's precise location and allow enough time to get there
- Dress appropriately for the workplace that you are visiting
- Turn off all devices such as cell phones and headsets and keep them tucked away
- Show enthusiasm and try to learn as much as possible
- Introduce yourself to various people and ask for follow-up contact information for anyone you would like to contact later for more details
- Be respectful of people's work time

After the job shadow:

- Send thank-you notes to the mentor and anyone else who gave time during the job shadow

- Make notes about the experience to revisit later or use for a school report on the job shadow
- Keep contact information handy with notes for following up when needed down the line[1]

Note

1. Sarikas, Christine. August 9, 2018. "Complete Guide: Job Shadowing for High School Students." PrepScholar, https://blog.prepscholar.com/job-shadowing-for-high-school-students.

Are there benefits of job shadowing when an internship is not an option? There are several. First, teens get a risk-free chance to observe different jobs and to learn about various choices within particular career fields to understand better what entering that career entails. It is much better to check into careers while still in middle or high school than to pursue a career later on and ultimately find out it is not a good fit.

Another good reason to job shadow is that teens can speak with and observe their mentor during the experience. Additionally, most job shadowing also includes meeting and finding out about other people and jobs at the company or organization. Teens have a chance to make connections, ask questions about what is liked and disliked about a job, and get advice about getting into that career field. It also gives teens a chance to know the staff so that later on, if a job or internship opportunity comes along, they will be remembered, especially if they can keep in contact.

A third reason job shadowing is valuable is that it allows a teen to see what it is like to do the work every day, interact with coworkers, have a supervisor, and overall, be part of a particular workforce. These observations will give a job shadower a handle on what to expect when applying for and taking on a job or internship.

Teens interested in setting up a job shadowing experience can ask their school guidance counselor or career counselor for leads. They might also consider contacting a business or agency's human resources department on their own to see if doing a job shadow might be a possibility. If you check into it with your supervisor and human resources specialist and find that your library is willing and able to host a teen who wants to do a job shadow, let the counselors at your local middle and high schools know that you are available to do so.[31]

SIDEBAR 1.2 NEW LIBRARIAN VANTAGE POINT

Realizing that librarianship was not only a career I could work toward but one that required a master's degree changed my life priorities quickly. However, while I was excited by my new goal, I did not want to commit to the financial and emotional toll unless I was sure it was what I wanted. I had to get creative and decided to use the contacts formed during a lifetime of frequenting my local library to request a job shadowing opportunity.

The difference between an internship and a job shadow is the level of commitment and pressure. With an internship, you have to put in a significant amount of time, and you might have external requirements to meet, such as assignments for course credit. On the other hand, job shadows provide you a brief, concise snapshot of the everyday working life of a professional in the field. You will get a firsthand experience of what they do day-to-day. Your conversations will be interrupted by patrons or colleagues as the workday goes on, and it is not going to feel like you had enough time to answer all of your questions, which is okay. That is the best part. You can have a concrete understanding of your true interest in the profession in a single day. Do you leave wanting more, wishing you could come back the next day? Or was it not quite for you? Either way, there is no wrong answer, and nothing is wasted—job shadowing can help young adults make the right decision.[1]

Sierra Pandy
Job shadower at the Poudre River Public Library District in Fort Collins, Colorado, and recent MLS graduate

Note
1. Pandy, Sierra. August 4, 2020. Email message to author.

High Schools and Internships

As with job shadowing, some teen internships are offered independently of school involvement. However, internships can often play an important role in high school career education. In some high schools, internships are a requirement for graduation. In others, they may be an elective. Either way, if your local high school encourages or assigns internships for credit, let the principal or guidance counselor know that you might be willing and interested in taking on a teen library intern.

Often, schools seeking internship opportunities for their students struggle to find good placement matches for them. Because this can be a time-consuming and challenging endeavor, some schools even have internship coordinators on staff. These coordinators connect with businesses, agencies, and organizations in the community to see who might be willing and available to commit to a student internship.

Perhaps such a coordinator, the guidance counselor, or other school faculty member might contact your library and ask if you might consider taking on a teen intern. Usually, if someone does, it is because a teen expressed interest in a library-oriented opportunity. On the other hand, if your local high school already knows up-front that you are available as a mentor for teens curious about a library career, that will most likely save steps and be much valued. Remember, though, before you reach out, you will want to make sure that your supervisors and administrators approve such an offer. You will also want to have a plan in mind for what a teen internship would look like before approaching your superiors with this prospect.

In the former scenario, the person coordinating internships at a local high school might contact you, your library director, or your direct supervisor to place a student at your library. If your administrator receives a request and the proposal is considered, vetted, and approved, you might be asked to take on the assignment. If you understand the concept of and procedures for teen library internships ahead of time, you will be one step ahead of the game and more comfortable accepting the mentorship.

What are good reasons for pursuing and taking on a school-coordinated student internship? There are several:

- Spending time in a professional setting enhances academic learning in a way that no advanced placement course can. Being present and observing in a professional setting is

worthwhile in itself, but interns often take on additional active and valued roles that help them learn and grow.
- An easily overlooked benefit of internships is their boost to school culture. The internship process livens up the school year, especially for seniors. Teachers and coordinators enjoy helping students explore their passions, and the positive attitudes that can result from internships can flow into the whole school.
- Internships can help students developmentally. For example, a student who has trouble focusing might respond well to being responsible for working with young children, or a perfectionist might discover ways to compromise when facing real deadlines.[32]

Future Ready Schools®

In recent years, the concept of "future-ready" schools has taken flight, and it further supports the idea of encouraging teen internships. Through it, educators are encouraged to ensure that students are not learning in a vacuum in the classroom but are putting what they learn into practice to navigate their adult lives successfully. When a school maintains a future-ready philosophy, its educators are encouraged to be innovative and ensure that each student graduates from high school with the agency, passion, and skills to be a productive and responsible citizen. In such a setting, district and school leaders collaborate to advance evidence-based practices and rigorous and engaging student-centered learning environments. Central is the inclusion of vision, attentive teaching, goal setting, human interaction and relationship focus, and technology. Essential to this learning environment is promoting positive experiences outside of the school and through libraries.[33]

One way that educators do this is by integrating the concept of work-based learning. Students can encounter this in a series of interconnected facets. At their most effective, these facets can lead to an internship experience. This explanation will help you to understand how the concept can unfold:

> Work-based learning brings the classroom to the workplace and the workplace to the classroom. This instructional strategy provides students with a well-rounded skill set beyond academics and includes the soft skills needed to succeed in college and the working world. Businesspeople guest speak in classrooms, host college and career skills workshops, and participate in mock interviews. Students can tour worksites, network with, and shadow business professionals. Work-based learning culminates in an internship that allows students to apply their classroom skills and learn more about what it takes to succeed.[34]

Future Ready Schools has a helpful website through which they offer free information for educators, librarians, and anyone else needing to learn more about promoting and instilling youth leadership skills. These resources include a variety of pertinent and supportive webinars.[35]

How the concept of "future-ready" specifically fits into teen *library* internship situations will be illustrated in the next chapters.

Legal Considerations When Hiring Youth

Any time a minor is hired, employers must follow particular rules and policies that vary by the youth's age at the time they are offered employment and from state to state. Before planning an internship, you will need to investigate what guidelines you need to follow. How you will manage the proper protocol should be included in a proposal for approval to submit to your administrators before an internship plan is finalized.

Keep in mind that according to the Fair Labor Standards Act (FLSA), federal law restricts the type of employment minors may perform and the equipment they may use. The regulations regarding minors' employment are specific and fall into two categories. One is a set of restrictions applicable to sixteen- and seventeen-year-olds. There are more explicit limitations for younger workers ages fourteen to fifteen, including hourly restrictions.

Most states have also enacted child labor laws, and these cover work hours for minors. Even though the FLSA does not limit how many days per week minors can work, some states do, and this takes into account different hours for work performed on school days, days preceding school days, and more relaxed hours during the summer unless teens are enrolled in summer school.

Teen interns do not command significant compensation, but you will want to pay them as fairly as you can within funding constraints. At times, according to the FSLA, teens may also legally be paid a subminimum wage of $4.25 per hour during the first ninety consecutive days of employment if they are under the age of twenty. However, some states have enacted higher minimum youth wages. Check the applicable rate in your locality.[36]

You will want to fully understand the particular limits at your library, city, and state before you get the green light to design an internship. You need to consult with your human resources coordinator and legal expert regarding hiring underage teenagers for internships at or through your library. Even if you are hoping to choose a teen who is already eighteen and no longer a minor, you will still need to find out what guidelines to follow for a young adult intern.

The United States Department of Labor has a useful online resource to which you and teens can refer for internship policies and regulations. It is called "Youth Rules!: Preparing the 21st Century Workforce."[37] For easy access to a myriad of pertinent information about legally hiring a teen and working as a teen, check out its numerous useful links that address any concerns an employer or young employee might have regarding youth on the job. A toolkit for youth is provided, plus a special section for employers, parents, and educators. In addition, there is the contact information for the labor department in each state. There is also an app that can be downloaded.

Because, as noted, youth labor requirements differ so much from state to state and from community to community, and because federal laws must also be regarded, this book cannot include all the information you need to know to develop a legal teen internship for your locale. Again, it is highly recommended that you follow the advice given in this section and that you verify how to handle a teen internship with your local legal representative, your human resources advisor, and your own state's set of laws.

An Overview of the Types of Experiential Learning

To sum up this chapter, here is a review of the various kinds of experiential learning formats that can benefit high school age students and older teenagers. Remember, *experiential learning* provides direct experience through which teenagers learn and use skills and reflections to apply the new ideas gained from career exploration and their classroom learning. It includes internships and service learning, regular jobs, and various practicum opportunities.

FIGURE 1.3
Cheyenne Jones enthusiastically describes her accomplishments as a teen intern at the Auburn Public Library in Georgia. Jones was hired by the library through a grant from the Public Library Association. Credit: Zach Miller.

You can decide on the best fit for your local teens and what you can offer by considering the following definitions:

- A *volunteer* is a person who performs a service willingly, without pay or credit, to support a cause.
- *Service-Learning* is curriculum-based, or it satisfies organizational membership requirements for contributing to the community. It emphasizes hands-on learning while addressing real-world concerns.
- *Civic Engagement* offers a broad concept of community involvement and awareness that can include advocacy, service-learning, volunteerism, and political participation to develop community-based knowledge, values, and skills.
- *Capstone/Project-Based Learning* is the culmination of learning in a particular subject area or focus. A student generally works on a single large project for an academic major or as part of a particular schoolwork assignment.
- *Externships or Job Shadows* provide an initial exposure to a career for a brief period, such as one day a week or a couple of hours per week, by having students or others interested in that career observe, follow, or "shadow" an experienced employee or professional. Externships may include academic credit when connected to a course.
- A *Student Employee* is hired to provide services to an organization regularly in exchange for compensation, not academic credit.
- *Internships* are a form of experiential learning that may or may not carry credit for school and can be paid or unpaid. They combine new knowledge of a career with practical ap-

plication and skills development in a professional setting. Internships allow young people to gain valuable applied experience and make connections in professional fields they are considering for career paths while giving employers the opportunity to guide and evaluate aptitudes.[38]

As you have seen in this chapter, there are many experiential learning types. This book focuses on internships, but there are other ways you can approach this topic. You can also adapt the concept of "internships" in several other fashions, depending on your community's needs, what funding you can secure, and what your own library can offer. Keep in mind that the ideas in this book can be adapted to fit any number of the choices you have for offering young people the advantage of career exploration while they are still teenagers and in high school, or even, perhaps, just entering college.

Here is an inspiring vantage point from a dedicated and successful teen internship mentor and supervisor to complete this chapter. It is a perfect segue into the next chapter.

SIDEBAR 1.1 LIBRARIAN VANTAGE POINT

I tell many interns I will never let them fail. I will watch them struggle to find answers and deal with large crowds and demands, but I will never let them fail. Each intern is here to succeed and learn how to become a marketable future employee. We hope that will be in the library field, and it is true of at least one intern, but putting a price on an experience that teaches professionalism when most other students will learn a different skill set in a box store or fast-food restaurant, really gives that student a leg up in the workforce that they have yet to enter.

As a mentor, you will go over things twice. You may go over a concept or a task three times. We librarians have been in the workforce for many years and are used to being professional, having certain standards, and working for long hours at a time. These interns are likely not. Be patient. Be supportive. Be honest with them, and they will be honest for and with you.

I never wait for my interns to ask questions; instead, first, I ask some questions, such as, "Is there anything you need? Does everyone understand the program? How can I or the staff help to support you? Is there a project you think you might want to work on?" I have found that by asking questions, the interns start asking questions. Sometimes this has led to great conversations about how libraries operate, in-depth questions about customer service, or sometimes just a follow-up question that they have about something they are working on but don't feel comfortable asking because they don't want to be embarrassed.

All of this takes a lot of effort, but you get from your interns what you put into challenging them. One day, I was not able to make it to work. I sent my supervisor as well as my interns a video on how to use baking soda and water to make a paste, which was to be used to clean the flat carts in our department as a project. It turns out that the interns loved learning to do something new, and every staff member commented on how clean the carts were (we had been cleaning them for over ten years, but the paste made a huge difference). I later discovered that my supervisor only got the interns the supplies, and the teens took care of everything else.

This program has produced confident self-starters for nearly a decade, and I hope to continue growing it so more students have the opportunity to experience all the large and small things we do to keep libraries going. Who knows, we may even produce a few librarians and possibly even a few folks who will be our next library leaders.[1]

Patricia VanArsdale
Hussey-Mayfield Memorial Public Library
Zionsville, Indiana

Note
1. VanArsdale, Patricia. February 21, 2020. Email message to author.

Notes

1. Kyler, Nina J. [n.d.] *Internship Guide: A Resource Toolkit*. Regional Office of Education # 17, De-Witt, Livingston, Logan, McLean Counties of Illinois. Contact https://roe17.org/contact-us or Regional Office of Education #17, 201 E. Grove Street, Suite 300, Bloomington, IL 61701, to obtain a copy.
2. Kyler, *Internship Guide*.
3. Office of Career and Technical Education. [n.d.]. "Youth Internship Program Framework." South Dakota Department of Education, https://doe.sd.gov/cte/documents/YI_Manual.pdf.
4. Mendieta, Erick. January 19, 2018. "The Benefits of Internships: A High School Student's Perspective." Yoh Blog, https://www.yoh.com/blog/the-benefits-of-internships-a-high-school-students-perspective.
5. Vets Guide. [n.d.]. "High School Students Can Benefit from Internships." VetsGuide, http://www.vetsguide.com/high_school_students_can_benefit_from_internships_40017097.html.
6. Rebora, Anthony. May 2019. "Honoring the Teen Brain: A Conversation with Thomas Armstrong." *Educational Leadership*, p. 26.
7. Rebora, "Honoring the Teen Brain," pp. 24–27.
8. Cook, Priya. June 2019. "Growing Urban Conservationists." *Parks & Recreation*, p. 39.
9. The Studio Museum of Harlem, https://studiomuseum.org/.
10. Wave Hill, https://www.wavehill.org/.
11. "Teen Night (Ages 13–18)." 2020. Metropolitan Museum of Art, https://www.metmuseum.org/events/programs/met-celebrates/teen-night.
12. Matthews, Nadine. June 7, 2018. "NYC Teens Take Over the Metropolitan Museum of Art." *New York Amsterdam News*, http://amsterdamnews.com/news/2018/jun/07/nyc-teens-take-over-metropolitan-museum-art/.
13. Kardys, Jack. June 2019. "Park Afterschool Programs: A Vital Community Resource." *Parks & Recreation*, p. 8.
14. Simonton, Stell. December 3, 2020. "Integrate SEL by Focusing on Strong Relationships in Diverse Environment, Report Says." Youth Today, https://youthtoday.org/2020/12/integrate-sel-by-focusing-on-strong-relationships-in-diverse-environment-report-says/.
15. Carroll, Kathleen. August 26, 2019. "Teenage Brains Are Elastic: That's a Big Opportunity for Social-Emotional Learning." EdSurge, https://www.edsurge.com/news/2019-08-26-teenage-brains-are-elastic-that-s-a-big-opportunity-for-social-emotional-learning.
16. Clark, Alexis. 2020. "Social-Emotional Learning: What You Need to Know." Understood, https://www.understood.org/en/learning-thinking-differences/treatments-approaches/educational-strategies/social-emotional-learning-what-you-need-to-know.
17. Robert Wood Johnson Foundation. July 16, 2015. "How Children's Social Competence Impacts Their Well-Being in Adulthood." In *Social and Emotional Learning: A RWJF Collection*. Robert Wood Johnson Foundation, https://www.rwjf.org/en/library/research/2015/07/how-children-s-social-competence-impacts-their-well-being-in-adu.html.
18. "What Is Connected Learning?" [n.d.]. Connected Learning Alliance, https://clalliance.org/about-connected-learning/.
19. Connected Learning Research Network, https://clrn.dmlhub.net/.
20. "Inclusive Internship Initiative." 2020. Public Library Association, http://www.ala.org/pla/initiatives/plinterns/guidelines.
21. Kyler, *Internship Guide*.
22. "What Is Connected Learning?"
23. Murphy Paul, Annie. November 4, 2013. "How the Power of Interest Drives Learning." KQED, https://www.kqed.org/mindshift/32503/how-the-power-of-interest-drives-learning.
24. Murphy Paul, "How the Power of Interest Drives Learning."
25. Murphy Paul, "How the Power of Interest Drives Learning."

26. Torpey, Elka. March 2015. "Clusters, Pathways, and BLS: Connecting Career Information." U.S. Bureau of Labor Statistics, https://www.bls.gov/careeroutlook/2015/article/career-clusters.htm.

27. *Connecting Youth & Business: A Toolkit for Employers*. 2014. Opportunity Nation, https://opportunitynation.org/wp-content/uploads/2014/06/ON_Youth_Business_Toolkit.pdf, p. 138.

28. Apprenticeship.gov. [n.d.] "What Is the Difference between an Apprenticeship and an Internship?" United States Department of Labor, https://www.apprenticeship.gov/faq/what-difference-between-apprenticeship-and-internship.

29. "Co-op Program." [n.d.]. Mercy Career and Technical High School, https://www.mercycte.org/cte-programs/co-op-program.

30. Moon, Kristen. April 10, 2019. "Why Job Shadowing Is Secretly the Smartest Way to Spend Your Summer." NICHE, https://www.niche.com/blog/why-job-shadowing-is-worth-your-time/.

31. Sarikas, Christine. August 9, 2018. PrepScholar, https://blog.prepscholar.com/job-shadowing-for-high-school-students.

32. Levine, Eliot. 2010. "The Rigors and Rewards of Internships." *Educational Leadership*, pp. 46–48.

33. Future Ready Schools, https://futureready.org/.

34. Handugan, DeAira. 2019. "*Understanding Skills Training and Development: A Program Evaluation of Nontraditional High School Internships*" Thesis, Concordia University, St. Paul. Retrieved from https://digitalcommons.csp.edu/cup_commons_grad_edd/350.

35. Future Ready Schools.

36. Gere, Anne-lise. May 15, 2017. "Summer Work and Internships for Minors—Tips for Success." GERE Consulting Associates, https://gereconsulting.com/summer-work/.

37. "Young Workers." [n.d.]. United States Department of Labor, https://www.dol.gov/agencies/whd/youthrules/young-workers.

38. Bridge. [n.d.] "Employer Guide to Structuring a Successful Internship Program." Bryant University, https://career.bryant.edu/resources/files/RI%20Employer%20Guide%20Good%20Internships%20are%20Good%20Business2%20(3).pdf.

2
Why Have Teen Library Internship Opportunities?

For many decades, libraries dedicated to youth services have provided valuable volunteer library experiences for young adults and have encouraged active and involved teen library participation. These kinds of experiences have been the foundation for many young people to go on to productive careers in many areas, including in schools and public libraries. Additionally, these participatory opportunities have created lifelong readers and library users and supporters who often steer their children to reading and library use in like manner.

Throughout those decades of getting teens involved in their libraries, there have been many essential developments that channeled this meaningful element's progress. Teens have had such opportunities as volunteering, promoting books and reading to their peers, serving on teen councils and library advisory boards, and taking on leadership roles such as planning and running programs or tutoring, serving in focus groups, building material collections, and creating displays.

In the last number of years, library internships for teenagers have become a positive new trend added to the mix of participatory involvement experiences that libraries can offer. Additionally, other kinds of opportunities provide a taste of what a library job entails, such as shadowing and getting paid to do individual programs on topics on which teens may be experts.

Providing Settings for Positive Youth Development

As discussed in the last chapter, any learning environment for young people needs to center attention on connected and social-emotional learning to positively hardwire the teen brain. Libraries are indispensable in promoting these concepts when they encourage positive youth development. This focus is so imperative that the Young Adult Library Services Association of the American Library Association has specifically addressed these elements in its training tools' goals and outcomes and to which youth librarians and other library staff working with teenagers can aspire. Encouraging, developing, and providing all kinds of internships for teens in communities, including libraries, can become a valuable catalyst for fostering these concepts.

How specifically do these competencies apply to providing teen library internships? Here are ten ways that astute librarians who work with teenagers in school and public libraries can satisfy these competencies:

- Build knowledge of teen growth and development to create and run teen library internship programs to meet teens' needs as they gain hard and soft skills that will take them successfully into their job and career futures.
- Recognize the importance of relationships and communication with teens as internship supervisors and mentors, who support teens individually and in groups to expand self-concept, identity, coping mechanisms, and positive interactions with peers and adults.
- Provide high-quality, developmentally appropriate, flexible internship environments that allow teens to have learning and growth experiences on the job, whether formally or informally.
- Partner with others from the library and possibly with compatible agencies in the community to plan, implement, and evaluate beneficial and meaningful internship opportunities, whether formally or informally.
- Encourage youth engagement and leadership by designing internships that offer appealing and significant library employment opportunities with teen input and feedback as essential elements.
- Build respectful and mutual relationships with appropriate community organizations, library customers, and families to promote optimal growth and development for teens as they enhance library services quality through their teen internship experiences.
- Actively advance cultural competency and responsiveness by creating inclusive, welcoming, and respectful internship experiences in a library or partnership setting that embrace diversity.
- Teach teens how to ensure access to a wide variety of library resources, services, and programs for and with fellow teens and others, especially those facing challenges to access, by creating a thoughtful and supportive internship opportunity.
- Help teens discover their internship work's impact and gauge their personal growth and development through an internship plan that includes data, various forms of feedback and evaluation, and continuous improvement.
- Through careful discussion and positive, ethical examples, ensure that teen interns have a chance to develop enlightening knowledge and useful experience on the job by carefully preparing, informing, and communicating with them during internship supervision and mentoring.[1]

As you have seen and will see in this book's examples of libraries (and other agencies) that are already doing or have done successful teen internships, the supervisors and mentors who are illustrated demonstrate most, if not all, of these qualities and competencies as part of their provision of teen internships. It is especially important that they all encourage teen intern ideas, advice, and responses that become intricate parts of the internship program processes, from well-thought-out interview systems through final evaluations through improving further internship experiences in the future. By making teen library internships available, librarians aiming to master these competencies can put them into play while improving their abilities in working with teens. The helpful and inspiring examples given in this book can help you follow suit.

Teen Library Internships Can Cultivate Partnerships

Some teen library internships occur with a school, university, special, or public library as the experience's singular provider. Yes, outside funding may be and often is involved, but even with the support of an external funding source, the library or library system itself sets the internships in motion and is responsible for seeing the entire internship process through.

On the other hand, in some circumstances, a teen library internship may take place as a partnership between a neighboring organization, community government, a school district, or a local business. Throughout this chapter and in chapters 4 and 5, you will find out about several ways that libraries can partner to host teen library internships and ultimately help teens constructively discover the world of work. Together, the partners can build the positive skills, confidence levels, and workforce preparation knowledge bases that are crucial for teens as they move into adulthood and the adult job market. It is a win-win prospect for the teens who are aided in building and preparing for their futures and the adults who want to welcome them into their career fields in the upcoming years.

There are many avenues for seeking teen internship partners. As mentioned in chapter 1, one of the most prominent leads for this kind of relationship is local schools or school districts. If this prospect is appealing to you, check with guidance or career counselors at schools in your community to see if they include an option for students to do internships outside of school. You might be surprised to find that they are anxious to include your library in the list of internship choices they offer from which teens can choose.

You might consider brainstorming with other youth library staff members to gather suggestions for potential community collaborators for teen internship outreach opportunities or cooperative efforts. These might include neighboring businesses, nonprofits, or service organizations. Another way you might partner is right within your own library. Plan work schedules and experiences with other departments or library branches to give teens a broad scope of exposure during the time they spend with you.

Promoting Library Careers

One of the many worthwhile reasons for offering teen library internships is to give interested teens the chance to learn about libraries and potential library careers, up close and personal. Even teens who are active in their libraries as regular visitors or volunteers are usually not provided with an in-depth opportunity to find out what paid library work entails. Teen interns are typically a true part of the library staff for the periods they are hired, and through that time spent helping to run their libraries, they discover whether they are drawn to further exploration of the library world. Even if teens decide in the long run not to aim for an actual library career, they still frequently develop an understanding of what libraries are all about, learn how to use them more effectively, share what they know with others, and advocate for them.

Although teens do go on to careers in other areas at times, some teen internships work out so well for both the teenagers and the libraries that the libraries end up hiring the teens as regular employees. This has happened in several libraries and can set teens on an employment path they might not have considered before. As a matter of fact, in 2018, this is exactly what occurred with a teen intern from the Auburn Public Library in Georgia, where she is now a regular staff member. Likewise, in 2019, after teen internships concluded at the Baltimore County Library in Maryland and the Alameda County Library in California, the same scenarios also came about. You will read more about these three internships in chapter 4, but for now, know that internships do often succeed in leading fresh new faces to the library field.

TEXTBOX 2.1 TEEN VANTAGE POINT

When I was first hired as an intern at the Owings Mills Branch of the Baltimore County Public Library, I was ecstatic. My excitement never died down throughout the entire internship experience. I was given the chance to travel, meet like-minded individuals, create a project based on the community's needs, and was even able to see the impact of that project directly.

During my time at the library as an intern, I was given the opportunity to explore every aspect of how the library functions. My duties ranged from shelving and checking in books to helping in the bookmobile, and I discovered my eagerness for serving the community. After the internship ended, I was hired as a permanent staff member when a position was available.

To say that working at the library makes me happy would be an understatement. As a teenager, feeling welcomed in a space and having the ability to make positive change to help those in need gives me a sense of purpose. I feel that sense of purpose every day in my workplace, knowing that even the smallest tasks carried out could improve a person's view of the library.[1]

Sade Wilkins El
Baltimore County Public Library, Maryland

Note

1. Wilkens El, Sade. August 25, 2020. Email message to author from Anna White.

Here is another superb example of a teen intern moving forward to a permanent regular library position at Hillsborough County in Florida. As a partnership with Hillsborough County Schools, the county's Redefining Internships for Student Empowerment (RISE) program gives local students entering their senior year in high school a chance to gain workforce skills by being placed in two-month-long jobs with various county departments of their personal choice. The teens get essential professional development instruction in writing resumes, job interviewing, networking, and other fundamental employment and employment-seeking elements through weekly coursework. RISE interns also expand their government career exploration by getting firsthand looks at other county operations outside of their assigned departments during weekly field trips. As they spent time learning and on the job, each intern earned $10.50 per hour.[2] As of this writing, forty students have completed the RISE program in Hillsborough County. The county had previously offered some internships, but the RISE program heightens its reach.

In the summer of 2019, because RISE department matches are tailored to each intern's interests and skills, library fan Victoria Tims was happy to be placed at the rebuilt C. Blythe Andrews, Jr., Public Library, where she spent a great deal of time throughout her childhood.

FIGURE 2.1
Sade Wilkens El shares her thoughts at the Public Library Association's Inclusive Internship Initiative wrap-up meeting in 2019. Wilkens El was hired for a permanent position after her internship. Credit: Zach Miller.

After Tims received her diploma at Middleton High School in the spring of 2020, she became the first RISE graduate hired by the county. In August 2020, at age seventeen, she became a full-time library associate at the Seminole Heights Branch Library of the Hillsborough County Public Library Cooperative, where she does many of the familiar tasks to which she was assigned as an intern.

During her RISE internship, Tims's supervisor, Raishara Bailey, noted that Tims was a great employee who carefully followed directions and was eager to discover how the library operates. She is glad that Tims is now a regular fellow employee at the library system, even if she works at a different location.

Tims was glad to have completed her internship in 2019 since the 2020 RISE internships were canceled due to the coronavirus. However, the county plans ahead and intends to recruit RISE teen interns once again for the 2021 summer season.[3]

From these illustrations, remember that one of the most fulfilling parts of a library career is introducing others to it, especially young people who have yet to settle where their lives will lead them. Often, teens overlook a library career as a possibility, and when they do, they are usually unaware of the many options they have within its parameters. Having teen library interns develops overall work skills and ethics. It allows librarians to contribute to libraries' future workforce. There are few things as rewarding as seeing a protégé happily enter a field of which you are extremely proud and want to promote to those with interests and abilities that can help make it prosper.

TEXTBOX 2.2 TEEN VANTAGE POINT

The biggest impact this internship had on me is the benefits from stepping out of my comfort zone. I am an introvert, and for the longest time, I struggled with getting out of my comfort zone. Through this internship, I was free to create a program I wished to see and view the world in a different light. In learning all that goes into planning, preparing, advertising, and presenting an event, I was able to practice being a leader in a public setting. Throughout the challenges, I did not stay stuck in my shell. Instead, I learned to be flexible, adapt, and have a backup plan. Most importantly, I was shown the behind-the-scenes of how a library worked and realized that this is what I want to do in the future.

Yasmeen Chavez
Alameda County Library, California

Note

1. Chavez, Yasmeen. August 21, 2020. Email message to author.

FIGURE 2.2
At the September PLA wrap-up event in Washington, D.C., for the 2019 Inclusive Internship Initiative, Yasmeen Chavez from the Alameda County Library is shown speaking about her internship project. She was hired as a permanent library employee following the internship. Credit: Zach Miller.

TEXTBOX 2.3 LIBRARIAN VANTAGE POINT

One intern returned for several years. I learned that she was president of her school Anime and Manga club and that she was very knowledgeable about authors, artists, and titles that were being translated or adapted for an English-speaking audience. This intern spent many shifts evaluating the current manga collection. Items that she reviewed included the titles, authors, and artists of the manga; the total number of items in a series; the number of items held by our library; and the current status of particular manga. For the latter, she determined if titles were still being released or if the author/illustrator had gone on an extended hiatus. This intern created a similar list for anime by consulting a number of anime award lists and researching the availability of these titles.

She is currently in college and plans to pursue a master's in library science, which she recently told me was likely due to her many years of volunteering. While I cannot argue this point, I do believe this decision was made in part to the education and inside look at library operations she received, even if it was in a single department.[1]

Patricia VanArsdale
Hussey-Mayfield Memorial Public Library, Zionsville, Indiana

Note

1. VanArsdale, Patricia. September 29, 2020. Email message to author.

Library Internships Help Teens to Develop Soft Skills

Besides allowing teens to gain work experience in a library area that attracts them, a good internship experience also gives teens a way to develop essential "soft skills" that will be needed in their future employment and relationships. Research shows that a well-planned internship will enable teens to build initiative, teamwork, analytical skills, and various communication skills by its conclusion.[4]

As Linda W. Braun, a library consultant and past Young Adult Library Services Association president, says, "For teens to be truly job-ready, libraries should provide services that support the traits and soft skills valued in the workplace, in addition to technical knowledge and proficiencies." She explains that although technical abilities such as creating resumes, exploring career options, and learning to connect with potential employees are important, they do not mean that a teen is *job-ready*. Being job-ready means that not only do teens possess technical know-how like these elements and more, but they learn to develop the soft skills of professional and cooperative behavior, good communication, resolve, and autonomy.[5]

For example, at the Providence Public Library in Rhode Island, they have a teen leadership program called Teen Squad. Teen Squad provides recurring classes that target work-readiness, contemporary skill development, and interest exploration for teenagers. As a competency-based program, teens partner one-on-one with teen services library staff to identify learning goals, design learning plans, and encourage teens to develop responsibility.[6]

Under the auspices of the Teen Squad leadership opportunities, the library supports a summer learning internship called My City, My Place that integrates history, technology, and career skills development for the hospitality and tourism industry. As one participating intern stated, "Providence Public Library and the My City, My Place program taught me a lot of valuable skills and really helped me to discover that public speaking is something I am good at."[7]

For these internships, forty teenagers are hired for the summer to research their city's history and tourism highlights. As part of their internship assignments and by engaging in teamwork, they learn to use audiovisual mediums to promote information and marketing plans relating to these topics. As they go, the interns receive mentoring, coaching, and feedback from both library staff and local communications professionals. Their internships culminate in promotional presentations for a panel of experts representing local tourism agencies, the area newspaper, and the library's marketing department.

Notice that these teen interns had not been working in the library itself but *through* the library's teen services section in partnership with other significant community businesses and organizations. It is a fine choice for library teen internships to function in this manner and the alternative of having teens working as part of a library staff itself. Variances are all acceptable when a library supports and runs teen internship programs, if those teens hired are learning the key elements of reporting to work regularly and on time and practicing other professional behaviors that allow them to develop the valuable soft skills that they need.[8]

Job Fairs, Website Links, and Career Planning Workshops

Another way that libraries can encourage career exploration and foster teen internships, apprenticeships, and other hiring opportunities is by holding job fairs and career workshops at the library, participating in occupational fairs being held at and with local middle and high schools, and providing links to potential employment prospects through the teen library web pages on library websites. Find out if you can add such a section to your library's teen page; if your local schools would like to include library staff representatives at their career and vocational fairs; and if there is local internship and job information that teens can access through a list you post with recent openings and details.

Here are some instances of libraries that have been doing job and career outreach to teens, offering valuable information that teens need for occupational exploration and experiences:

- The District of Columbia (D.C.) Library website has been a superb example of how webpage advertising functions. They have provided a teen page called Opportunities for Teens, which has listed several ways young adults can actively participate as volunteers in the library and ways they can find paid work options. Teen volunteers have earned school community service credits while Teen Council applicants have been hired for hourly pay. The website has also promoted the annual Mayor Marion S. Barry's Summer Youth Employment Program, which includes library work.[9]
- The Mix at San Francisco Public Library has offered a page with opportunities for teenagers. It has featured both volunteer jobs and internships at the library and in the Bay Area, including through San Francisco YouthWorks, which has provided paid internships in city government offices, libraries, recreation facilities, and the Mayor's Youth Employment Education Program.[10]
- The Baltimore County Public Library partnered with Junior Achievement's Inspire Career Fair, which took place for over three days and hosted more than three thousand eighth graders from Baltimore County schools. During the fair, library staff used virtual demonstrations to enthusiastically show what it is like to work in today's libraries,

whether using 3D printing, recommending books, or practicing additional methods. The young teens could peruse the Career Fair; ask questions about skills, education requirements, and various career particulars; and connect with library staff members and other area professionals.[11]

- The New Orleans Public Library planned a Summer Internship and Job Fair in March to help teens find employment over the summer. To prepare for it, they publicized requests to local businesses to let them know about any jobs or internship opportunities they would be offering and encourage them to participate in the fair.[12]
- At the Oakland Public Library, they offer a Youth (ages twelve to twenty-five) Job and Paid Internship Fair early in the year. The Fair gives young adults a chance to meet potential employers, connect with youth agencies that offer paid internships, and have a consultation to perfect their resumes. They also provide a link to the library's Oakland Has Jobs page on Instagram.[13]
- As a partnership between its Youth Commission and the Memorial Library, the Village of Arlington Heights in Illinois held a job fair at the library for high schoolers in February 2020. During the fair, local businesses offered teens jobs with flexible hours, and area organizations promoted their volunteer, internship, and other opportunities. Before the job fair took place, the library held a preparatory program to learn about and practice good interviewing skills.[14]

The pandemic has recently prohibited holding many of the job fairs and other activities like those presented here (see chapter 7). Consider providing similar resources like these online at your library to support the cause of promoting prospects for teen career exploration when conditions are not safe. Later on, you might be able to alter these events to in-person formats.

Even if you cannot fund and support a teen library internship right away, you may be able to start small endorsing the idea by holding events with the businesses, agencies, and organizations in your community. Try planning a teen career workshop or program. You could also use a job fair to publicize any teen volunteer opportunities you might have already established at your library. But how do you do these things successfully? These tips are a good start:

- Enlist interested teens, perhaps from a library teen council or advisory group, to help plan the program, select the professional speakers for it, and market it to fellow teens. When teens buy in and partake in program design and publicity, you see better results.
- Most professionals from a community will not charge a fee to participate in these kinds of events. Usually, they feel like they are giving back to the community and fostering interest in their career fields by taking part.
- Career counselors recommend that teens have a chance to interview professionals informally in occupational areas to which they are drawn at such events. Encourage the professionals who agree to participate in your workshop, program, or job fair to interact with the teens in addition to giving a talk about their job. This might lead curious teens and willing professionals to partner for some job shadowing or maybe even an internship.
- Be sure to have a list of the career clusters available and related information that teens can peruse, even if there is one or a limited number of professionals represented. There might be some career fields that teen attendees never knew about or considered. If teens ask questions and want more details about a particular area not represented at the event, find appropriate follow-up information for them. Also, let teens know about books and online resources that they can follow up with on their own to learn more about educational requirements, job seeking, interviewing, starting a new job, and more.

- Vet the prospective professional speakers ahead of the event to ensure they are good communicators who are knowledgeable, appealing, and adaptable.
- Ask presenters to bring hands-on examples from their work to show and explain, and then schedule a question and answer time. This will help teens feel more involved and engaged, give them an insider's view into the requirements and options for a particular career, and make the program seem more of an interactive event than a lecture.
- Have snacks and drinks on hand. Both teens and adult speakers will appreciate this touch.
- Take photos, and let the professionals know how they can access them. Remember to check your library's photography policy before proceeding.
- Be sure to publicize your event well. Ask teachers and guidance counselors to promote the program in their school and to parents. Let local youth-serving organizations, agencies, and businesses know what the library is doing and see if they will let their clients know. You might even encourage a school field trip to the library for the event if the scheduling can be coordinated. Recruit teens who frequent your library and those involved in your library teen council, if you have one, or a similar group, to assist in creating the publicity and advertising the event to their peers.[15]

To Pay or Not to Pay, That Is the Question

There are many kinds of library and other internships for teenagers, and compensation varies depending on the program's purpose and what financial backing is available. Most teen internships provide a salary or a stipend, which gives hired teens a chance to earn a paycheck. For some, this might be the first time they are paid for work. Some internships offer gift cards or other compensation rather than a paycheck. Some internships may be unpaid, but the teens earn school credit or service-learning hours.

If you decide upon an unpaid teen internship, whether because of library policy, lack of funding, or other reasons, be mindful of the criteria of the United States Department of Labor Wage and Hour Division for unpaid internships:

- Even though it includes the employer's facilities' actual operation, the internship is like training given in an educational environment.
- The internship experience is for the benefit of the intern.
- The intern does not displace regular employees but works under the close supervision of existing staff.
- The employer that provides the training derives no immediate advantage from the intern's activities; on occasion, its operations may be impeded.
- The intern is not necessarily entitled to a job at the conclusion of the internship.
- The employer and the intern understand that the intern is not entitled to wages for the internship.[16]

Another kind of teen work opportunity in or through libraries could be apprenticeships, mentioned in chapter 1. These jobs are typically done for pay, whether by a stipend or through an hourly wage, and they are usually arranged to take place during an extended period. Although a few have tested the waters, libraries have not traditionally offered apprenticeships to high school students. This might be the next frontier of teen involvement in libraries, however, and if you think it could be a good fit for your library, try arranging an apprenticeship by coordinating with your local high school career or guidance counselor. This would be an excellent place to start exploring the idea.

Returning to internships, teens can earn money from library internships depending upon funding sources. When you create your teen library internships proposal and intend to offer monetary or other compensation, it is important to investigate potential financial support and to have a plan ready to pay for teen employment. This plan would be included in the approval request and presentation for your administrators and others who might need to sign off on the idea.

SIDEBAR 2.1 TEEN VANTAGE POINT

I've been volunteering at the library going on four years. Two of those years have been as a summer intern. The internship process allowed me to grow in skill sets I didn't know I needed in a library setting, such as thinking on my feet when problems arose, developing technical skills (for example, through the internship, I was able to make a tutorial library walk-through pamphlet for the Inspire Database), and learning how to communicate with the public.

I am very grateful to the library and its workers for giving me the opportunity to work with them and giving me a whole new skill set. I have learned leadership, accountability, and work ethics as well, which have helped me in all other aspects of my life. It is my hope that, through the internship positions offered in the future, others can benefit as much as I did.

Bethany Worrell
Hussey-Mayfield Memorial Public Library, Zionsville, Indiana

Note
1. Worrell, Bethany. July 3, 2020. Email message to author.

For libraries that have provided payment for teens, compensation can have a wide range of formats, amounts, and funding sources. Here are some teen internship examples from recent years demonstrating what teens might be offered in compensation:

- For the Teens in Public Service internships in King County, Washington, a program that has been active since 1997, teens were hired by nonprofits at the minimum wage of $15.75 per hour in 2020. Funding is through donations.[17]
- At the Boulder Public Library in Colorado, teens have interned in the BLDG 61 makerspace. They become expert at the technology and machinery that help them create unique projects to benefit others. Those who are hired have earned gift cards for their work.[18] Find out more about these internships in chapter 4.
- In Texas, the Austin Public Library has, in previous years, offered teen summer internships, called Teen Mentors, through which teens created teen-led programs based on their interests and expertise and for which they were paid $8 per hour for twenty to thirty hours per week. The library has also offered $100 stipends to teenagers who serve as Teen Experts and who planned and ran individual programs and events for their peers.[19]
- The San Francisco Public Library has an inviting space for teens and a digital media lab called The Mix, which began with a planning grant from the Institute of Museum and Library Services and the MacArthur Foundation and is supported by the Friends of the San Francisco Public Library. A ten-week program called The Mix CORE has been offered to successful applicants ages thirteen to eighteen, for which they have earned a stipend.

The work program has provided job experiences to learn teamwork, find out more about libraries, and promote The Mix to teens around the Bay Area.[20]

- At the Adler Planetarium in Chicago, they have offered summer teen internship programs through which teens have taken on professional museum roles, including learning about and leading STEAM (science, technology, engineering, arts, and math) programs. Through the twenty-five-hours-per-week internships, which have run from June to August, teens have earned $14 per hour.[21]
- Students at Wakefield High School in Raleigh, North Carolina, have planned internships based on their own interests. Teens have often found their internship placement and sponsor independently, which could be at a library, or they have been able to get assistance from their school's career development coordinator. Once they had obtained a placement, students spent 135 hours at their internship, completed weekly journals, submitted time cards, and turned in final projects to earn high school credit instead of taking a class.[22]
- The Chicago Public Library has participated in a foundation- and donation-supported citywide employment program, After School Matters (ASM). Teenagers were able to enter pre-apprenticeships, apprenticeships, advanced apprenticeships (they must be at least fourteen and they earn stipends); assistantships (in 2020, earnings were set at $8.50 per hour and hires had to be at least sixteen); and internships (in 2020, teens would have earned $10.50 per hour, they had to be sixteen to eighteen years old, and they must have participated in three previous ASM programs). Teens have been hired in programs that focus on arts, communications, leadership, sports, and STEM (science, technology, engineering, and math).[23] Find out more about these Chicago internships in chapter 5.

As you can see, there are many options for internships that might be created and how to reward the hired teens, depending on funding and purpose. Internships can be designed and developed with many different plans, goals, and methods of compensating teen workers in mind.

Funding Teen Library Internships

There are many ways that libraries can fund teen library internships. Even unpaid internships often need monetary support. These are the primary ways that you might secure funding:

- Through grants given by state and national library associations and their partnerships
- Through grants provided by foundations, businesses, and agencies that want to boost the use of libraries and foster literacy among young people
- Through grants and awards given by local service organizations
- Through fundraising via Friends of the Library groups or other library fundraising endeavors
- Through regular youth services or teen services library budget allocations
- Through a combination of these funding sources

Before seeking funding, have a plan for the amount you will need and for what it will be used. You will need to find out your own library's policies and procedures for attaining funding from inside and outside sources. Consult with your supervisors and administrators to ensure you are on the right track. You might want to present several options to them from which you and they can choose. The next few sections describe some specific ways to apply for funding.

The Public Library Association's Inclusive Internship Initiatives

In 2017, the Public Library Association's (PLA) Inclusive Internship Initiative (III) was piloted to increase diversity in public librarianship. In 2018, the initiative provided funding to fifty libraries in thirty-five states for mentored internships awarded to high school juniors and seniors from diverse backgrounds. The internship award program was repeated in 2019 for libraries throughout the country. Grants coordinated by the Institute of Museum and Library Services were allocated from preprofessional Laura Bush Twenty-First-Century Library Program Grants,[24] which supported the PLA's initiatives. These internship opportunities are prime examples of what teen library internships should be and can be about.

Through the internships, the teens selected to participate gained exposure to and experience with various library facets, from administration to programming to user services. Before the internships were underway, all the lucky teenagers who received internship awards and their mentors attended a June kickoff event in a major United States city and a wrap-up event in a different major city in September. Travel costs to both events were paid for separately from the funding provided for internship stipends.

FIGURE 2.3
Aaron Vivanco speaks about his teen internship experience at the Laredo Public Libraries in Texas during the PLA Inclusive Internship Initiative wrap-up event in the fall of 2019. Credit: Zach Miller.

Requirements for mentors are as sensible and meaningful for the adults as the teen requirements are for the teens. Libraries applying must:

- Assign a staff person to serve as a mentor
- Identify appropriate teens
- Develop a connected learning project in conjunction with the intern
- Provide five hours or more per week of one-on-one intern mentoring and coaching
- Attend the spring and fall kickoff and wrap-up events for mentors and interns
- Share the successes, challenges, and opportunities across the III cohort, within the library, and to community stakeholders
- Comply with applicable nondiscrimination laws, including but not limited to those in the Assurances and Certifications, throughout the grant award and the intern application and selection process[25]

Although the 2020 internships were not able to take place due to the worldwide health emergency, early in the year, PLA anticipated that the internships would still be taking place and held a free, beneficial preparatory "office hours"-type of webinar in January. During the webinar, past librarian mentors who worked with previously hired teens through the initiative shared details about participating in the program and answered questions. PLA staff reviewed the application process, deadlines, program requirements, and answered questions.[26]

TEXTBOX 2.4 THE INCLUSIVE INTERNSHIP INITIATIVES

As noted, the Inclusive Internship Initiative (III) is a PLA Program, supported by a grant from the Institute of Museum and Library Services (IMLS) and the Laura Bush Twenty-First-Century Library Program. It has been funded from 2017–2021. The internships are widely varied and extremely meaningful and interesting. You will read about several in the two upcoming chapters. Here is a reflection on the internship programs and their reach from PLA:

Consider that public librarianship is an overwhelmingly white, female field, which is not reflective of the diversity of the communities served by libraries everywhere. The III is designed to introduce high school juniors, seniors, and incoming first-year college students from an extensive array of backgrounds to potential careers in librarianship.

PLA has required an application process each year for the libraries interested in being considered for internship support. Any public library in the United States has been eligible to apply. The brief application has asked questions surrounding community profile, library efforts to support inclusivity, and mentor availability. An effort has been made to build a diverse library cohort, with representatives from different library sizes and geographies. Rural and tribal/pueblo libraries were particularly encouraged to apply. To date, 152 interns from 117 libraries across forty-two states have participated.

The selected libraries were responsible for choosing their interns. PLA encouraged a broad approach to "diversity," asking libraries to think about which community groups were not well represented in their library. Year by year, this led to a genuinely multifaceted representation of cohorts extending beyond racial markers. III has welcomed interns who are neurodiverse, transgender, housing insecure, DACA status, and directly touched by the justice system, to name just a few real-life intern backgrounds and experiences.

Mentors could be from any library department, not just from teen services. The mentors tended to trend more diverse than the profession at large and provided valuable leadership and supervisory opportunities. PLA provided training to selected mentors on recruiting for diversity.

Each participating library received a stipend of $3,500 for the summer. The bulk of this money was to spend on internship salaries. PLA strongly believes that interns should be compensated for their work. Unpaid internships exclude potential participants, which is especially damning when focusing on building more inclusive spaces. Paying an intern also signifies their work matters and that this experience is to be treated as a job. Funds were not allowed to support mentor time.

Each internship year, the full group of interns gathered in June, at the start of the internship, for a kickoff event. The kickoff was rooted in conversations about identity, inclusion, and equity and gave space for complex conversations that were key to understanding the program's overall purpose.

Over two kickoff days, the group received brief master class presentations from select mentor volunteers. These presentations introduced interns to a range of library services beyond traditional reading, such as ones covering topics like "PRM Clothing Exchange," "Makerspaces," "STEM Engagement," "Outreach to Immigrants and Refugees," and "Teen Mental Health." The kickoff provided valuable networking and real-life understanding for the interns, many of whom had not traveled before or met people from different parts of the country. Mentors also formed practitioner networks that have lasted beyond their internship hosted summers.

Interns and mentors were tasked with designing a community-oriented project to examine and document their own communities' stories over the summer. The master classes' purpose was to get creative juices flowing as mentor-intern pairs came up with projects that advanced intern interest and meeting library goals. The interns were also encouraged to explore key aspects of their identity in their project development.

The structure for constructing their project ideas was modeled on the IMLS's Community Catalyst program. The Community Catalyst Initiative seeks to inspire and challenge museums, libraries, and their partners to transform how they collaborate with their communities. PLA believes it is important for interns to have a personal stake in developing their projects. This demonstrates trust while bringing new ideas and possibly new audiences into library programming.

Over the summers, mentor-intern pairs worked locally to implement their projects, while PLA provided ongoing support through webinars and social networking. The variety of projects included digital literacy training for non-English speaking seniors, a Period Action Drive, civic engagement for teens, translating library materials, bringing library services to local hospitals, and hosting social justice movie nights.

The sustainability and scalability of the intern-led projects were a surprise to PLA. Mentors from across the cohorts got new program ideas to implement. Some libraries were able to sustain the interns' projects beyond the summer, recognizing the value of the teens' contributions.

The full group of interns reconvened in the fall for a wrap-up event. At the wrap-up, each intern gave a five-minute presentation describing the personal impact from their participation in III, the impact on their host library, and the impact on their community. PLA also provided sessions on college and career readiness, which put the internship experience into the context of an ongoing learning opportunity.

Mentors spent an average of ten hours a week in direct contact with interns. Mentors were encouraged to introduce the interns to activities outside their immediate project responsibilities through arranging "shadowing" with colleagues, bringing the interns to programs and outreach events, and introducing the interns to key stakeholders and decision-makers. Some libraries formed mentoring teams to offer more expansive opportunities for the interns while sharing the time burdens.

PLA conducted a robust survey program. Pre- and post-surveys were issued at the kickoffs and wrap-ups. Interns were surveyed on their perceptions of librarianship as a viable career and more practical knowledge related to project development. Mentors were surveyed on their perceived leadership skills development and overall library changes in meeting the needs of diverse users.

It is too early to tell if any interns will pursue careers in libraries since the first class of interns will just graduate from college. However, several interns have found ongoing part-time work in their libraries while others work in their college libraries as work-study students.

Overall, III has been a huge success. New generations were introduced to libraries' vital work while building real-world skills. Library mentors developed leadership skills. Libraries tapped into underserved audiences in meaningful and sustainable ways.[2]

Mary Hirsh
Public Library Association

Notes

1. Community Catalyst Initiative. [n.d.]. "About the Initiative." Institute of Museum and Library Services, https://www.imls.gov/our-work/community-catalyst-initiative.
2. Mary Hirsh. June 29, 2020. Email message to author.

YALSA/Dollar General Teen Library Internship Grants

For many years, the Dollar General Literacy Foundation has generously provided grants to schools, public libraries, and nonprofit organizations to assist in implementing and expanding literacy-oriented programs for youth. Part of this time, their grants focused on Summer Learning Resource Grants and the Teen Summer Intern Program Grants. The purpose of these grants has been to combat the "summer slide," which often causes youth to experience learning setbacks if they are not given challenging opportunities to continue progressing during the summer before the new school year begins. (You can read more about this concept and how it relates to the pandemic and other emergencies in chapter 7.)

FIGURE 2.4
Mary Hirsh presents teen intern Yasmeen Chavez from the Alameda County Library with a certificate of recognition at the fall 2019 PLA Inclusive Internship Initiative event. Credit: Zach Miller.

During the grant years, Dollar General provided its twenty-five summer learning grants of $1,000 each to libraries in need. The funding was used for resources and services to teens who were English language learners, struggling in school, and lived in socioeconomically challenged communities. Further, they gave an additional twenty-five teen summer intern grants of $1,000 each to libraries that offered teens a place to develop hands-on job skills while supporting the execution of the summer learning programs and allowed the teen interns who were hired to collect stipends.[27]

The Young Adult Library Services Association (YALSA) of the American Library Association facilitated these grants for library teen interns. (Several of them are featured in chapter 4.) The last year that YALSA partnered with Dollar General to award these grants was 2019. However, that does not mean that Dollar General ceased to provide grants that can be applied to teen library internship opportunities.

In 2020, Dollar General revised how they offer grants to nonprofits, schools, and libraries. First, they began providing summer reading grants that support the creation or expansion of summer reading programs. Criteria for these grants are that they will target young children through seniors in high schools who are new readers, below-grade readers, and readers who need assistance in expanding their capability despite learning disabilities.

FIGURE 2.5
Teen interns Nayana Thompson (left) and Morea Lee (right) help measure, pour, and make glitter calming jars during the Adult 101 Life Skills for Teens Mental Health program. Their internships were funded by a YALSA/Dollar General grant. Credit: Janet Monterrosa.

Other grant opportunities that Dollar General is funding are Youth Literacy Grants. These grants are designed to assist in implementing or expanding existing literacy programs; purchasing new technology or equipment to support literacy initiatives; and purchasing books, materials, or software for literacy programs.[28]

Savvy youth services or teen services librarians can recognize that these recent grants, which aim to "fund the power of learning," could be applied to incorporating teen library interns to run such learning and literacy programs. If you are hoping to offer any teen library internship opportunities and seek funding, you might consider applying for one of these grants through which you would have teen interns address the program criteria that Dollar General requires. After all, chances are your library is already providing or anxious to provide programs that address literacy concerns in your community.

You might want to keep tabs on the Dollar General website to notice any potential teen internship funding opportunities that fit your plans while meeting the company's current requirements to promote literacy among youth. Do not forget that Dollar General also supports other nonprofits. If your school or public library is interested in partnering with another organization that operates nearby with a similar focus, it might make your chances of being awarded a grant even stronger.

Other Grant and Funding Options

There are scores of other options for grants and monetary support for your teen library internships. Some of these could be from large businesses or organizations. Still, you might also investigate small and local business support, professional associations, and foundations that would be willing to fund learning experiences for youth.

One good example of foundational support is the Ezra Jack Keats Foundation Mini-Grants. The foundation offers up to $500 to seventy schools and public libraries every year. The grants are given for creative and innovative activities that enrich a local youth experience. They aim to give teachers and librarians support for special projects or activities outside the standard curriculum and engage youth in meeting curricular goals. The foundation has given monetary support for a wide array of projects that foster creative expression, cooperation, and community, and they are always open to new and inventive ideas. They want unique programs that enhance learning experiences and offer significance, which can be evaluated and fun while offering youth a sense of achievement and pride. Why not tie in a teen internship to an imaginative proposal? The foundation seeks innovative programs that can:

- Develop required academic skills in a creative and exciting way
- Allow educators to collaborate across disciplines
- Inspire students to work hard toward a desired goal, applying necessary skills and knowledge to the project and the team
- Involve whole families and bridge generations to benefit the larger community
- Allow youth to explore their own culture and learn about others[29]

There are many other grants to be had that could be applied toward teen library internships. You might wish to explore these possible sources online. For example, the USA Grant Watch website posts an array of updated links to apply for the funding of literacy projects[30] and out-of-school youth program grants.[31] Another resource for finding grants is the publication *Youth Today*. They have a section through which you can research available grants, and often the focus of the funding is for library, literacy, and summer/after-school learning endeavors.[32]

Another resource for funding teen library internships can be through your state library or library commission. Find out if your state agency has such a youth internship support option for which you can apply. You might be surprised to see that grant funding exists through it. If not, the youth coordinator at the state library or library commission may be able to help connect you with potential funding sources.

An excellent illustration of this kind of in-state funding comes from Nebraska. For many years, the Nebraska Library Commission has provided funding to accredited Nebraska public libraries for youth internships and other teen-oriented library endeavors. As of this writing, they seek applicants for 2021 internship grants. They serve as administrators for additional monetary support to their funding from the Institute of Museum and Library Services under the Library Services and Technology Act provisions.

The Nebraska internship program introduces high school and college students to an exciting array of opportunities at Nebraska libraries. The internships are intended to function as recruitment tools and aids to youth considering the library as a viable career opportunity. The program accomplishes this by providing public libraries with the finances—up to $1,000 per library or branch—to present stipends to the student interns. In past versions of this program, student interns have helped the libraries expand programs, complete projects, improve websites, and increase social media use while bringing fresh ideas into the library.

As you have most likely noticed from other examples, every grant initiative has a list of fulfillment goals to be met by recipients. The Nebraska Library Commission grant likewise requires several targeted goals. Libraries that receive the grants must involve their interns in real library work that takes advantage of their experience and interest. Each internship must give the youth a snapshot of library work's positive aspects and help instill this work as a viable career. To accomplish this, interns are expected to be given enlightened views of libraries and librarians' roles, an understanding of behind-the-scenes library operations, and insights into the role of technology in libraries. The award libraries are encouraged to use the financial assistance they receive for interns to expand a program, complete a project, and bring fresh ideas to the forefront. During the internships, recipient libraries are expected to record data and keep other evidence to show that communities have benefited from their internship experiences.[33] Again, these requirements greatly resemble those of many other grants for teen library interns.

Finally, remember your Friends of the Library (FOL) group as a potential source for funding internships. With a strong, well-planned proposal, you might be pleasantly surprised at their willingness to support such a venture if they have enough money available or they can conduct a fundraiser. If you do receive such support, be sure to send the group a report of the results with thanks. A bonus would be if you would ask interns to come to a FOL board meeting or membership meeting and give a presentation on their internship experiences—an opportunity for teens to express their gratitude in person. As someone who has been on both sides of this sort of funding interaction—as a teen services librarian and a FOL board member—I know firsthand that FOL groups really enjoy hearing from the young people for whom they have provided money.

Never fear if you have tried to gain funding and have not been successful. Perhaps you could glean the needed cash from a creative library fundraiser, or, as already mentioned, you might decide to offer an internship without a stipend or wage. Many teens would welcome the opportunity to learn and grow through such an opportunity, even without pay. However, be sure to provide perks of some sort, such as T-shirts, snacks, a fine dispensation (if your library still charges fines), a thank-you finale of some kind, and lots of praise. A regular teen services programming budget is often sufficient to cover an unpaid internship program. You will find some good examples of effective unpaid library teen internships as you read on.

Getting Library or Other Approval to Offer Teen Library Internships

As with any programs or projects you want to propose at your library or through a partnership, you will need to seek approval from the powers that be before moving forward with your teen library internship idea. On the other hand, occasionally, an internship opportunity will be directed to your administrators, and they will ask you if you are willing and able to take it on. In this case, you have preauthorized approval, which is great. However, when you and your coworkers are the sources for having teen interns as a promising idea, you will need to pursue your superiors' approval to begin your actual plans. This also means you will need to find out ahead of time if in-house funding can be provided or if you may be given the go-ahead to apply for a grant.

Be mindful that in some library settings, there is a person in human resources you need to coordinate with as well. Likewise, if your city or town has a designated grants coordinator, you will most likely need to apply for outside funding through and with that person. Additionally, if you are looking for FOL funding, you will need to present a proposal to your local group to see if they can help.

When developing a teen internship proposal (or any proposal for consent), there are several steps to follow:

- Figure out how funding might be secured. You may need to include this in your proposal or make an initial, separate proposal to address monetary support.

- Start with an introduction that offers background information about the reasons for conducting the internship and expressing its importance. You can use information from this book to develop a strong proposal.
- After that, state how the teen internship(s) will benefit the library, the community, and youth.
- List the internship objectives and stakeholders. What do you expect each stakeholder to get by offering the internships?
- Next is the plan of action section in which you describe the specific steps and timeline that will be followed to see the internship through and how the funding that is provided will be utilized.
- The management plan section allows you to outline who would oversee which aspects of running and evaluating the internships.
- Subsequently, you will create a conclusion where you restate and underscore the value of the plans you are suggesting and how the internships would progress.
- Finally, if you have used any resources (like this book) or if you have conferred with others who have previous knowledge and experience that helped you put together your proposal, credit these at the end.[34]

Discuss with those who need to provide approval how and when you will state your case and ask them to add you to the appropriate agenda. Prepare proposal documents ahead of time and distribute them to the involved parties. Determine who will need to be there when the proposal is presented and who will need to speak about it and respond to questions. Find out how soon you can expect a decision so that you can move forward promptly when approval is given.

Your proposal will most likely be approved as submitted or with adjustments made as needed. Then you are on your way! If, conversely, your proposal is denied, ask what you might do to revise and resubmit it if there is time. It is worth the extra effort to keep your teen internship idea alive, if possible. Ultimately though, if the final word is that your proposal has not been approved, ask for reasons why and request to resubmit another proposal later.

Intern Advisory Group

If you are able and would like to offer teen library internships as an ongoing opportunity, consider developing an intern advisory group of previous interns to assist you in training and advising you and new interns. You might ask interns at their final evaluation sessions when their internship time is complete if they would be willing and able to serve on such a committee or board.

A good example of one such advisory group is from the Teens in Public Service (TIPS) program in Washington State's Puget Sound area. TIPS, which has been going strong since 1997, is a not-for-profit organization funded by local and national donors and dedicated to developing future leaders committed to their communities. TIPS selects teenage leaders for paid community service internships and pairs them with charitable organizations over the summer.

In 2020, TIPS began its first ever Youth Advisory Committee, comprised of past TIPS interns who volunteered to help optimize their successors' internship experiences. The alumni committee members focus their time as advisers to bring forth innovative, engaging initiatives for future summer programs. They guide TIPS changes as they use their committee platform to collaborate and effect change for the next class of TIPS intern leaders. One of their especially important recent roles was to convince TIPS to continue the 2020 summer intern season in an adjusted format because of the coronavirus crisis rather than cancel the program.[35]

Libraries can think about putting together a similar corps of "intern alumni" and asking them to serve as advisors for similar purposes. This would be especially appropriate in a multibranch library system that has an ongoing teen internship program at several locations, but it would also work with individual interns from year to year. Even if the teens or young adults now live at a distance, they may be willing to participate remotely.

If you are planning a proposal for repeated internship approval, ask previous interns for their endorsements after their own successful experiences, or to perhaps attend a proposal meeting in person to give their testimonials if they are available.

Whether you keep in touch with former interns either formally or informally, their previous participation in internships can be invaluable in moving your current teen internship programs forward. They can give you ideas, comments, and feedback from the perception of those who have been there. As another example, the University of Washington Libraries learned that the advice of preceding interns is a huge benefit in the progress of their teen internship program of the moment. They even invite back past interns to serve as mentors if they are interested.[36] This could be another way to incorporate their valuable input and viewpoints.

Notes

1. Young Adult Library Services Association. 2020. "Teen Services Competencies for Library Staff." American Library Association, http://www.ala.org/yalsa/guidelines/yacompetencies.

2. "Featured Job: Summer Youth Intern (High School)." February 4, 2019. Hillsborough County, Florida, https://www.hillsboroughcounty.org/en/newsroom/2019/02/04/featured-job-summer-youth-intern-high-school.

3. "RISE Intern First to Join Hillsborough County." August 7, 2020. Hillsborough County, Florida, https://www.hillsboroughcounty.org/en/newsroom/2020/08/07/rise-intern-first-to-accept-full-time-job-with-hillsborough-county.

4. NACE Staff. July 19, 2017. "The Key Skills Employers Develop in Their Interns." National Association of Colleges and Employers, https://www.naceweb.org/talent-acquisition/internships/the-key-skills-employers-develop-in-their-interns/.

5. Braun, Linda W. January/February 2019. "Career Readiness for Teens." American Libraries, p. 72.

6. "Teen Programs." 2020. Providence Public Library, https://www.provlib.org/education/teen-loft/programs/.

7. "Teen Loft." 2020. Providence Public Library, https://www.provlib.org/education/teen-loft/.

8. Braun, "Career Readiness for Teens," p. 72.

9. "Opportunities for Teens." [n.d.]. DC Public Library, https://www.dclibrary.org/teens/opportunities.

10. "Job & Volunteer Opportunities." [n.d.]. The Mix at SFPL, https://themixatsfpl.org/jobs-and-volunteer.

11. Kopa, Angelique. February 20, 2020. "Your Library and Junior Achievement." ALSC Blog, https://www.alsc.ala.org/blog/2020/02/your-library-and-junior-achievement/.

12. "Seeking Summer Internships & Jobs for Teens." 2020. New Orleans Public Library, http://nolalibrary.org/page/311/seeking-summer-internships-jobs-for-teens, last accessed March 1, 2020.

13. "Youth (12–25) Job and Paid Internship Fair." 2020. Oakland Public Library, https://oaklandlibrary.org/events/main-library/youth-12-25-job-and-paid-internship-fair.

14. Village of Arlington Heights. February 3, 2020. "Teen Job Fair Held February 4 at Arlington Heights Memorial Library." *Daily Herald*, https://www.dailyherald.com/submitted/20200131/teen-job-fair-held-february-4-at-arlington-heights-memorial-library.

15. Wyckoff, Amy, and Marie Harris. November/December 2018. "Career Workshops for Teens." *American Libraries*, 50–53.

16. TeenLife. June 6, 2014. "The Value of a Summer Internship for Teens." TeenLife Blog, https://www.teenlife.com/blogs/value-summer-internship-teens.

17. "TIPS Internship Program: Frequently Asked Questions." 2017. Teens in Public Service, https://teensinpublicservice.org/tips-intern-faqs.

18. Keasler, Christina. August 6, 2019. "Colorado Teens Use Makerspace to Create Accessible Board Games." *School Library Journal*, https://www.slj.com/?detailStory=colorado-teens-use-makerspace-to-create-accessible-board-games.

19. Tuccillo, Diane P. 2020. *Totally Tweens & Teens: Youth-Created and Youth-Led Library Programs*. Lanham, MD: Rowman & Littlefield, p. 46.

20. "More About the Mix." [n.d.]. The Mix at SFPL, https://themixatsfpl.org/more-about-the-mix.

21. "Teen Opportunities." 2020. Adler Planetarium, https://www.adlerplanetarium.org/learn/teens/teen-opportunities/.

22. Pannoni, Alexandra. May 30, 2017. "Learn How Teens Can Get High School Credit for Internships." *U.S. News & World Report*, https://www.usnews.com/high-schools/blogs/high-school-notes/articles/2017-05-30/learn-how-teens-can-get-high-school-credit-for-internships.

23. "Programs." 2020. After School Matters, https://www.afterschoolmatters.org/teens/programs/.

24. Hirsh, Mary. September 24, 2019. "2019 Inclusive Internship Initiative Concludes in D.C." *American Libraries*, https://americanlibrariesmagazine.org/blogs/the-scoop/2019-inclusive-internship-initiative-concludes-dc/.

25. Deutsch, Laurence. January 7, 2020. "Host Libraries Sought for 2020 PLA Inclusive Internship Initiative." American Library Association, http://www.ala.org/news/member-news/2020/01/host-libraries-sought-2020-pla-inclusive-internship-initiative.

26. Deutsch, Laurence. December 23, 2019. "PLA to Host Free 'Office Hours' Webinar for Prospective Inclusive Internship Host Libraries." American Library Association, http://www.ala.org/news/member-news/2019/12/pla-host-free-office-hours-webinar-prospective-inclusive-internship-host.

27. Lam, Anna. September 13, 2018. "YALSA Opens Up 2019 Summer Learning and Teen Intern Grant Applications." American Library Association, http://www.ala.org/news/member-news/2018/09/yalsa-opens-2019-summer-learning-and-teen-intern-grant-applications.

28. "Funding the Power of Learning." 2020. Dollar General Literacy Foundation, https://www.dgliteracy.org/grant-programs/.

29. "About Mini-Grants." 2020. Ezra Jack Keats Foundation, https://www.ezra-jack-keats.org/h/about-mini-grants/.

30. "79 United States Literacy Grants and Grants for Libraries." 2020. USA Grant Watch, https://usa.grantwatch.com/cat/22/literacy-and-libraries-grants.html.

31. "114 United States Grants for Youth." 2020. USA Grant Watch, https://usa.grantwatch.com/cat/41/youth-out-of-school-youth-grants.html.

32. "Grants." 2021. Youth Today, https://youthtoday.org/category/grants/.

33. Nebraska Library Commission. 2020. "2021 Library Internship Grant Program: Grant Overview." Now Hiring @ Your Library, http://nowhiringatyourlibrary.nebraska.gov/internship/InternshipApp.asp, last accessed September 1, 2020.

34. Schreiner, Erin. 2019. "How to Teach Kids to Write a Proposal." Classroom, https://classroom.synonym.com/teach-kids-write-proposal-7735080.html.

35. TIPS. March 4, 2020. "Introducing TIPS Youth Advisory Committee." Teens in Public Service, https://teensinpublicservice.org/tips-news/2020/3/4/introducing-tips-youth-advisory-committee.

36. Flynn, Kian A., and Elliott Stevens. September 9, 2020. Video chat with author.

3
Developing Teen Library Internships

BEFORE YOU PUT TOGETHER an internship plan, it is important to decide what the opportunity will look like. There are several kinds of internships that you can offer to interested teens. Depending on the school or public library setting and the needs and goals of the library, here are some internship formats you can consider:

- A year-round internship that matches the school year's length could work best for a school library but might work for a public library as well. Another arrangement could be fall/winter or winter/spring. These might take place for about ten hours a week, but you would have to decide the best time frame for both the library staff and a teen's schedule.
- A seasonal internship might occur during winter or spring break at a public library, though most libraries sponsor internships during the summer when school is out for a few months. These could range from ten to thirty hours per week, again depending on the internship's parameters and the library's goals.
- A micro-internship might take place on weekends, during evenings, or for a very limited time frame. These might only be three to five hours per scheduled day, following the internship plans. For teens who want to use their internship time to create and run a program for peers or other library users, this might be the best arrangement. Some university libraries, which you will read about in an upcoming chapter, have two-week internships with full-length workdays during the scheduled dates.
- Virtual internships can be short-term or long-term, depending on the internship focus. Teens would complete their internship at their own pace, on their own time away from the library, but coordinate with a mentor as they proceed. In times of pandemic or other emergencies, this would be a good way to provide internship opportunities. Learn more about this in chapter 7.[1]

Job Descriptions

You will need to generate a job description and the internship application form. A good approach is to make a tentative outline of it to include with your proposal and then develop the actual description once the position is approved. Check with your administrators to see if this approach will be acceptable at your library.

Whatever format you are required to use or decide to use, make the information clear and to the point so teen applicants understand up-front exactly what they will be doing and encountering if they are hired. Concise yet complete is the way to go.

Here is a job description as an example from the Jefferson County Library in Port Hadlock, Washington, that shows what such a document might contain. You will also find more examples in the appendices that illustrate other formats. One includes the job description as part of the application flyer. (See appendices A, B, and E.)

TEXTBOX 3.1 JEFFERSON COUNTY LIBRARY

Job Description
Classification Title: Teen Intern
Classification Summary:

This is a temporary, nine-month position. The Teen Intern will work in a public library setting, gaining hands-on experience and valuable skills. Work schedule is flexible; hours up to four hours per week, usually two days per week, two hours per day. Work is performed under the general supervision of the teen services coordinator or youth services librarian.

Distinguishing Characteristics:
A teen who is at least sixteen years old and currently enrolled in school.

Primary Duties and Responsibilities—General: (The following are not intended to serve as a comprehensive list of all duties performed in this classification.)

- Collaborate with teen services coordinator for program planning, marketing, and facilitation of teen programs
- Help to implement "Make Do Share" philosophy
- Serve as mentor to Teen Advisory Board
- Assist with the creation of social media content
- Help with ordering for and weeding of YA collection
- Assist with special projects

Knowledge and Abilities:
Knowledge of:

- Library services
- Young adult/teen literature

Ability to:

- Be friendly and welcoming to all teens/patrons
- Be punctual, arrive on time, and be prepared for work
- Establish priorities and organize workload
- Interact positively and effectively with teens, other patrons, and staff

- Provide information to patrons in a tactful and courteous manner
- Determine appropriate action within clearly defined guidelines
- Work cooperatively with others
- Communicate effectively both orally and in writing

Minimum Qualifications:
Minimum age is sixteen.
Physical Demands:
Must be able to stand, sit, or remain in a stationary position for extended periods of time; move about inside and around the library; organize and arrange resources inside and outside of the library, including organizing books and other library resources on library shelves with a height of up to 6.5 feet; relocate and move carts weighing up to 150 pounds and boxes and bags weighing up to fifty pounds; and communicate with library staff and patrons.
Work Environment:
Work is generally performed inside in a library environment. Work is performed in varied schedules, including weekends and evenings. May have some exposure to angry or hostile patrons.[1]

Note

1. Bahlmann, Scott. February 23, 2020. Email message to author.

You will find it beneficial to coordinate the job description design with your human resources specialist or another administrator. It is important to get input from someone knowledgeable about and in charge of job descriptions to assure that your creation is legal and covers all important points required in a job description for your library.

Applications

After pondering the previous chapter's advice, once you have decided on an internship design and job description and have everything approved, producing an application form is the next step. An appropriate application for the specific teen internship at your library is essential. You may want to choose an online application form, a printed application form, or both—depending on how you wish to receive the completed applications. Requiring a parent or guardian signature will impact your decision.

You will need to develop content that prepares the applicant for the library and internship program expectations while allowing any required demographic and logistical data to be recorded. This might include age, gender, socioeconomic status, and any other sought information. Some items may be added but be indicated as optional for respondents.

Additionally, it is a good idea to determine what skill sets, previous experiences, and interests teens possess that would be beneficial during the internship. On the other hand, as applicable, elucidate any concerns about potential transportation barriers while traveling to and from work, safety issues, and any additional information that you feel should be included.

You will need to set a timeline for releasing the application and a deadline for its submission. Allow at least one to two weeks for this, but more time if necessary, such as where you would like to see academic records or transcripts with the application. Be sure to clearly explain how and where the application should be submitted, the dates of service and orientation, and when interviews and notifications will occur.

**TEXTBOX 3.2 SAMPLE CONTENT
FOR A TEEN LIBRARY INTERNSHIP APPLICATION**

[Name of Library]
[Internship year/dates]
[Concise overview of age requirements; internship duties; work dates and times; expectations, targeted outcomes, and evaluation methods; wages, other compensation, or, if unpaid, describe the benefits; work location(s) information; staff/coworker information; interview process]

Please fill out this form completely and return it by the deadline of [date]. Interviews will take place [time period]. Notifications of the internship interview results will be by [date].

Applicant information
Full Name:
Date of birth:
Mailing address (number/street/city/state/zip):
Phone number (with area code):
Current email address:
[Note: You will be contacted by email. Remember to check it. Notify us of any changes.]
Grade in high school:
Name of high school:
Current cumulative GPA:
Parent or guardian's name:
Parent or guardian's full address:
Parent or guardian's phone number (with area code):
Parent or guardian's email address:
Please answer the following about your needs, background, and interests.

- Will you require any special accommodations during the interview process?
- Tell us about your educational experiences, volunteer experiences, and extracurricular activities.
- What experiences have you had in working with people of different ages and from different walks of life?
- What are the dates and times you are available each week during the internship period?
- Do you have any scheduling conflicts or restrictions?

References
Please provide two references with contact information from adults (teacher, librarian, coach, employer, etc.) not related to you who would be able to explain your ability in academics, work, volunteering, or extracurricular activities.

Reference #1
Full name:
Email:
Phone number (with area code):
How do you know Reference #1?

Reference #2
Full name:
Email:
Phone number (with area code):
How do you know Reference #2?
Items to attach to (or upload with) your application

- Your latest high school grade report
- Your resume
- A cover letter in which you briefly explain the reasons you would like to be selected for this internship, what you hope to learn from the experience, your personal goals, and any special knowledge or skills that you can offer.

Signature of applicant:
Date of application:
Signature of parent or guardian for those under age 18:
Date of signature:
Click "submit" [for an online application] or print and mail/return in person to:
Teen Internship Search Committee
Such and So Public Library
Address
City, State, Zip

Make sure that teens understand that they must commit to the time and effort that the internship entails. Usually, in the summer or during other vacation periods, this is not as crucial, but remember that teens are also occasionally enrolled in summer classes or other special activities during these times away from school. During interviews, clarify with teens to assure that they are not taking on a responsibility that is too much to handle by accepting an internship offer. You might ask applicants to fully detail what their schedules look like during the internship period. One way to work around any conflicts might be to offer schedule choices for work hours, settings, or locations rather than asking teens to come in at particular times and to a specific library if your internship design allows it.

Again, as with creating a job description, you will need to check in with your human resources specialist and administrators for approval before crafting and releasing an application. Plan carefully to allow enough time for your application to be approved. A flyer and FAQ information sheet could be approved at the same time if you would like to incorporate them as well.[2]

Remember, completing an application and submitting it completely, clearly, and as instructed is a skill that teens may need to have in the present and will need in the future as they get older. Make sure you apply care and consideration for this need when you design and put your application form together. Teen applicants will not only be seeking to become your successful candidate, but they will be learning an important lesson about job searching in the bargain.

For more examples of teen library internship applications and job descriptions, the appendices in this book. (See appendices A, B, and E.)

TEXTBOX 3.3 TIPS FOR TEENS ON APPLYING FOR INTERNSHIPS

Teens applying for internships would benefit from following the advice in this section. It would be worthwhile for libraries sponsoring internships to share these tips with interested teens who are applying. This information could be included on informational flyers and application forms and discussed during any career preparation programs being offered at your library:

- To increase the chances of obtaining an internship, it is essential to be as professional as possible, even as a teenager seeking a first job. Teens need to know how to prepare a neat and complete application, speak well, and dress.
- Strong interview performance, academic performance, and references are the top qualities sought in high school internship applicants because they reflect progress toward professionalism.
- To prepare for an internship opportunity, teens need to work hard to maintain good grades as best they are able. This demonstrates determination and focus.
- Teens should be ready to ask for recommendations from teachers, coaches, and employers who know them well and will provide complimentary remarks. It is a good idea for teens to keep an up-to-date list of potential references and their contact information, and for teens to inform those being asked to serve as references that their positive comments may be requested in the future.
- Creating a resume that includes key information like part-time work experience, professional objectives, a high school GPA, extracurricular activities, and any notable awards or recognition is indispensable. Even though teens might not yet have an experience that is directly relevant to their chosen career area, it helps to include as much related information as possible. Doing this when applying for an internship highlights their seriousness about potentially getting into the field of interest.[1]
- Teens who have never created a resume may be stumped about how to proceed. They are often unsure about how to write the resume and in what format to create it. They are often worried that they do not have any real credentials or experiences to write about. Using a handy resume tool can be a great help.[2]
- One good resource is the Resume Generator at the ReadWriteThink website. With two different formatting options, this generator guides students through the creation of a resume that can be saved and edited and includes written and audio tips that provide extra support.[3] One of the formatting options is specifically for teens

who have yet to develop more experience. It provides tips on leveraging the current know-how that teens already have to design a resume that is still impressive.[4]

Notes

1. Vets Guide. 2014. "High School Students Can Benefit from Internships," https://vetsguide.com/high_school_students_can_benefit_from_internships_40017097.html.
2. Patel, Jason. March 28, 2019. "How High School Students Can Land a Great Internship." NICHE, https://www.niche.com/blog/how-high-school-students-can-land-a-great-internship/.
3. ReadWriteThink. 2020. "Student Interactive Resume Generator." National Council of Teachers of English, http://www.readwritethink.org/classroom-resources/student-interactives/resume-generator-30808.html.
4. Patel, "How High School Students Can Land a Great Internship."

Publicity for Teen Internships

It is productive to post notices for teen library internships on the library website and especially helpful for a publicity blurb to appear on the teen web page if one is available. In addition, public library internships can be advertised at local high schools. If yours is a school library internship, you might choose to get promotional details about it on the school announcement mediums and through the school counselor or vocational guidance specialist.

It is also a great idea to let local newspapers and radio stations know about the internship opportunities to promote them through their media sources. You might be surprised that community news resources are glad to report on these opportunities for teens to get work experience and explore potential careers. Such stories are usually considered positive and uplifting community news, and these outlets are anxious to share them. Of course, you will also want to promote your internships on various kinds of social media and through general library publicity, such as email blasts or newsletters, in addition to what appears on the website.

At the Sonoma County Library, they promoted their teen library internship on the library website in detail, in addition to a short piece included on the library blog. Besides reaching out directly to teenagers in the community, they also encouraged adults who knew a promising teen to "send them our way,"[3] and they later added a blog post following the internship to describe the results.[4]

In addition to the blog post, the publicity for the Sonoma County Library's position—which gleaned fifty-six applicants—is given here as an example of a very comprehensive teen library internship application announcement. Learn further details of this internship in chapter 5.

You will benefit by aiming to leave no stones unturned as you seek teen interns. The more teens who apply, the better, even if you need to allow more time to review applications and set interview schedules. Your promotion of the internships will attract the best candidates to choose from and provide another avenue for teens to learn what programs, classes, and activities the library has to offer; to gain valuable interviewing experience even when they are not the successful candidates; and to let them know about any alternative openings you may have for teen volunteers, tutors, or other youth leadership opportunities.

PAID TEEN INTERNSHIP opportunity at Sonoma County Library - Help spread the word!

Submitted by kdeweese on April 24, 2019 - 3:03pm

Do you know a motivated, public-service minded high school student who is looking for a unique summer job? Send them our way! Sonoma County Library is looking to hire a teen between the ages of 16-19 who reflects the diversity of our community for an exciting paid internship!

Sonoma County Library was selected to participate in the Public Library Association's **Inclusive Internship Initiative** (III), which offers a paid, summer-long internship at the library to a high school student between the ages of 16-19 (entering Junior, Senior, or First-Year College). Through III, students from diverse backgrounds are introduced to careers in librarianship.

This summer, our III intern will work with mentor staff in the **Sonoma County History & Genealogy Library**, a community resource that manages local history and genealogy collections. It is located behind the Central Library in downtown Santa Rosa. The SCH&G Library acquires, organizes and makes available to the public materials that document the unique characteristics and communities of Sonoma County. There is also a required travel component – the selected intern must be available to attend (all-expenses-paid) trainings in Chicago (June) and Washington D.C. (September).

Follow this link to apply, and for full details about this internship. Applications are due **by May 7, 2019**.

Thank you for helping us to share this opportunity with teens in our community!

FIGURE 3.1
The Sonoma County Library's promotional publicity for its teen library internship posting. Credit: Sonoma County Library.

TEXTBOX 3.4 PLA INCLUSIVE INTERNSHIP INITIATIVE PROGRAM

Sonoma County Library was selected to participate in the Public Library Association's Inclusive Internship Initiative (III), which offers a paid, summer-long internship to a high school student at the library. Through III, students from diverse backgrounds are introduced to careers in librarianship. We are currently recruiting for a motivated, public-service-minded high school student between the ages of sixteen and nineteen. Could you be our III intern?

Our Library

Sonoma County Library serves our communities in fourteen locations. Though the Library explicitly supports diverse communities in its policy through a Statement of Inclusivity (2017) and a Resolution in Support of Undocumented Residents/Immigrants/Dreamers (2018), its staff does not mirror community demographics. Only 10 percent are Spanish-bilingual. There is a critical need to recruit and support local talent, particularly from underrepresented communities, in order to serve the County well. The III program is a pathway program developed to increase diversity in public librarianship. Since its inception, more than one hundred high school students at eighty libraries across the country have learned about careers in librarianship. We are excited to share our love of libraries with a teen representing the diversity of our local community.

History and Genealogy Library

This summer, our III intern will work with mentor staff in the Sonoma County History and Genealogy Library (SCH&G), a community resource that manages local history and genealogy collections. It is located behind the Central Library in downtown Santa Rosa. The SCH&G Library acquires, organizes, and makes available to the public materials that document the unique characteristics and communities of Sonoma County. Our collection strengths include local women's history, architecture, agriculture, urban planning, and arts and culture. We have substantial family history research materials, including books, journals, and databases. Our collections of maps and photographs are among the most popular.

Internship Tasks and Responsibilities

In addition to learning what it is like to be a librarian in a public library setting, the History and Genealogy III Intern can expect to learn about organizing, describing, and using archival and historical materials. The intern may assist with helping the public, community engagement, social media outreach, and event planning. They will have the opportunity to learn and participate in:

- Creating inventories and finding aids;
- Communicating our resources and services to the public;
- Designing and promoting a library program or event;
- Identifying community needs; and
- Expanding the library's reach.

The Library's extensive Strategic Plan will provide guidance for the intern's project, offering a range of goals that can support both professional exploration and meaningful community service. Interns will spend dedicated time writing, reflecting, and sharing about their experiences. With their mentors, interns will develop a connected learning project to be completed over the summer, based on their interests. Joanna Kolosov is an archivist and librarian interested in preserving the web and protecting cultural heritage materials. Zayda Delgado is a librarian and archivist interested in bringing local history to life for new audiences.

Did we mention you get to travel?

The selected intern must be able to participate in two trips (all expenses paid!), together with other teens in the intern cohort, for the kickoff and wrap-up events.

- Kickoff event in Chicago, IL: June 13–15
- Wrap-up event in Washington, D.C.: September 20–22

Pay and Hours

Interns will be paid $15/hour, with a maximum of 225 hours worked over the course of the internship.

Qualifications

Interns should meet the following qualifications:

- · Must be entering their junior or senior year of high school or first year of college;
- · Attention to detail, ability to prioritize tasks, and passion for helping people;
- · Willingness to learn and develop new skills; and
- · Interest in history and culture (preferred but not required).

How to Apply

The application form, in English and Spanish, is linked below. Please fill out the form and submit by Tuesday, May 7. The application may be submitted either online through the Google Forms link or by email (send as attachments).

Please contact Kathy DeWeese, Zayda Delgado, or Joanna Kolosov with questions.

- PDF Application (English/Spanish)
- Online Application (English/Spanish)[1]

Note

1. "PLA Inclusive Library Internship." 2019. Sonoma County Library, https://sonomalibrary.org/iii.

Interviews

Imagine: You have carefully reviewed all the applications for your teen internship position(s). You have weeded out the applicants who do not fit the criteria you have set, and you are left with a group of candidates who *might* fit the bill. Now it is time to schedule interviews to get the intern (or interns) on board.

Be sure to schedule enough time to interview all potential teen interns. Even if your time is at a premium, which it probably is, you will want to figure out a way to conduct interviews with all of the top prospects, even if there are more than you expected. You do not want to miss that perfect match because you did not take the time to interview everyone who might be just right. Also, choosing the wrong teen who might not be ready to take on an internship can be more trouble than it is worth, so you want to make sure that your decision is a good one.

Finding that great match can be a huge benefit for you and the library. Besides the positive aspects of providing mentorship and coaching for a receptive teen, you will be getting an extra set of hands to help. The right teen can assist with regular library duties and projects, produce some new and innovative programs or activities for your library clientele, or become a shining light for drawing other young people to the library. However, choosing someone is not necessarily an easy task. You might realize, especially if you have done previous adult employment interviewing, that teen applicants coming to the table can potentially arrive without a good deal of work experience or professional skills to make them stand out. The key to successful teen internship interviewing is asking the most effective questions.

It will help to pose questions that will glean the best answers when there might not be many past experiences as a gauge. Still, you want to learn as much as you can about the teens' skills, abilities, interests, and personality to determine who will be the most suitable fit for the job.[5]

Keeping all that in mind, here is a group of possible questions to select from that you might want to ask or adapt:

FIGURE 3.2
The flyer for the Sidney Johnson Summer Internship at the St. Louis County Library is appealing and clearly states the essential details for interested teens. Credit: St. Louis County Library.

- Do you think that what you have learned in any of your high school classes might help you during this internship?
- Can you tell us about any volunteer or community service experience you have had?
- Do you participate in any extracurricular activities, and why are they important to you?
- What experiences have you had with teamwork?
- What skills, knowledge, and experience do you want to get from this internship if you are a successful candidate?
- What skills do you already have that you might be able to use during an internship?
- What are the reasons you are interested in this internship?
- What do you know about our library? Have you participated in activities and programs here?
- Are you clear about the internship requirements and responsibilities?
- Are you interested in library work for your future job?
- Do you have goals for after graduation? If so, please describe them.
- What do you like to do for enjoyment?

As you ask these broad-based questions, ask teens to elaborate on their responses as needed and to use specific examples whenever possible rather than allowing them to give simple yes or no answers. Even though teens have little or no job experience, focus on the internship's expectations, the candidate's practical skills, and how they will fit into your library organization. If you follow these tips, hiring your intern will most likely prove successful.[6]

Let teens know your decision as soon as possible after it is made. Contact the teen (or teens) you want to hire and those who were not selected according to the timeline for notification that you previously determined. Be positive in your conversations, even with those teens who were not successful candidates. Give the teens who were not chosen—including ones you did not interview because they did not make the cut—any information about alternative opportunities you might be offering, such as job shadowing or volunteering—more about the latter in a second.

TEXTBOX 3.5

Betsey Brannen, children's services supervisor at the Frederick County Public Libraries in Frederick, Maryland, shared her staff's top eight tips for libraries that plan to hire teen interns:

- Require those interested candidates to drop off their applications at the library. While email or online submission is easiest for applicants, requiring a quick visit to the library gives you an immediate snapshot into the individual on a relaxed basis. Did they drop off the application and run? Did they hang out to snag a library card? Are they a familiar face?
- Offer an opportunity for those not chosen to receive some feedback on their application and interview. Not only is it valuable for them, but it forces you to step outside of your comfort zone and provide constructive feedback.

- Be honest with the amount of time you expect from the intern. Teens do not reside in a vacuum, and it can be frustrating to find out that their caregivers are expecting them for a family vacation that may take place in the middle of their required work time.
- Set boundaries with your teen interns in the workplace. If the teens get a lunch break, will they feel welcome to take it in the break room?
- Be specific about their daily job tasks and goals. Make sure to have plenty of additional work to do if you find your intern completes their tasks in a more than timely fashion.
- Welcome them when they arrive, and thank them when they leave. Yes, they were hired to do a "job," but learning workplace culture concepts is equally as important as the job they were hired to do.
- The exit interview is just as important as the entrance interview. It can provide you with valuable information for the following year's internship.
- Collaborate with the workforce development or job coordinator at your local school. They will know the work permit protocol's ins and outs (should your state require it), and they will also have information about comparable internships and jobs in your area.[1]

Note

1. Brannen, Betsey. October 7, 2019. "2019 Teen Summer Intern Program: Tips and Tricks to Make Your Internship Program Successful." YALSA Blog, http://yalsa.ala.org/blog/2019/10/07/2019-teen-summer-intern-program-tips-and-tricks-to-make-your-internship-successful/.

The Teen Internship Candidates Not Hired

When you select teens via the interview process to be interns at your library or through a partnership, there will most likely be other teens who must be turned down for the positions. You will want to contact the teens who were not picked and give them the news in a positive manner that will make them feel appreciated. After all, those teens tried their best, and you want to encourage them to try again another time or to seek out opportunities elsewhere.

You might also consider offering alternatives to teen internship candidates who were not hired if you are able. Some libraries suggest that the teens who were not selected for the internships take on volunteer positions instead. At the Hussey-Mayfield Library, they have a Teen Volunteer Corps in addition to their internships. The interns train the teen volunteers as part of their duties. The letter sent to the teens not chosen as interns is upbeat and makes them feel special and important even though they did not secure an internship. This may not be the reality in the adult work world, but with teenagers, we are trying to offer positive direction and growth experiences, so in these instances, it makes sense to do so.

TEXTBOX 3.6

Here is an example of a rejection letter that still encourages teens to be engaged in the library:

Dear (Name of Teen),
Thank you for your interest in being a teen intern. Your qualifications are excellent, but we had more applicants than open positions and are unable to provide you a position as a teen intern at this time. However, we do have a position for you in the Teen Volunteer Corps. You can be a valuable addition to the Teen Volunteer Corps program, and we hope you will volunteer on the first floor every Monday from 4:00 to 6:00 p.m.

Training will be held on Thursday, May 25, from 5:00 to 7:00 p.m. in the Lora Hussey Room. Pictures will be taken, but you can bypass this since you have already had your photo taken.

We will start by eating free pizza, learning about customer service, going over a few notes, then splitting into two groups where each group will learn the details about their specific program.

If you wish to volunteer and cannot attend, please call the library and let our staff know so we can make arrangements to have you trained as soon as possible. We hope to make this an exceptional summer program for all students involved, and we look forward to meeting you.

Any camps or vacations listed on your application have been recorded. It is not required, but we encourage any missed hours to be made up by picking up another shift anytime during the summer. Please see the attached sheet for instructions on how to drop or pick up a volunteer shift. Your scheduled shift (listed above) has already been entered. In early July, another letter will be mailed to your home with information about the Perfect Attendance Party, which will be for anyone who volunteers eighteen hours or more over the summer.

Thank you again for your interest in the Teen Intern Program, and we hope to see you on Thursday, May 25, for training.

Patricia VanArsdale
Teen Librarian (phone and email)

Note

1. VanArsdale, Patricia. September 29, 2020. Email message to author.

Permission Forms

If you do not know what permissions might be necessary, check with your human resources specialist and library administrators to find out what parental/guardian forms, if any, will be required. In the case of making your own forms for the internship, ensure that whatever ones you might create are approved according to library policy and legal advice. Your library may already have forms for you to use or templates to use as examples.

In general, permission forms may include the following information:

- Intern's name and date of birth
- Description of the job and an outline of specific activities and tasks that require permission, including any travel
- Medical release
- Custody release
- Emergency contact information with relationships
- Medical information, including health issues, medications, and insurance
- Photography, recording, or social media permission
- Signature(s) and date

Permissions will vary by library, of course. If a teen is expected to participate in an outside event such as one of the PLA gatherings or an out-of-town conference, a separate permission form from the agency hosting the event may be required. Again, consult those in charge of legal issues at your library to ensure that any permission forms you need are correctly designed.

The Internship Plan Handbook: An Indispensable Resource

Once you have your teen interns on board and their scheduled work time is approaching, it is time for training. One of the best tools you can use is an internship plan handbook. If you are asking, "Why create an internship plan handbook?," the answer is that there are several good reasons. First, once you have finally received funding and approval for teen internships at your library, it will help to produce a handbook for both teen interns and the library staff to follow. The handbook gives directions, information, and answers needed to complete internships successfully from both points of view, eliminating confusion.

You might ask yourself if putting together an internship plan handbook is really worth the effort. The idea of gathering all the material and information you will need might appear overwhelming and tedious. However, all the planning and preparation you do up-front to develop your internship program framework will lead to a worthwhile resource.

Consider engaging fellow staff members in helping you to write up the content and edit it, figure out useful diagrams and illustrations to match the text, and get the document into a workable format. This could be online, in a binder, in a folder with sections, a combination of these formats, or using whatever tool or tools you decide would most benefit you, your library staff, and your teen interns.[7] If you have had teen interns in the past, you might consider asking them for content advice in putting together the handbook.

One library creates a handbook that includes specific information sheets for individual tasks that teen interns take on each summer, including step-by-step instructions for programs, snipped images to illustrate points, scripts, and assigned duties for a few teens who will be working together. Your handbook could be standardized and updated each new internship season or made individually for each unique internship experience. How you devise the handbook can be as simple, complex, or flexible as need be. You might have one handbook for teen interns and another for library staff working with them, or one main handbook combining both teen information and adult information.

How to Design an Effective Handbook for Teen Interns

The following sections offer an outline of suggested topics and content to consider for putting together a teen internship handbook. Again, you might give teen interns a printed document that they can refer to as needed; you might make it with digital content that can be easily adjusted or decide that you want teens to have access to both.

Welcome/Introductory Page

The best way to begin a handbook for teen interns is by writing an introductory page to welcome them. Depending on the setting for the internship, it is a good idea to start with a greeting from the library director, high school principal, or another administrator who can make them feel appreciated from the top. They will feel more at home in their new job, valued, and inspired to do their best. It will enhance their willingness to contribute to the best of their abilities during their time with you.

History of the Library and Mission Statement

Chances are, on your library's website, there is a synopsis of the library's history. Sometimes, with a particularly celebrated or otherwise notable library, there might even be a more extensive narrative of its past. Library users often find this background information insightful and appealing. Likewise, most libraries post their mission statement and related information online and in public places so that users are aware of the library's outlook and goals.

When you put together your teen internship handbook, a nice touch would be to include a brief history of the library and its mission. This will give teen interns a more in-depth perspective of the library's purpose, focus, and what the library stands for. It will be a way to motivate them further as they recognize their role in helping the library carry out its principles.[8]

Orientation

Orientation should occur either at a designated time before the actual internship begins or on the intern's first day. I am sure you are aware that this is a crucial starting point when hiring anyone, and it is especially important for teen interns. For many of them, this might be their very first job, and a well-planned and organized orientation will start them off on the right track. The whole point of offering an orientation is to acclimate interns to the library, its background, and its purpose. Interns also get an overview of the internship and find out about the foundational resources they will need to succeed.[9]

If you have more than one teen intern, it is a good idea to schedule the orientation so that all of them can attend together. This way, they get to meet and engage with the other teens working at the same level of responsibility, perhaps even as teammates. It will also save you time because you will hopefully not need to repeat the orientation more than once. Even if you have several teens working at different library branches for the summer or other times, a general orientation for everyone at once is sensible. If this is the case, then each intern can have a shorter, less intensive orientation at their individual branches following the general one.

Consider using presentation software to create the orientation session. This can be useful for interns to access online afterward if they want a refresher on any topics you cover. Further, it would help an intern who cannot attend with the other interns to review independently later. It will also help another staff member to use in your place if you are not available for training.

If possible, have your library director or someone else from administration stop by to greet the interns in person. This special touch will make the interns feel very important and appreciated, in addition to the welcome message included in their handbook.

When an internship program is being repeated, think about asking previous interns to come by and share their viewpoints about the time they spent working at the library. It might be reassuring and insightful for teens to hear from peers who have had a previous similar experience and to know what it is like from their perspective.

It is a good idea to go over the entire teen internship handbook with the teens at the beginning of the orientation. Have them look through the sections of the handbook along with you, point out each one's purpose, explain how to use the checklists, and review any contact information for supervisors that is provided.

Give interns a tour of the library where they will be working. If you are meeting at the main library branch or other centralized library location beforehand with several interns assigned to various branch locations, you may still want to give all of them a tour of that central facility. They will enjoy hearing about multiple settings, stretching their legs, and seeing the library from different vantage points—the larger main library and their smaller "home" one—and better envision how the library system is connected.

If you have space, designate a specific spot or workstation for your teen intern. At the library where I last worked, we had a special work area for volunteers to use, complete with a computer, other equipment, and materials that they would need to do their jobs. When we had interns, they also used this workspace. Your teen interns will feel even more important and comfortable if they know where their own desk area is—even if it is shared—and that the supplies they need are either kept there or are easily in reach. In providing such a space, be sure to include a visit to it as part of the orientation. In the case of more than one intern using the same space, give each person a separate drawer or cubby to keep their own things, if possible. Make sure desk mates have an opportunity to meet each other before they begin accessing the space.

For purses, cell phones, or other valuables that teens cannot leave at home, have a designated spot to keep valuables. Make sure teens know how to get into it, and if a key or combination is needed, they know who the backup person is if they have trouble opening it.

Show teen interns any badges they will be required to wear when on duty and where they will be kept. If you have T-shirts that they will be expected to wear, explain when and where they will need to wear them. Be sure the interns receive them in time to ensure that the shirts fit and for the teens to prepare them at home for first wearing.

Visit the break or lunchroom and tell teens what supplies are there for their use and about any staff protocols they need to follow when using the area, such as an expectation to clean up after yourself, do your dishes, and label any food put in the fridge with name and date. If you can provide snacks and drinks for them to enjoy at times, teen interns will greatly appreciate it. Be sure that the interns are invited if there are any all-staff parties or celebrations. Finally, remember to plan a thank-you gathering at the end of the internship to emphasize teen accomplishments and honor them. It can be kept small and economical or be a bit more extravagant. Either way, teen interns will feel happy that you were grateful for their work.

> **TEXTBOX 3.7 TEEN VANTAGE POINT**
>
> I participated in the internship program at the Hussey-Mayfield Memorial Library for three summers. The internship normally occurs starting around May or June and ends in August.
>
> I had to submit an application, and I went in for an interview. To apply, one also needed one year of experience as a volunteer with the summer reading program.
>
> Patricia VanArsdale is the librarian in charge of the program and the supervisor. She would set up the teen summer reading program each year and give interns different tasks for days when it was slow. By the end of the summer, interns would delegate tasks and lead volunteers.
>
> There is training provided and a guidebook if the interns have questions about what to do. Patricia created the guidebooks. She made sure to stop by during each intern's shift to answer questions and talk to the interns and volunteers.[1]
>
> Kathleen C.
> Hussey-Mayfield Memorial Public Library, Zionsville, Indiana
>
> **Note**
>
> 1. C., Kathleen. July 20, 2020. Email message to author.

Intern Job Description, Responsibilities, and Expectations

Although the internship job description is included in the advertisements for an intern position along with the application form, you will also want to place a copy in the internship handbook. That way, the teen who secures the job can check the description as needed.

If you have multiple teen interns, you may have several different work duties and job descriptions for the various individuals. When you place them in the handbook, interns can refer to the job descriptions and remember who is assigned to which tasks. In the next chapter, you will see that some libraries with more than one intern have them tasked with various programs, activities, audience age groups, and everyday responsibilities, depending on their job descriptions. As discussed earlier, you will want to make your job descriptions as clear and concise as you are able, especially when several teens have both similar and differing assignments.

It might help to create checklists for any work topics where you find them appropriate. Teens can check off tasks and assignments they have completed, keep tabs on the days/hours they addressed them, and make notes as needed. When based on the job description elements, the checklists allow the teen interns and the supervisor to monitor work accomplishments and progress. The checklists and associated comments will also be handy later when completing and discussing follow-up evaluations and providing references. Copies of completed checklists can be kept in a folder and scanned and stored electronically for future reference.

It is a good idea to have teens sign in and out when they come to work. This will teach them about a responsibility that is usually required in adult workplaces. There is a good chance that you may do this yourself, and you need to turn in a time sheet to be paid. It is a helpful practice for teens to keep careful notations of their work hours. You might want to create a form that can be filled out to record their work time and accomplishments and which they will need to complete, sign, and turn in on a set schedule. This might be an alternative to a checklist or a derivative of one. You can use a template included in the appendices to help you make such a form. (See appendix D.)

It is also important to clarify how and when teen interns will receive their compensation. If interns are getting weekly paychecks, what dates can they expect them? If they will receive a stipend, at what point will they get it, and how will it be delivered? If they are getting a gift card, what amount, what kind of card is it, and when can they expect it? If the library is unable to offer monetary pay, but interns are receiving a T-shirt, a free book, other reward, service-learning hours, or school credit, be sure to explain that during interviews and clarify it in advance of the internship start date. No matter what teens are getting as compensation, remember to praise them for jobs well done, teamwork, improvement, and being a good sport as their work indicates.

Library Policies and Procedures

A section on library policies and procedures is a must; however, you do not want to make it too cumbersome. A bulleted list might be the most effective way to present this information.

Be sure to refer to your library's vision and mission statements. You might think that teens would consider this boring, but what is more likely is that, to them, it will seem as if they are official and belong—which they do! These kinds of statements are usually positive, short, and to the point and will give teens a good feeling about being a part of such an uplifting enterprise. Tell teens how you interpret these statements and ask for a brief discussion on what the statements might mean to them.

Meet with your supervisor or human resources specialist to help decide what policies and procedures should be part of the handbook. You will probably want to include information about ethical standards, library rules, and workplace harassment policies while using terminology accessible to teenagers. Some of the rules may be simple yet important, such as a policy that all employees and volunteers must always wear a name badge when on duty.

Let teens know about the library's dress code, what is appropriate attire for their particular job, and any exceptions to the policy. For example, if a teen is observing and assisting with a school visit or a library storytime, they may be asked to wear a less casual outfit than might usually be permitted.

Be clear with teens about social media, photography, and other library policies. Ensure they know that they are encouraged to be friendly, kind, and welcoming to library customers, and also restrict personal phone calls and conversations that take time away from work hours.

Make sure that interns know about library hours, holidays when the library is closed, days not required to be at work, and special events like staff meetings in which they will be included.

Teen interns also need to know who to contact if they have a problem or a complaint, especially if they notice someone breaking library behavior rules or if anyone or anything has made or is making them feel insecure, uneasy, or unsafe. Their mentor or mentors might be the best first-line contact, but if a mentor cannot be reached or if your library has other requirements, depending on a potential situation, let them know whom to call upon and when. Be very clear and reassuring that reporting an incident is essential and that all library staff members are required to report such occurrences to their supervisors.

Library Tools, Materials, and Equipment That Interns Will Use

If teen interns are using library equipment and materials for their jobs, you need to include instructions here and during the orientation. Most libraries will have teen interns using items such as audiovisual equipment, computers, and printing and copying equipment.

If teen interns are expected to use a 3D printer for any reason, be sure to give them careful instructions and monitor their use until you and they feel comfortable. 3D equipment can be tricky, but once teens get the hang of it, they will enjoy using it. Most teens, especially those who are computer-savvy, catch on to these printers way sooner than most adults!

Giving teens a temporary library email address, if feasible, will make them feel important, and they will get staff messages that they need to have while they are employed. Make sure they are given login information during their orientation, and you might want to include reminder hints in this handbook section. Let them know that if they have any trouble with access to let their supervisor or mentor know right away, and make sure they know the rules library staff must follow when using work email.

FIGURE 3.3
Interns Marcus Bennett (right) and Zach Rude (center) direct incoming Teen Council member Emma Weisler to her station as the group begins to set up for a life-size Candyland game. Bennett and Rude used a detailed list with instructions and a timeline while empowered to be in charge of training the council members as they arrived and monitored quality control. Credit: Patricia VanArsdale.

If teens are doing check-in and shelving, add directions for procedures to follow and steps to take. When doing check-in, they may be required to sort books in a particular order onto carts or sorting shelves, so insert directions on how to proceed. When shelving, give the teens directions, include them in the handbook, and have them shelve a few small sample areas to test their ability and check their performance before giving them a large shelving assignment.

When running or helping to conduct programs, teen interns may need to set up audiovisual and other equipment and know how to troubleshoot. Include simple directions in their handbooks, give them an overview during orientation and before a program, and supervise to ensure they understand how to use the equipment before leaving them to run the show.

In cases where teen interns will be helping with children's programs, let them know where all the props, costumes, and other materials are stored and give them lessons on how to use them. For costumes, make sure they know how to put them on, take them off, and store them properly, plus give them instructions on how to keep themselves cool when wearing some of the heavier costumes. You might need to supply frozen blue ice or other items to keep costume wearers safe and comfortable. It helps to require those in heavy costumes to be accompanied by another teen intern or a volunteer and arrange a signal for the costumed teen to use if they find themselves in heat or other distress.

You will also want to give teen interns advice on how to act around children when wearing the costumes. Some children are fearful of costumed characters, while other children can be overly affectionate with them. Teens need to know how to deal with both and draw in children who are not particularly frightened but might need a little encouragement to come closer. It is difficult to talk and see while in the costumes, so interns need to know to stay silent and use motions to communicate instead. The noncostumed partner accompanying the teen in costume can assist by interacting with the children and parents and providing guidance for the "character" as they move around.

For items that might have safety concerns, such as paper cutters or glue guns, include precautions in the handbook. Observe teen interns using any iffy equipment before allowing them to assist or work with the items independently. Check to see if your library has special rules and requirements about teen volunteers and interns using such equipment.

Before you prepare this section of the handbook, make a list of all the potential items your teen interns will or might be using. Think about what teens need to know regarding where the materials are stored and how to access them, use them properly and effectively, clean and otherwise care for them, and put them away correctly. Create checklists of the items they will be using with basic details about care and use and a place for them to write notes.

Make sure that teen interns know to inform library staff of any problems with or questions about materials and equipment.

Evaluations and Feedback

In this section of the handbook, you will want to let teens know that evaluations will be coming during and at the end of their time interning with you. Include a general overview of the evaluation process and what teens can expect that you will be asking of them. Will they be doing a self-evaluation along with an evaluation of working with library staff and other teen interns? Will a midpoint evaluation be required? Decide ahead of time how you wish to proceed. Also, let them know that you will be evaluating from your point of view, and that you, and perhaps other library staff, will be meeting with them at the end of the internships for exit interviews.

There are templates for creating a daily activity log and an intern self-evaluation form in this book's appendices. You may want to include a sample of the form they will be using later so they can see it in advance. (See appendices C and D.)

Coming up ahead, chapter 6 will address the topic of teen internship evaluations much more thoroughly.

General Information and FAQ Sheets

You may want to include "general information" and "frequently asked questions" pages for teen interns to quickly peruse as needed. Think about what you would like to add to such resource pages. The idea is to give teen interns a tool for easy reference, help them be confident, and save time.

Design this section to be informational and user-friendly. Of course, if teens notice that the information they need is not there, then the resource can encourage them to seek the guidance of another employee or supervisor.

Incorporate general commonly asked questions for any workplace, such as holiday schedules, payroll questions, contact information, and where essential materials are located. Put down as many minute questions as you can think of specific to your library or other internship work location. For example, if your library uses identification badges to access the building, you would want to have a question addressing what to do if you misplace or lose your badge.[10]

Creating this resource would be a good opportunity for you to brainstorm with coworkers to make sure you do not miss anything important. Make the document an evolving one that can be updated as needs arise. Listen to and consider questions teens ask that have not already been part of the resource, keep notes, and make necessary additions as you discover them.

Another addition may be a detailed information sheet on various topics that interns need to know about and use. For instance, at the Hussey-Mayfield Memorial Public Library in Indiana, teens are given information sheets that cover specific topics for their internship assignments, such as:

- Dealing with difficult people
- Closing procedures checklist
- Prize scripts to call winners
- Doing reminder phone calls to customers
- Participating in a scavenger hunt
- Tasks for certain days
- Schedules
- Other instructional documents as needed[11]

Glossary of Library Terms

It can be very helpful to add a brief glossary of library terms so teen interns can be in the know. As library staff members, even temporary ones, they will hear conversations and be asked questions by library users that they will want to answer. You will need to include terms that they may encounter during their time working for you, but at the same time, you do not want to overwhelm them. Ensure you are selective about the terms you choose and let the teens know that if they are unsure of these or any other terms, to ask a library employee for clarification.

Think about some terms you frequently use that teens might not understand but may encounter when assisting library customers or running programs. Many online resources will help you get definitions to adapt for teen interns. Here are some suggestions to get you started:

- Barcode—A small white label with black stripes that a computer can read, found on library cards and library materials, and used to check out items from the library.
- Bibliography—A list of documents (books, articles, reports, etc.) relating to a specific subject or person.
- Biography—A written account of a person's life.
- Book Drop—A place to return books borrowed from the library.
- Book Truck—A cart used to hold books before reshelving and transporting books and other library materials to the shelves for reshelving.
- Call Number—A combination of letters and numbers assigned to all books and most other items in the library that gives the material's location on the library shelves.
- Carrel—Study area for one person.
- Catalog—A listing of all the materials a library owns. It includes books, periodicals, movies, sound recordings, and more.
- Check Out—To borrow library materials for use outside the library.
- Circulation Desk—A place where users check out, renew, return, place holds, retrieve print reserves, and inquire about the status of library materials. Sometimes called "check out desk."
- Database—A collection of information arranged into individual records to be searched by computer.
- Hold—Items checked out by one borrower and requested by another patron. A hold is placed on the item, and upon its return, it is reserved for the person requesting it.
- Hold Shelf—A special self-service area of shelves where library customers can pick up coded items they have placed on hold.
- Icon—A small picture or symbol representing something else.
- Interlibrary Loan—A service that allows library users to access materials that the library does not own by borrowing a copy from another library.
- Stacks—The shelves on which the library's materials are stored.
- Virtual Library—Also known as an "electronic library" or "library without walls"; the library website serves as a virtual library.
- Withdraw—The process of removing items from the collection because they are outdated, unneeded duplicates, or in very poor physical condition. Also known as "weeding."[12]

As with other library jargon, if there are acronyms or abbreviations your library regularly uses, for example, "OPAC," you will want to include those in your glossary as well.

Contact Information for Teens to Connect with Supervisors and Coworkers

Let teen interns know who to contact in case of emergency or illness. Give them several names and phone numbers of people to whom they can reach out, cell phone numbers for text messages if possible, and email addresses. Include instructions on when to make contact and in what circumstances. Are they going to be late for a good reason? Is there illness in the family? Has the teen been injured?

You might also consider giving teens a list of coworker teen interns if they will not be working solo. When they must be absent or need to trade, you can encourage them to contact fellow interns who may be willing to switch or take an extra shift to keep the schedule running smoothly. At the Hussey-Mayfield Memorial Library in Indiana, they give the teen interns a welcome letter explaining the contact list and its use.

TEXTBOX 3.8

When you take on your interns, you will want to send out a welcome letter that gives general information to get started. Here is an example:

Hello Intern!

Welcome and thank you for being a valuable part of our team. I want to take a minute to explain what you have in your hands. First, you will notice pictures and phone numbers of our interns. Please treat this as a staff phone list. These numbers should be used to contact your fellow interns regarding intern-only activities. When summer is over, we ask that you shred or throw away the list since the numbers were not given directly to you by the number's owner. You have this list at home, so you can swap, trade, or contact another intern to take a shift you cannot make.

Also included is the intern schedule with the days and times you will be volunteering. Those who volunteer Friday and Saturday evening notice that you are scheduled from 2:00 to 4:55 p.m. The library closes at 5:00 p.m. on those days, and we ask that your ride be here by 4:55. We want to ensure that staff is not staying late to ensure you have a ride home, as we do not like leaving students here unsure when their ride is coming to pick them up.

If you need to adjust, you will need to confirm the change with the other participant and then notify Patricia by email. Patricia will confirm by email that the change has been made. If Patricia does not confirm the email, she did not get it. An intern schedule will soon be created using SignUpGenius, to show the latest switches.

You will also notice an intern availability sheet. This is to show you who is available which days and times. For example, if you volunteer the morning shift on Monday, June 17, and cannot make it, do not call Andrew, as he is only available to volunteer the evening shift. At this time, feel free to begin working with other interns to adjust your schedule as needed. Just know that the schedule will not be confirmed until Patricia verifies that a change has been made.

I am really looking forward to an awesome summer with some fantastic interns. If you or your parents have any questions, please feel free to call me, email me, or stop by any time.

Patricia VanArsdale
Teen Services Librarian
(phone number and email address)[1]

Note

1. VanArsdale, Patricia. September 29, 2020. Email message to author.

A Timeline Overview to Creating an Internship

Every internship design will have unique qualities and will be planned and run according to the individual library's needs and desires. In general, though, here is a timeline that you can use to help develop a teen library internship step-by-step. It places the elements discussed in this chapter and previous chapters into a format you can use to make a checklist:

- Develop a vision, a plan, and a timeline.
- Choose the library location or locations or places outside of a library location that would be internship sites.
- Figure out costs and potential funding sources.
- Decide who would serve as a mentor, supervisor, advisor, or in other roles deemed necessary. If your internship is a partnership, be sure all parties will be represented in supervisory designations.
- Get program support and approval from funders and your library administrators.
- Bring together an advisory committee of human resources specialists, library staff, and administrators as needed.
- Figure out administrative, technological, office, and support material issues. Who will take what roles in seeing the internship through, and how?
- Design internship forms, especially applications, and get them approved.
- Determine what publicity will be needed and how it will be distributed.
- Create an internship plan handbook that can be used by the teen(s) who are selected.
- Set the application process into motion.
- Interview qualified candidates and make choices.
- Conduct orientations and training sessions for interns.
- Monitor intern progress and arrange midpoint evaluations.
- Conduct end-point evaluations and meetings.
- Plan, organize, and hold culminating activities or events to honor your interns.
- Debrief administrators, human resources, and those who have sponsored the internships with funding, materials, or in other ways.[13]

TEXTBOX 3.9 TAB TEEN INTERNSHIP, SAMPLE CURRICULUM

The internship program and curriculum described here began in 2013 as a Teen Advisory Board (TAB) members-only incentive at the La Vista Public Library in Nebraska. It went on for several years, and it was featured in an article in *School Library Journal*.[1]

The TAB members had dedicated their time to library- and city-related volunteering tasks since TAB's inception in November 2010. Many of the teens regularly expressed the desire to work in libraries or become librarians themselves. Teen services librarian Lindsey Tomsu created the library's teen internship program in 2013 to offer those interested TAB members a chance to participate in a ten-week, in-depth, college-level intensive educational opportunity that they could use for National Honor Society requirements and college and job applications as a real internship experience. Her internship design is significant because it employs a true, well-balanced curriculum.

Although Tomsu has moved on to the Algonquin Area Public Library District in Illinois, she revisited doing a teen library internship at her new library in 2019. Details of that experience are related in chapter 5. In the meantime, here is an overview of the original program and curriculum as described by Tomsu, which may help you to prepare your own in-depth teen internship curriculum if you are interested in something so ambitious:

"After our TAB was created in November 2010, many of the members eventually started offering their own time as TAB volunteers for the teen programs. Starting at that time, if one of my TAB members attended a TAB meeting or helped, I kept track of their volunteer time, which in 2016 amounted to over 1,400 hours. By adding the TAB Teen Internship program, the teens had another incentive open to them to help extend their library knowledge and teach them more specific aspects of the profession in addition to regular volunteering.

"The idea of starting an internship program for members of TAB was not only as another incentive, but also to actively encourage those members who were interested in librarianship by fully immersing them in an intensive, but educational and entertaining, ten-week-long internship that showed them as many aspects of the profession as possible.

"The actual internship began when summer reading began, all of the tween and teen programs of the season were planned and scheduled, and the internship could serve as a college-level learning opportunity concurrently. When I initially created the program, I spent a few months building an actual curriculum for the internship, which I went back to and revised each year before the new batch of interns began—to make sure the readings were current and the assignments were still vital and being enjoyed by the interns.

"The interns would arrive every Tuesday and Thursday at 8 a.m. Just like any responsible employee, they had to "clock in" and be on time. The library had shared a building with the Sarpy County location of the Metro Community College, and Metro booked us a room during the summer for our internship classroom time. From 8 a.m. until 12 p.m., the teens and I participated in the educational part of the internship. This involved lectures and presentations, lively discussions, readings done before class, and the completion of any in-classroom assignments besides those few prepared at home. From 11:30 a.m. to 12:30 p.m., the interns took breaks for lunch. Afterward, we set up for the tween programs, which ran from 1:30 p.m. to 2:30 p.m. We then prepped for and ran the afternoon teen programs, which were held from 3:30 until about 5:00 p.m. Following that was program take down and then an intern break for dinner. At 6:00 p.m., we began our evening program. The interns helped clean up after that program, and they would leave around 8 p.m. Occasionally, the interns were required to be at the library on other days for after-hours programs or weekend programs.

"Interns under consideration for selection must have completed an application, and then, if they were able to meet the schedule, they came to an interview with me and the previous summer's interns. Once interns were selected for the internship, they received an official offer letter in the mail. Their parents, most of whom marveled at the opportunity afforded by such a program, read over the expectations and signed for their approval. Parents were also required to sign a driving waiver allowing their teen to be in a car driven by me to our various library field trips and for shopping purposes. For whatever reason, if a parent did not want their teen participating in the program, this is the stage at which they removed themselves from consideration and declined the offer.

"Once I had received their completed paperwork, the interns received their workbook of materials in early May. This included a detailed work schedule showing their hours, an internship expectations guideline sheet, and their unit-by-unit collection of materials, including a calendar with due dates, copies of their readings, and assignment packets. Once they received their materials, they could begin their readings, take notes, and ready themselves to talk about their responses for when the internships began.

"The internships themselves were broken up into eight units of materials over ten weeks, with two additional all-day movie-a-thons which did not allow for our usual classroom time. The eight units consisted of the following topics:

- Introduction to Libraries and Librarianship: The interns learned about the history of libraries throughout time; reviewed their internship expectations; learned basic library terminology; learned about public service; and saw how libraries are managed.
- Programming: The interns observed how I go about planning programs for teens. They learned where ideas come from and how programs go from an idea to reality. They were expected to help with all the summer reading programs in general. The interns were responsible for planning the content of the Teen Storytime Program, which involved choosing books and picking a craft, plus the brainstorming, budgeting, shopping, and running of their teen program for Guilty Pleasures Night, during which they were the 'librarian for the evening' and for which they were introduced as such and ran the entire event.
- Circulation: The interns learned how the circulation staff operates. They learned how the library opened in the morning, about the circulation system, how to sign someone up for a library card, how to check in and check out books, and about the importance of patron privacy and confidentiality.
- Reference: The interns discovered what goes on at the reference desk, how the computer lab works, where items are in the library, how to conduct a reference interview, and how to do reader's advisory.
- Collection Development: The interns learned about the collection development policy; the process of collection development; were introduced to various review sources; found out how materials are ordered, cataloged, and processed; learned how to shelve materials; learned about challenge issues; and were taught how to weed books.
- Teen Services: Many of the teen interns were interested in how teen services are provided, so there was a special unit focused on serving teens. This included teen collections, programs, spaces, and so on. The interns learned about other aspects of teen librarianship as well, such as grant writing, schedule making, displays, marketing, and so on. They also helped to start planning for the following school year.
- Miscellaneous Topics: As the interns sat down with several librarians, they learned a bit about different kinds of library jobs and some of the duties they entail. In addition, the library director discussed the challenges of running a library, how budget issues are dealt with, how a partnership with Metro Community College worked, and took interns to various city meetings when feasible to see what a director did at them. The interns also took field trips to Sump Memorial Library in Papillion, Bellevue Public Library, and Baright Public Library in Ralston to see how libraries vary from one another. They had a detailed library field trip checklist to complete during their visits. At Bellevue, they also sat in on the children's storytimes to compare them to storytimes at their own library.
- The Future: In the final unit, the interns learned about resume writing, interviewing, college applications, and what they would need to do if they were interested in pursuing a career in library science.

"The core milestones of the internship included the following:

- Understanding the history and future of libraries
- Learning about different types of libraries

- Visiting other area libraries and seeing how they are the same or different from their home library
- Brainstorming, planning, budgeting, and presenting their own teen programs
- Learning how to shelve books
- Learning basic circulation tasks
- Learning how to do booktalks
- Learning how to conduct reference interviews
- Writing book reviews
- Creating book displays
- Understanding censorship issues
- Learning how to do collection development and weeding
- A 'Soak a Book' assignment, which involved purposefully water-damaging a book and attempting to repair it
- Creating a resume[2]

Lindsey Tomsu
Algonquin Area Public Library District, Illinois

Notes

1. Tomsu, Lindsey. November 2, 2015. "A Model Internship Program." *School Library Journal*, http://www.slj.com/2015/11/teens-ya/a-model-internship-program/.
2. Tomsu, Lindsey. September 18, 2020. Email message to author.

Notes

1. "Internship Plan Handbook." 2019. Parker Dewey, http://info.parkerdewey.com/internship-handbook?hsCtaTracking=570d2f87-3e56-41ec-b4b6-79c615045c58%7Cc7f34a38-c109-46f6-96bd-c19937726e29#to-go.
2. Youth Made Toolkit. [n.d.]. "How to Develop a Local Youth Manufacturing Internship Program" SFMade, http://sfmade.org/wp-content/uploads/YouthMade-Toolkit.pdf.
3. DeWeese, Kathy. April 24, 2019. "PAID TEEN INTERNSHIP Opportunity at Sonoma County Library—Help Spread the Word!" Sonoma County Library, https://sonomalibrary.org/blogs/news/paid-teen-internship-opportunity-at-sonoma-county-library-help-spread-the-word.
4. Gore, Kat. October 2, 2019. "Sonoma County Completes National Summer Internship Program." Sonoma County Library, https://sonomalibrary.org/blogs/news/ma-county-library-completes-national-summer-internship-program.
5. Smith, Angela. 2020. "The Best Interview Questions to Ask Interns." The Muse, https://www.themuse.com/advice/the-best-interview-questions-to-ask-interns.
6. Smith, "The Best Interview Questions."
7. "Internship Plan Handbook."
8. "Internship Plan Handbook."
9. "Internship Plan Handbook."
10. "Internship Plan Handbook."
11. VanArsdale, Patricia. September 29, 2020. Email message to author,.

12. "Glossary of Library Terms." 2020. Upstate University of South Carolina Library, https://uscupstate.libguides.com/glossary.

13. Kyler, Nina J. [n.d.] *Internship Guide: A Resource Toolkit*. Regional Office of Education # 17, DeWitt, Livingston, Logan, McLean Counties of Illinois. Contact https://roe17.org/contact-us or Regional Office of Education #17, 201 E. Grove Street, Suite 300, Bloomington, IL 61701, to obtain a copy.

4

A Close Look at Public Library Teen Internships

THIS CHAPTER FEATURES DESCRIPTIONS of a selection of teen library internship positions of many kinds that have been held in and through public libraries. As you read about these examples, you will see various types of teen internships and the funding that endorses these valuable work experiences. You might want to use these as motivation and a catalyst to design your own library teen internship plans. Additional internships in other settings, formats, and through notable partnerships are covered in the next chapter.

As mentioned earlier in this book, many of these teen internship illustrations were from the years just preceding the coronavirus pandemic. Several of them were scheduled for 2020 but needed to be rescheduled, canceled, or reworked. Some examples are still included in this chapter with appropriate notations about their destinies. Keep in mind that, in addition to a pandemic, all kinds of emergencies could potentially occur that would affect all library staff members, together with volunteers and interns. Alterations that might be made in such circumstances are addressed in chapter 7.

As you learn about this array of actual teen library internships, you will notice that they reflect much, if not all, of the information and advice from the beginning of this book, and you will see connections to them as you read the last two chapters. Use the recommendations I have given along with their inspiring, time-tested examples to devise or improve your teen internships.

Alameda County Library, Newark Public Library Branch, California

As one of the Public Library Association's (PLA) Inclusive Internship Initiative grant recipients in 2019, the Alameda County Library in California offered a summer internship to a deserving teen. Yasmeen Chavez, the teen who was hired, is impressive in her own right. She was raised in a family where Spanish was her first language, and she worked hard to learn English and tutor her two younger sisters. She also graduated in the top 10 percent of her high school class and received the Michael Gendreau Community Services Scholarship for the reading and tutoring volunteer work and volunteer program assistance she did at the Newark Public Library starting in her sophomore year. She aims to continue working with the education of young people in the future to help them be the best they can be.[1] She was a natural to become a successful internship candidate.

As explained earlier in this book, each PLA intern and mentor pair was expected to attend a kickoff and wrap-up event in a major city after their grant was awarded. The grant criteria included a requirement that each intern would create a community-based project that reflected the intern's interests and the library's goals, and on which the intern would make a presentation at the national wrap-up event. Mentors needed to spend at least five hours a week on direct intern support. A requirement was that interns were only allowed to spend 25 percent of their time on administrative tasks like copying, filing, scanning, and so on, to keep employment duties professional and relevant. Another fundamental focus of the internship was that it needed to introduce the intern to the ins and outs of careers in librarianship. Additionally, mentors must have practiced leadership skills, and the host libraries must have developed new audiences through outreach and programming plans with their interns.

Chavez designed her internship project with these things in mind and according to her personal goals for the future. Her project aimed to help children, ages eight to twelve, who became English-language learners after recently arriving in the United States. Chavez wanted to help them gain confidence in their verbal fluency of the English language so that they would have the ability to persevere through the difficulties of the language barrier.

The program consisted of four equally important parts: making name tags with silly prompts to encourage conversation; the first center, which consisted of informal one-on-one conversations with prompts to guide them; the second center, which focused on making crafts and planning in small groups to fashion little performances that encouraged teamwork and effectively speaking to one another to accomplish a goal; and finally, the actual performances, which the children presented to the entire class.

Although the multifaceted program involved speaking to one another in English to practice the language, that element was implicitly incorporated, so children did not feel pressured to

Itinerary

	Day 1	Day 2	Day 3	Day 4
(Silly) Name Tag (5 min)	Nickname	Favorite Animal	Favorite Character	Favorite Food
Center 1 (5-7 min)	Get-to-Know-You Questions	Funny Story	The Best Day Ever Personal Story	What did you do today?
Center 2 (20 min)	Draw a Story	Make props and practice	Make puppets and practice	Bring, draw, or make something from your culture
Performance (20 - 25 min)	Share your Story	Skit	Puppet Show	Cultural Show and Tell

Backup Games: Pictionary, Headbandz, Taboo, Telephone

FIGURE 4.1
The outline of the project plan created by Yasmeen Chavez at the Alameda County Library's Newark Public Library Branch. Credit: Yasmeen Chavez.

speak it well. They were comfortable in a group with children who also struggled with learning English. They were able to practice it in a welcoming environment where everyone understood what they were going through. They were also able to make friends through their experiences, which helped them gain much-needed support in their struggle with language barriers.[2] Chavez presented the outline of her program and these results at the PLA wrap-up event.

As mentioned in chapter 2, after Chavez's successful and impressive internship, she accepted a permanent position at the Alameda County Library.

Auburn Public Library, Auburn, Georgia

The Auburn Public Library hosted three successful teen internships in 2018 and 2019. The one from 2018 and one of the ones from 2019 were funded through a grant through the Public Library Association's Inclusive Internship Initiative. After the 2018 internship's success, the library was anxious to host another, plus an additional one. The second internship in 2019 was funded by a Dollar General summer internship grant given through the Young Adult Library Services Association (YALSA).

Applications, which included a personal statement and a teacher reference, were accepted during four weeks in 2018. Applicants who submitted all required materials and indicated that they were available to work all summer long, minus no more than one or two weeks off that could be rescheduled, were interviewed. There were four teens out of twelve who met the criteria.

The successful candidate was a high school senior, Emily Brooks (now Emily Friel), a star soccer athlete and high academic achiever who provided not one but two recommendations with her application. She worked from May 21 to August 3 for thirty-five hours a week for ten weeks, including two weekends in June and September in Chicago and Washington, D.C., respectively, for the PLA kickoff and wrap-up events. The library was given $3,000 to fund the internship, and Brooks was paid $10 per hour. Library manager Bel Outwater served as her mentor and said hiring an intern for a paycheck created buy-in and a good incentive for working in the library. She conducted Brooks's orientation, did most of her training, and accompanied Brooks to each of the PLA gatherings.

For the internship, Brooks designed a connected learning project that she worked on all summer and upon which her presentation at the September wrap-up would be based. She came to her interview with an idea for her connected learning project already formed, based upon her love of history. Her plan was to create an oral history project to preserve the many stories and anecdotes that were passed down through the generations of families that have lived in Auburn for decades, some dating back to before the Civil War.

As Brooks pursued her project, she got to experience some local events. One was the Gwinnett County Bicentennial Torch passing through Auburn in July. Another was the dedication of a donated historic fuel pump from a gas station that once sat where the Auburn City Hall is currently located and now resides on the building's front porch. Outwater, as Brooks's mentor, learned that her grandfather actually worked for the donating family at the seed mill that they owned in addition to the gas station, something that she learned from attending the event with Brooks.

Brooks's oral history project is continuing at the library due to the teen's careful planning and laying of a solid foundation during her ten-week internship. Outwater says that this project is one that other libraries could readily implement.

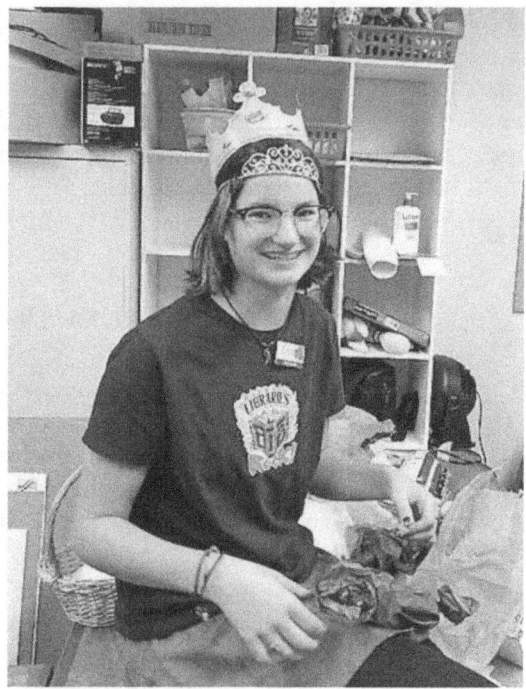

FIGURE 4.2
Emily Brooks celebrates her eighteenth birthday during her internship at the Auburn Public Library in Georgia. Credit: Bel Outwater.

In addition to her excellent project, Brooks learned the basics of library work in circulation, reference, shelving, and customer service. She followed through with the internship expectations by developing and displaying good work habits, creating and finishing her connected learning project, and filling a need for supplementary library staff during the hectic summer season. Through it all, she discovered the important role of the library in the lives of teens and the whole community.

The library turned in the required survey responses to PLA that evaluated its overall success to culminate the internship. When completing the survey, the library considered Brooks's achievements on the job, including the effective completion of her connected learning project. As a result of her internship, Brooks was offered a part-time position at one of the neighboring branch libraries. A year later, she returned to the main Auburn Library to become their new teen services coordinator. A secondary benefit of keeping her on the staff is that if the library has any questions about the oral history project, they know who to ask!

A subsequent PLA internship took place May 28 through July 27 the following year with the same kickoff and wrap-up weekend attendance requirements as there were the previous year. As was the case in 2018, the intern needed to develop an original connected learning project and aim for specific goals to be met according to PLA instructions.

During the summer of 2019, the library also offered a second, part-time teen internship. The additional internship was desirable because of the great success of the 2018 experience. The library realized that a full-time job was a large commitment for many teens, even if it was only for the summer. The second job's focus was providing a part-time work opportunity for a teen to gain practical experience in a safe environment with room to learn and take risks. The position was dubbed the YALSA/Dollar General Part-Time Teen Internship due to its funding source. For this position, the library applied for and was the recipient of a Dollar General grant administered through the YALSA.

This time, the library accepted applications for three weeks, during which the positions were publicized on social media, in the library, and at the two county high schools. Applications were expected to include a short personal statement about why teens were personally interested in working in the library along with a teacher reference. All applicants who submitted properly completed applications, the required components, and indicated their availability for the entire eight-week summer internship period (with a potential allowance of one or two weeks that could be rescheduled) were considered. Both internships were advertised together, and applications were submitted concurrently. The library interviewed a total of twenty-one applicants from a pool of twenty-seven, with most of the interest expressed in the part-time position.

With the $3,000 PLA grant, the full-time intern was paid $10.50 an hour for thirty-five hours a week for eight weeks. The $1,000 grant from YALSA/Dollar General provided the part-time

FIGURE 4.3
Teen interns Cheyenne Jones and Christina Miller pose with mascot Scout from the Auburn Public Library in Georgia. Credit: Bel Outwater.

intern $8.25 an hour for eight weeks at fifteen hours a week, higher than the minimum wage. The intern received $985, and $15 purchased a name tag (for which the library would have paid, but the grant covered it).

Assistant library manager Holly Burrell served as the mentor for the 2019 full-time PLA intern, Cheyenne Jones. She was responsible for doing Jones's new employee orientation, training her, and traveling with her to the PLA kickoff and wrap-up events in the spring and fall to Chicago and Washington, D.C. Along with Jones, Burrell did the orientation and training for the part-time intern, Christina Miller.

The training involved learning the essentials of library work in circulation, reference, shelving, and offering customer service, and helping Jones plan her connected learning project. After the orientation and training, Miller was supervised by Bel Outwater since she was responsible for reporting to YALSA and Dollar General at the end of the internship period. Other library staff supported Miller as needed with library-related tasks.

The goal for the part-time opening was to hire the teen, then allow the teen's interests and talents to shape the course of the internship. When sixteen-year-old rising high school senior Miller interviewed for her first paying job, she was a shoo-in. She had already been a library volunteer and teen advisory group member since she was twelve. She came to her interview incredibly prepared with pages of notes and dressed more professionally than the librarians had ever seen her, a sign that she was taking the opportunity seriously. Her work ethic was impeccable, but since she was rather quiet, the librarians encouraged her to help plan and execute teen programs with her peers. They discovered that her gaming hobby could be translated into multiple successful teen programs such as a Dungeons and Dragons session and virtual reality play.

At the end of Jones's PLA internship, the library submitted the required survey responses to PLA evaluating its overall success. The library described Jones's accomplishments on the job, including the successful completion of her connected learning project. YALSA also collected a survey response to evaluate the Dollar General grant. In addition, Bel Outwater wrote a blog post for YALSA about the success of Miller's internship.

The library targeted outcomes for the internships to help teens develop critical job force skills, from interview preparation to constructing an effective resume. To that end, they held a resume workshop during the application acceptance periods for interested teens. Other addressed skills were adhering to a work schedule, keeping track of work time, and interacting well with customers. The more ambitious goal was to observe the individual teens, find out their talents and interests, and play to those strengths.

TEXTBOX 4.1 LIBRARIAN VANTAGE POINT

Christina helped us with a little of everything over the summer. We offered a program every day of the week, including a free lunch program for youth eighteen and under. She helped hand out summer reading prizes, take pictures, shelve, and interact with patrons at the information desk. But where Christina really shone was in helping lead teen programs.

Our teen programs, for twelve- to nineteen-year-olds, took place on Thursday nights. One of our more popular programs that we repeated several times is Virtual Reality. We have a forty-inch television set up in our teen section, and an Oculus Rift system hooked up to it. Christina assisted with the setup of the device, and by the end of the summer, she could operate it better than any staff member! She helped download updates, choose games, and we stepped back and let her run the show with the other teens. She was fair, making sure everyone got turns and keeping the audience engaged in the fun. She also ran her first-ever Dungeons and Dragons campaign sitting in the Dungeon Master chair for a group of seven very excited teens (we almost had to throw them out of the library at closing time!).

Having an extra person to help during the summer was amazing, but seeing Christina step up and lead programs was an extraordinary experience. We provided her with tools and opportunities, and she performed beyond our highest expectations. We labeled our teen summer learning program a success for many reasons (higher participation, higher attendance), but watching Christina bloom with confidence was a highlight of the summer. Thank you, Dollar General and YALSA, for allowing us to be a part of your program—it changed lives.[1]

Bel Outwater
Auburn Public Library, Georgia

Note

1. Outwater, Bel. October 21, 2019. "2019 Teen Summer Intern Program: Summer Learning to Summer Leading at the Auburn Public Library." YALSA Blog, http://yalsa.ala.org/blog/2019/10/21/2019-teen-summer-intern-program-from-summer-learning-to-summer-leading-at-the-auburn-public-library/.

Baltimore County Public Library, Owings Mills Library Branch, Owings Mills, Maryland

The Baltimore County Public Library offered a teen library internship in the summer of 2019 (along with attendance at the weekend-long Chicago kickoff and Washington, D.C. wrap-up sessions in the spring and fall) with funding from the PLA Inclusive Internship Initiative. As was the goal for other PLA teen internships, the job focused on introducing youth from diverse backgrounds to library careers while helping librarian mentors develop their leadership skills.

The paid internship in 2019 incorporated a range of meaningful work opportunities in the library system. Although the Owings Mills branch hosted the internship, Sade Wilkens El, the teen selected through an application and interview process, also spent time at the Woodlawn branch; in the library system's Collection Development, Marketing, Virtual and Media Services departments; and with its Youth Bookmobile. These experiences were in addition to the community-based connected learning project created and run by the intern herself.

Librarian Cody Brownson-Katz and branch manager Anna White partnered to recruit, interview, and hire Wilkens El. Brownson-Katz was her primary mentor and met weekly with her throughout the summer. However, in practice, they discovered that the entire branch staff, plus many other coworkers throughout the library system, became invested in Wilkens El's internship and in assuring her chosen project's success.

> ### TEXTBOX 4.2 LIBRARIAN VANTAGE POINT
>
> I attended ALA Midwinter in Seattle in 2019 and heard past mentors and interns speak about their experience. We had a goal to grow teen services. Since our branch is not within walking distance of a school or neighborhood, we primarily engaged with teens in the community through outreach at our local high schools. A paid internship seemed a great way to connect with students in our area.
>
> Our management team also wanted to take meaningful action toward making the profession—and our staff—more diverse. We hoped that the experience of going through the PLA Inclusive Internship Initiative program could help us advocate for additional paid internships at Baltimore County Public Library in the future and give us some ideas for how to structure a successful internship experience.[1]
>
> Anna White
> Owings Mills Library branch manager, Baltimore County Public Library, Maryland
>
> **Note**
>
> 1. White, Anna. August 25, 2020. Email message to author.

The internship in 2019 was structured based on the PLA requirements of a community-based connected learning project, regular mentoring sessions, communication with other interns in the cohort, and journaling about the experience. As noted, built into the plan were opportunities for Wilkens El to learn about different library departments, especially those involved in her project. She attended community meetings, assisted with outreach and special events, wrote a public blog post for the library website, and created a video about her community project for the library staff intranet.

These are the outcomes that Brownson-Katz and White outlined and targeted for their teen intern:

- To introduce the intern to a variety of career paths in public libraries
- To learn about the different ways that libraries serve and interact with their communities
- To learn and practice workplace and customer service skills
- To gain valuable project management skills
- To help the library branch engage with youth in the community in a new way
- To pave the way for a future internship program for the library system
- To provide supervisory experience for emerging leaders on the staff

The overall results were so positive that the internship experience was used to advocate for more paid youth internships at the library system. The library had planned to host additional interns at several branches during the summer of 2020 through Baltimore County's Summer Youth Employment Program, but this had to be canceled due to the pandemic. Still, the library hopes to plan for more internships in the future.

FIGURE 4.4
Sade Wilkens El shows the products that were donated to battle period poverty for her internship project at the Baltimore County Library. She organized a PAD Packing Party for teens as a key part of the project using the donations. Credit: Cody Brownson-Katz.

Monetary compensation for teen interns was an essential component of the PLA initiative. After the results of the 2019 internship experience, the importance of offering such an opportunity to teenagers and the benefits to the library was enhanced. Library staff believes in communicating to interns that the work they have done in the library is significant, and this is reinforced by providing a paycheck. Doing so helps to level the playing field and ensures that internships are available to qualified young people who may not be able to give up a summer job with wages to pursue a valuable experiential learning opportunity.[3]

> **TEXTBOX 4.3 TEEN VANTAGE POINT**
>
> Sade Wilkens El's Internship Project Blog Post:
>
> Did you know that one in four women in the United States struggled to afford period products last year? Pads and tampons are expensive but can't be purchased with funds from government assistance programs such as the Women, Infants, and Children (WIC) program and the Supplemental Nutrition Assistance Program (SNAP). Coping with menstruation is especially challenging for people living below the poverty line or experiencing homelessness. For women who are already struggling to make ends meet, it often means a choice between food or menstrual products every month.
>
> This lack of access to menstrual products is called period poverty, and it's not just a problem in underdeveloped nations. In Baltimore County, "there is a definitive need for these items amongst individuals experiencing homelessness," according to Homeless Outreach Coordinator Maggie Carnegie of Prologue, Inc., which distributes menstrual products on a weekly basis.
>
> Period poverty often goes unaddressed because of the taboo around menstruation. So, let's talk about periods! The Owings Mills Branch is hosting a Period Action Drive (PAD) to collect pads and tampons for people in need from July 15 to August 29. All donations will be distributed to Prologue and the Community Crisis Center. We're inviting girls in grades six through twelve to join us for the PAD Packing Party on Thursday, August 29, to package the donations into kits that provide products for a complete monthly cycle. It's a safe space for girls to openly discuss any problems they are facing, give back to the community, and learn more about period poverty.
>
> Baltimore County Public Library has many materials on periods, self-esteem, and other wellness topics for teen girls.[1]
>
> Sade Wilkens El
> Baltimore County Public Library
>
> **Note**
>
> 1. Wilkens El, Sade. August 22, 2019. "Fighting Period Poverty: Be Involved." Baltimore County Public Library, https://www.bcpl.info/blog/2019/fighting-period-poverty-be-involved-at-the-library.

Brooklyn Public Library, Brooklyn, New York

At the Brooklyn Public Library, there has been a unique opportunity for teens called the Librarians for Tomorrow Teen Internship Program, which started in 2017. It has been a groundbreaking, practical internship plan for high school students from diverse backgrounds who were enrolled in grades ten through twelve and expressed an interest in library careers. The project was made possible by an Institute of Museum and Library Services grant and the support of the Brooklyn Library's Gala Philanthropic Auction.

In reviewing applications, the library looked for committed and enthusiastic teens who were willing and able to learn, work, and help others. A moderate to fluent English proficiency was required, and bilingual capability was desirable. Teens who were hired needed to have the signed consent of parents or guardians to participate.

The most recent Librarians for Tomorrow internships were set from November 2019 through June 2020, based on a pre-pandemic schedule. Internships had been planned to be completed as they were in previous years, as follows:

Teens chosen for the internships were scheduled to work five to eight hours per week during time out of school for a total of 135 internship hours. This included twenty-five to thirty-five hours of training plus field trips focused on library, college, and career skills. Hands-on work experience rounded out the remaining 100–110 hours.

Teen interns worked behind the scenes to design original programs and projects, welcomed people to the library, provided customer service, and assisted with various library events and activities such as reading to children, robotics, and cooking.

Each intern received a stipend for their work and accrued volunteer hours and gained valuable experience for resumes. With the support of mentors, teens built academic, college, and career readiness skills. They got to know and interact with like-minded teens from across New York City who were also making a difference through their libraries. Finally, each intern was required to create a capstone project based on their own special interests that tied in with the library's mission.[4]

Cabell County Public Library, Huntington, West Virginia

One of the libraries chosen for Public Library Association's Inclusive Internship Initiative funding in 2018 was the Cabell County Public Library in Huntington, West Virginia. The library selected a sixteen-year-old rising junior from Huntington High School to receive the award. She spent her summer employed in the youth department at the library and was able to work closely with young children from the community. The experience was her introduction to being in the workforce and earning a paycheck for the first time and gave her food for thought in deciding on a public service major for college.

Breana Bowen, the assistant director for youth services, explained that from among the hundreds of impressive applications the library received, the successful teen candidate was their best choice. The teen had already been a loyal library volunteer for three years, from the time she was in middle school, and she intended to continue as a volunteer when her internship was over.

In addition to her other work responsibilities, the teen developed a Multicultural Mondays program. She gave people from the community, representing diverse backgrounds, a forum to teach others about the unique aspects of their cultures. Her work was instrumental in giving others, especially parents and children, exposure to other cultures they might not have otherwise known.[5]

Charlotte Mecklenburg Library System, Charlotte Mecklenburg Counties, North Carolina

The Charlotte Mecklenburg Library System has many teen volunteers at twenty branches. As part of their teen summer participation offerings, they have provided teen summer internships for several years, supported by YALSA/Dollar General grant funding. The three internships in

2019 targeted their Sugar Creek Library, a well-used county branch in a low-income area with a lower recruitment and retention rate of teen summer volunteers. The library felt that it would be a perfect location to have internships that would increase teen involvement and dedication while helping to ensure the success of the summer reading program.

Once they were hired, the teen interns assisted with a summer reading kickoff event, where they operated a STEAM activity station. They also prepared summer reading materials for the children's department, managed summer reading registration, oversaw book displays, and helped to run programs. In addition, they had shelf-reading assignments, which included pulling duplicates from the library collections, processing materials for book sales, and aiding the circulation staff each day by pulling morning hold requests and handling deliveries.

Throughout the summer, the teen interns contributed 229 hours of work during which they successfully collaborated with each other and fellow staff members, and there were no problems with the teens sticking with their jobs. The Sugar Creek Library benefited positively from their internship roles while the teens found their work personally satisfying.

Teens were able to shine in ways that enabled them to use their unique personalities and skills effectively. One intern, Treyson, found that wearing the Clifford the Big Red Dog costume at the summer reading kickoff was hot, but he did not mind because it made the children happy to see him in it. Another intern, Aleah, enjoyed playing and interacting with children in-between shelving in the children's room. She also discovered the personal joys of reading more, using the library's hold system, and finding out that she enjoys both ebooks and audiobooks. The third intern, Kaliyah, who aspires to become a graphic designer, spent some time with and got tips from a staff member who is also an artist, a connection she might not otherwise have been able to have.

Hayley Burson, the teen librarian, attributed each teen intern's success and dedication to keeping the tasks enjoyable and varied. She was pleased to see that each teen demonstrated growth as they did their jobs, learned a great deal of new and good things about the library, and found their niches in the process.[6]

Gadsden Public Library, Gadsden, Alabama

For the summer of 2019, the Gadsden Public Library hired three teen interns. Two of the internships were funded by a YALSA/Dollar General grant, and the third by library fundraising.

Fifteen teenagers applied for these positions. Each had to complete an application and come to an interview. Library staff sought candidates they felt would get the most benefit from a library employment opportunity. They were the most adept at being interviewed and would fit in well with the Young Adult Department.

There were several particulars for teens who were applying. They did not need previous experience, they must have been enrolled in a school within the county district, and they needed to supply multiple references. During their interviews, teens were asked to reply to a series of questions. They were asked why they wanted the internship experience, what they hoped to do and be in five years, what they considered one of their favorite books, and what they felt were their greatest strengths and weaknesses. Through this process, the library staff members interviewing the teens could get valuable information about the teens' personalities that helped them select those they would hire. They discovered what the teens enjoyed reading, what they liked about school, and what they liked to do.

In addition, because they had good background information for the three teens chosen, they could tailor their assignments to those that each teen would do best. One intern had experience flying a drone and using a telescope, so he was scheduled to assist with technology-oriented and space programs. Another teen was adept at working with social media, and she was asked to take and caption photos and videos of library events. The third teen was interested in education and was drawn to working with youngsters, and she was given opportunities to assist with programs in the children's department. Each intern was expected to work five hours a week, in two two-and-a-half-hour shifts during the busiest times of the day.

Proper training to comprehend what library work is like before embarking on their new jobs was required for all teens. They spent a training day during which they toured the whole library, met their fellow library staff members, observed programs, learned basic policies and procedures, and were coached on professionalism. The teens were taught about the things libraries do and offer in addition to providing books and doing shelving, plus about the role of each library department. Even though the teens all attended the initial training day, the library staff knew that they would still need to update them about daily expectations. Each day, they received an overview with details on what they would accomplish, above all when programming was part of the schedule. Each day's instructions varied depending on assignments for that day, sometimes requiring a checklist as they completed tasks. The teens also learned that they were expected to shelve materials or get items ready for upcoming programs during downtime.

The interns became familiar with the teen programming schedule and assisted staff with set- up, cleanup, and running both passive and active events and activities, big and small, which ranged from gaming to art, and more. On weekdays, participating teens were given free lunches and snacks.

The library staff learned a great deal themselves as they supervised and worked with the teens that summer. They found that knowing the teens' strong and weak points was beneficial. Because two of the teens were active at school and had experience with children's birthday parties, they were able to balance several tasks at the same time, manage loud and energetic programs, engage readily in art projects, and deal well with other teenagers. Although they did not tell the teen interns to refrain from chatting with other teens while on duty, library staff did remind them to keep their conversations professional when representing the library during work time.

In contrast, library staff discovered that the third teen had trouble dealing with noisiness and too many people at once, which made his working in the busy and often loud teen area a problem. He was reassigned to a quiet setting and work that fit his personality—employing his precision skills to shelve books and scan materials. The library staff realized that they needed to address the nature of the work assignment locations during the future training and scheduling of interns.

Young Adult Librarian Nicole Tudor said, "The intern program turned out to be very successful. Both the teens and staff benefited from the relationship. The library had extra help during our busiest time of the year. The teen interns received beneficial experience which will help them as they join the workforce or go to college."[7]

Hussey-Mayfield Memorial Public Library, Zionsville, Indiana

For several years, Patricia VanArsdale, the teen and adult services assistant department head at the Hussey-Mayfield Memorial Public Library, has enrolled teen summer interns. Although they are currently unpaid, they are still dedicated and eagerly seek these positions that have a higher responsibility than regular volunteers.[8] The internship program has had a different number of teens each year, but that number often falls around eleven to fourteen students, which provides coverage for twelve shifts per week.

The internship program takes place each year during summer reading, which coincides with the last day of school when it starts. While the dates vary each year, summer reading usually begins either the Thursday or Friday before Memorial Day or the Tuesday or Wednesday after Memorial Day and then runs for eight to nine full weeks.

The internship program's focus was designed to provide an additional level of volunteerism for a select few teens who had shown excellence in their previous library volunteer contributions. The interns provided support for library staff in managing their more than thirty peer Teen Volunteer Corps members and for VanArsdale in the provision and overseeing of all teen programs, including the teen summer reading program in general. Interns worked more than forty hours during the summer, more than twice what is expected of the volunteers.

The first year of the internship program was 2012, thanks to YALSA and the Dollar General Literacy Foundation's support. The $1,000 grant that the library received was also awarded to them in 2013 and 2014. The grant could not go toward staff salaries but was used for stipends that were evenly divided among the interns.

Because it was so popular and successful, the program continued in 2015, 2016, 2017, 2018, and 2019 without the financial support of YALSA and the Dollar General Literacy Foundation grant, and interns served without pay. The program did not take place in 2020 due to the pandemic.

To be eligible as interns, applicants must have been previous members of the Teen Volunteer Corps program. They were also required to have had good attendance during their previous service; to have displayed good attitudes toward staff, patrons, and fellow volunteers; to have demonstrated good communication skills; and to have shown a desire to go above and beyond their typical volunteer duties of assisting with the summer reading program. If teens completed the Teen Volunteer Corps applications and indicated they were also interested in the Teen Intern positions, they were sent information to apply.

Applications for the Teen Volunteer Corps have been due in early April, while Teen Intern applications are due the week before the local spring break. These deadlines allowed ample time for reviewing, interviewing, contacting, and scheduling the entire pool of candidates. Communications about decisions, either by email or paper mail as specified by the applicants, were sent out on the same day that choices were made. Teens under consideration knew to expect additional, finalized information, including placement and schedules, in this correspondence. They also knew that mailings would be sent out in red envelopes to be easy to spot and not accidentally thrown away.

After examining teen intern applications, those who qualified were contacted to arrange short interviews with general questions. These interviews were meant, in part, to screen applicants and also to teach prospective interns about and let them experience the interviewing process. VanArsdale and her supervisor worked together to conduct the interviews and discussed which teens they wanted to choose afterward. In recent years, one aspect of the process was revised. Previous interns who were interested in returning were not required to interview. However, those specific teens were informed that they were still welcome to interview if they liked to practice for future job and career opportunities. Although no one has taken advantage of this opportunity so far, the option will remain in the future. On the other hand, good quality applicants who did not get an internship were placed into the Teen Volunteer Corps program if they were willing to take that alternative.

FIGURE 4.5
As one of her duties, a library teen intern trains Teen Volunteer Corps members about a portion of the Teen Summer Reading Program. Interns and volunteers were placed into small groups and rotated stations, providing intimate and in-depth training for each specific part of the program. Credit: Hussey-Mayfield Memorial Public Library.

> **SIDEBAR 4.1 TEEN VANTAGE POINT**
>
> Once you apply, then the library sets up an interview, which lasts about fifteen minutes. You talk about your strengths, what you enjoy doing at the library, and then the interviewers discuss the program and what you would potentially be doing if you are "hired" as an intern, though there is no payment.[1]
>
> Bethany Worrell
> Hussey-Mayfield Memorial Public Library, Zionsville, Indiana
>
> **Note**
> 1. Worrell, Bethany. July 3, 2020. Email message to author.

Each year, the selected interns have undergone a two-day extensive training before logging their more than forty program hours. Each intern was held accountable for their shift and was responsible for finding another intern who could trade shifts if they could not meet their schedule due to vacations, camps, other conflicts, or family obligations.

During the internship periods, VanArsdale has had each student fill out a record of the duties they have performed. She has provided a daily to-do list of tasks that needed to be accomplished on a per-shift basis for interns to undertake themselves or to delegate to volunteers. In addition, library staff members could delegate additional projects to interns when these tasks were finished. These plans included reshelving, doing inventory, prize desk setup, copying daily crosswords, straightening shelves and desks, pulling down old event posters, and putting up new posters. Interns also sign up participants for the summer reading challenge, pass out prizes, and do several additional tasks to assist the library staff. A variety of information sheets are given to the interns to stay on task. VanArsdale uses screenshots and other images as needed to make sure that the interns know exactly what to do.

Interns have greatly expanded training, responsibilities, and time requirements compared to a volunteer's expectations. Volunteers work two two-hour shifts per week, and they are responsible for manning the summer reading desk and shelving and doing inventory when things are running slow. Interns work two four-hour shifts per week, and in addition to the volunteer responsibilities, they are the leaders. They often delegate tasks to the volunteers and pull volunteers to help them with the projects to which they are assigned. Interns set up and tear down the prize desk and can enter the staff back room to retrieve prizes when those items run low at the desk. Interns can also facilitate library programs with some supervision, such as the video game hour or showing a movie and supervise library patrons during these activities. VanArsdale has played a very active role in offering guidance during summer reading, managing interns and volunteers, providing advice, answering questions, giving positive feedback on behavior, and offering tips to improve as interns are empowered to act independently.

The teens are expected to gain valuable work experience while contributing to the library. Volunteers gain experience in teamwork, work ethics, and organization. To that mix, interns add leadership, delegation, and on-your-feet decision-making. The library acquires the interns' and volunteers' assistance, which helps run the summer reading challenge and the many events associated with it, including craft events, movie events, and social events.

To illustrate one particular task delegated to interns, Matthew Health and Sam Stucky were just two of the interns who were instrumental in creating detailed directions for completing specific tasks for special projects interns. They put together step-by-step instructions on handling summer reading prize winner drawings and notifications, running "top reader reports," how to effectively remind upcoming program registrants, and more. They took photographs and made screenshots to help guide their fellow interns. The document they created was clear and useful for their coworkers.

Interns were expected to sign in for their shifts, correctly locate the sign in and out cards, record their time, and then come to the reference desk to introduce themselves to the staff member at the desk. The introduction portion of this task was a more recent, positive addition. This requirement was designed to inform the reference librarian which teen intern was assigned to the shift. At the same time, it gave the interns a chance to become comfortable speaking to unfamiliar adults.

Essentially, this requirement was a great opening to a meaningful connection for several interns. For instance, one intern would introduce himself and add, "I'm handy with computers, and I like looking stuff up if you need help with anything." This single sentence and others like it did wonders for both the intern, who was excited to help with a variety of further tasks over the summer, as well as for the staff member who was staffing the reference desk. After two weeks or so, staff members often found themselves checking the intern schedule wanting to know when a certain intern would be in, as they had a project or task that particular intern was going to enjoy. This small change resulted in happier interns and a happier, more productive staff. It also allowed staff to provide interns with additional feedback on the many parts and pieces of library jobs of which most people are unaware.

SIDEBAR 4.2 TEEN VANTAGE POINT

The library's summer internship was part of the Summer Teen Volunteer Corps Program. The program's focus was mainly to facilitate the summer reading event that our library hosts, where prizes are awarded for time spent reading. Interns were an intermediary between teen volunteers and library staff, and we received extra training and worked longer shifts.

Interns largely supervised and managed volunteers, plus helped in an organizational role, setting up the summer reading booth, supervising events, and dealing with other projects. Some of my projects included writing detailed instructions for uploading photos to a digital picture frame and designing library displays. My internship took place over the summers of 2015 and 2016, from early June to early August.

During my first interview, I remember asking about the difference between a volunteer and an intern. Patricia explained that since the volunteer program was so successful and important to the success of the summer reading program, they wanted to expand that program. Interns, she explained, would have greater responsibility and autonomy. They'd be helping run the show behind the scenes and be the go-to people when we hit a snag.[1]

Ty Allen
Hussey-Mayfield Memorial Public Library, Zionsville, Indiana

Note
1. Allen, Ty. May 29, 2020. Email message to author.

Each year, the internship program is evaluated using a group exit interview. This interview is often a two-hour, relaxed, organized discussion about the interns' experiences. For many, it is the first time they have seen each other for more than two minutes since they originally came together for their training two months before. Additionally, the internships have ended with individual exit interviews, during which VanArsdale and the individual interns have had an opportunity to review the entire experience.

After the interviews, VanArsdale discussed the answers with her supervisor to see if any changes could be made for the following year. She would then pull these notes back out in March or April of the next year to revisit the previous intern responses to see if changes or adjustments could be made. Anyone unable to attend the group exit interview was asked the questions during their final shift or emailed the answers later.

In addition to the exit interviews, interns have been responsible for keeping detailed lists of tasks they performed during their internships, being as specific as possible. For instance, they were told not to simply say "program prep" but to indicate particulars like "setting up tables and chairs for adult programs; cleaning out the popcorn machine; and shelving books." Each intern received a sheet to make their notes, and which they were encouraged to keep for their records (see a suggested form template in appendix D). This record allowed them to recall the abundance of tasks they performed on the job while providing VanArsdale with a written record of what they accomplished over the summer.

VanArsdale keeps copies of the lists of achievements for other staff members who would like to know what the teen interns have done so that they have something to consult when writing references. She also gives them to former interns and copies their parents to have the information readily available and apply it later as needed. One intern even told her that he could often reference his intern experience in an interview with a recent store chain because he had access to these notes, giving him an edge over other applicants.[9]

Finally, to illustrate how meaningful these internship opportunities were, here is a little story. One young lady biked to the library on two-lane back roads with no sidewalk or shoulder, showing her commitment to and enthusiasm for her internship. An exciting result of her experience was that, because her service was so personally meaningful, she decided to enter the world of librarianship after high school.[10]

Indian Prairie Public Library, Darien, Illinois

As a district library, the Indian Prairie Public Library serves parts of Darien, Burr Ridge, and Willowbrook, Illinois. As Natalie Williams, head of youth services, explained, the district applied for and thankfully received a YALSA Summer Intern Grant, funded by Dollar General. This funding allowed them to hire a teen at $10.50 an hour in 2019. Qualified teens who completed an application were required to undergo an interview process. Following the selection of a teen intern, staff provided orientation and training. Essentially, the teens who applied went through the same process as any new staff member.

An underserved area of the district is called Willowbrook Corner. During the summer, staff members from the Kids & Teens department have usually made weekly visits to the Willowbrook Corner Summer Camp at the Anne M. Jeans Elementary School. They presented activities to four different groups of approximately seventy children in grades K–5. In 2019, the successful teen summer intern, Carson, took on this responsibility with library staff.

For his internship, Carson planned and presented the activities for the children and guided various staff members, who rotated the task of accompanying him to the different locations. As Carson led them, children planted seeds and learned about gardening, created Makey Makey banana pianos, played with various musical instruments that the library circulates, constructed catapults, and completed several art projects. He taught them several cooperative group games such as Frogger, which he incorporated into his visits. On the last day, Carson delivered new books that participating children could keep as prizes.

Besides the Willowbrook Corner visits, the library staff organized a bus-sharing enterprise with a neighboring school district. The library uses the school's summer school buses and drivers to pick up the children from Anne M. Jeans Elementary School, bring them to the library, and return them to their summer camp. The library staff knew that transportation is not readily available for many families who find it challenging to get to the library. They wanted to experiment with new ways to reach the children and their families.

Using Carson's preplanned activities, children visiting the library were able to play games on the Nintendo Switch; use computers and tablets; create and sew in the makerspace called the WouldShop; make buttons; play with puppets; read; see their own artwork displayed in the Prairie Patch, the library's community garden; and so much more. Library staff received a great deal of positive feedback from the children when they visited, such as, "This is where I'm going to work when I grow up," and "Wow, I'm going to need at least three days to do everything I want in here." Carson proved to be an outstanding role model.

After the internship, both the supervisor and library staff working with the teen intern provided an evaluation experience that benefited both parties. The library acknowledged that their community, especially the Willowbrook Corner children, positively benefited from Carson's work. Likewise, they noted that the opportunity was beneficial for Carson himself, who gained experience interviewing, training, and working in the library.[11]

Laredo Public Libraries, Laredo, Texas

The Laredo Public Library hired a teen intern from June through September 2019, using funds provided by the PLA Inclusive Internship Initiative program. Analiza Perez-Gomez, Librarian IV, served as a mentor, and Ricardo Carrillo, the Circulation and Mobile Services Supervisor and Teen Advisory Board Facilitator, was the intern's direct supervisor.

Although having an application and interview process was optional according to PLA, the Laredo Public Libraries preferred to go through a definitive hiring course to make a selection. This process required an application, an essay, membership in the Laredo Public Libraries' Teen Advisory Board, and at least five hundred community service hours with the library. In this way, the most qualified and eligible teens from the community could have a chance at an application and interview experience. The successful candidate was a freshly graduated high school senior named Aaron Vivanco, now a student at Texas A&M International University.

Compensation of $3,500, an amount determined by PLA, was paid directly to Vivanco. Also covered by PLA was the all-expenses-paid travel for Perez-Gomez and Vivanco to attend and participate in both the Inclusive Internship Initiative opening event in Chicago and the closing event in Washington, D.C.

Rather than requiring a strict set of assignments for Vivanco, both the PLA staff and the Laredo Public Libraries staff were flexible about what he would accomplish. The internship plan was created based on the library's needs and the intern's interests and skill set. His community-based learning project, required by PLA, centered on introducing virtual reality technology into the library as a service that can be provided. He believes that adding virtual reality as a library service could spark curiosity about technology in children and teens and be the foundation of future pursuits. Through his internship efforts, Vivanco said that he learned a great deal about how a library operates and the process behind the events created for the public. He noted that he had been considering going into library work, but now that he knows and appreciates the library more, he is further inclined to do so.[12]

FIGURE 4.6
Intern Aaron Vivanco and librarian mentor Analiza Perez-Gomez from the Laredo Public Libraries in Texas attended the September wrap-up event for the 2019 Inclusive Internship Initiative in Washington, D.C. Credit: Zach Miller.

Throughout this process, the roles of the librarian mentor, the direct supervisor, and the other library staff were to guide the intern. At the same time, he learned the fundamental library duties as he planned and implemented his special project. To conclude, the internship was informally evaluated through conversations between the library director, the librarian mentor, other staff involved in the project, and the intern himself. Additionally, the intern reported his mentor's performance to the PLA staff.

Perez-Gomez said, "The outcomes for the internship were determined by PLA and included participation in the kickoff and wrap-up events. Other requirements were for the interns to complete a connected learning project and present it to their peers; develop job skills; practice public speaking; learn about new people and places; make new friends; and gain understanding of librarianship, including how the library fits into the community and why being a librarian is a fulfilling career."

She added, "All of the mentors/librarians selected by PLA were expected to guide their interns through the process and offer advice on their connected learning projects; develop leadership skills; build a network of peers; and demonstrate to their interns the 'Big Ideas' that are foundational to library services and programs. These ideas are access, confidentiality/privacy,

> **SIDEBAR 4.3 TEEN VANTAGE POINT**
>
> My experience with PLA was nothing like I've ever had before. It took me out of my comfort zone in that it was my first job-like opportunity, as well as in that it taught me more about all the different roles that come together in making a library operate and succeed in providing services to the public. But the time spent wasn't only limited to the library. I was also given the opportunity to meet and converse with people who have all kinds of different interests, ambitions, and goals. To be able to learn and share the knowledge that each of us had was incredible to do. PLA granted me an experience and opportunity that I would not have been able to be a part of if it weren't for them. It gave me job skills, allowed me to meet some amazing people, and also helped me think more about my own ambitions and goals in life.[1]
>
> Aaron Vivanco
> Laredo Public Libraries, Texas
>
> **Note**
> 1. Vivanco, Aaron. July 8, 2020. Email message to author by Analiza Perez-Gomez.

democracy, diversity, education and lifelong learning, intellectual freedom, the public good, and preservation."[13]

North Shelby Library, Birmingham, Alabama

During the summer of 2018, the North Shelby Library had eight high-school-age interns. Four of them were funded by a YALSA/Dollar General grant, and the Friends of the Library funded the other four.

The library staff created an application for the positions, posted it on their website, and distributed it at the local schools. The application included information about the teens' jobs to peruse, requested references, and required a commitment for the dates of training, the summer reading kickoff, and a scheduled intern-led STEAM program.

The library had forty-three teens who applied for the internships. Once the applications were received, the staff selected teens to be interviewed. Although a few chosen applicants could not meet the requirement to attend the three essential dates, it was still a challenge to interview twenty-eight of the remaining teens. These included members of the library's Teen Leadership Council who were automatically given interviews if they agreed to be present on the required dates. Despite interviews being limited to less than fifteen minutes each, it still took two evenings to complete them all. Besides the interviews, a basic shelving skills test was administered as teens waited to be called in.

Making the decisions to narrow down to only eight of these twenty-eight teens was not easy. The teens selected were hired to work thirty hours each, including their training time. Each of them would receive a T-shirt and a name tag, plus a stipend at the end of their internship period.

Once they were on board, the first step was to attend a three-hour training session. The training comprised a library tour, an explanation of work expectations, reviewing the pertinent parts of the library personnel manual, introductions of key staff, arranging job schedules, and the initial design of their STEAM program for eight- to twelve-year-olds. In addition to that program, the interns were assigned to assist with other programming and general library duties.

Their first task was to be at the summer reading kickoff and facilitate an activity relating to their forthcoming program. The activity they picked was creating a cardboard maze through which to navigate a Sphero robot. The eight interns separated into two teams of four, each team monitoring the maze for half of the time and then switching to assist with the special kickoff booths the other half.

After the kickoff event, each teen was scheduled for seven three-hour work shifts. Duties varied: setting up, helping to run, and taking down the children's craft and movie programs; setting up and assisting tween attendees with materials like Hue Animation and Snap Circuits during Tween Tuesday Tech programs; shelving library materials; and addressing special projects such as moving video games to locking cases.

The last internship project was completing the STEAM event that they began developing during their training session. The teens decided to include three activities in their program. They would do "Elephant Toothpaste," a marshmallow engineering challenge, and cardboard Sphero mazes. They were also responsible for setting up and cleaning up their program.

Once summer reading was over and the teen interns had completed all of their hours, they received their stipends. They also signed thank-you pictures for both Dollar General and the Friends of the Library.

The teen interns had many benefits from their work experiences at the library. They experienced applying for a job and being interviewed; learned about planning and teamwork as they executed their STEAM event; put positive workplace skills into practice as they observed being on time, followed the dress code, and registered their hours; used good communication skills to rearrange schedules as needed; learned to accept criticism; and made wise task choices. The teens also gained the library skills of shelving, planning and running programs, and completing special projects.

The teens also gained knowledge of the significance of evaluation. They collected and recorded attendee reactions for every program, which were all positive, and they also gave feedback on their STEAM program. After the STEAM program, the library staff held a short evaluation meeting with the interns, and they followed that up with an email to the interns asking for responses to twelve questions. The answers would be used for further improvement of the succeeding intern-created event.

The library staff considered the internship program a great success. Through it, many teen applicants who had not been active in the library before became aware of the programs being offered. Because of the good turnout of internship candidates, staff did not want to discourage the teens who were not selected, and they were very careful to turn them down in a positive fashion. As mentioned in the previous chapter, that is a challenge every library offering teen internships needs to consider when dealing with teen applicants.

Overall, the teens did a wonderful job with their library work experiences. They were a great help in numerous ways. In reflecting on the program, the young adult services librarian realized a need to address some of the program scheduling times better and allow the teens to practice their roles in the programs in advance to ease a few intern jitters. These were not major issues, and library staff planned to use this knowledge to improve the internship experiences in the future.[14]

Rancho Cucamonga Public Library, Rancho Cucamonga, California

The Rancho Cucamonga Public Library Summer Teen Volunteer Internship provided paraprofessional positions for teens to support the library's summer reading program while giving the interns the chance to build and enhance their employability in the future. The aim was to offer interns ample opportunities to learn new skills while honing existing skills through library staff members' supervision and mentorship during their internship period.

The internship was funded by a YALSA/Dollar General Teen Summer Intern Grant of $1,000. The Library's Teen Services staff, Brittany Garcia and Janet Monterrosa, applied for the grant in the fall of 2018 and received the award in early 2019.

The process for executing the internship began in the spring of 2019 when it was advertised through social media, flyers, email, and programming announcements from April 1 to May 1. Applications, available in both print and online formats, were accessible on April 15. Interested and qualified teens were asked to submit completed paper applications, which asked for parental signatures, in person between April 15 and May 1. Interviews were scheduled during the week of May 6, and offers for the positions were made the following week. The internship period was ten weeks long, lasting from May 20 to August 3.

The internship process was competitive and consisted of an application, a personal reference, and an interview. Applicants needed to be between the ages of sixteen and eighteen at the time of the internships. To qualify for a stipend, they had to commit to working all ten weeks of the program, especially for three important, large-scale events during the summer reading program. These events were the annual Star Wars Day in late May and the children's and teens' summer reading finales at the end of July. The entire application review process

FIGURE 4.7
Nayana Thompson (left) and Morea Lee (right) show their big smiles as they end one of their final shifts as teen interns at the Rancho Cucamonga Public Library. Credit: Brittany Garcia.

and interviews were handled by Garcia and Monterrosa, who took note of previous volunteer experience, understanding of the library's mission and values, communication skills, and summer schedule availability.

Eight of the twenty-three candidates were offered interviews using a ranking system. Interviews were held over two days. Garcia and Monterrosa asked the teen candidates about their strengths and weaknesses, why they wished to intern at the library, and their previous experiences. After these eight interviews, the two eventual finalists, Nayana Thompson and Morea Lee, were offered the internship positions.

The internships took place at three locations: the Archibald Library, the Paul A. Biane Library, and the Victoria Gardens Lifestyle Center. The majority of the time was spent at the first two locations, with one major event, the annual Star Wars Day, taking place at the lifestyle center. This special event was a required activity for the internship participants due to its large-scale nature.

Orientations were conducted at the onset, and exit interviews were given at the end of the internships. In-depth schedules were created based on each intern's availability and included sixteen hours of orientations and training. Garcia and Monterrosa, as the lead supervisors and mentors, provided the orientations and initial trainings; made and adjusted schedules for the interns and each library division; acted as liaisons between nonsupervisory library staff and the interns; provided opportunities for the interns to shadow library staff; and served as primary contacts for any questions, concerns, and social interaction. They also provided exit interviews and a letter of recommendation for each teen at the end of the internship.

The initial five-hour orientation that was conducted by teen services staff included an introduction to library policies and procedures; a tour of both library locations; discussions about each intern's personal schedule; basic information about the library and each of its divisions; introductions to library staff; and explaining the library's Code of Conduct and the California Labor Codes. This orientation mimicked the library's standard new employee orientation and onboarding process. Additional trainings were designed and delivered by each of the specific library divisions that worked with the interns during the ten-week program. The divisions participating were Teen and Tween Services; Children's and Family Services; Technology Services; Circulation Services; and Second Story and Beyond®.

An internship curriculum was developed with three goals in mind. The primary goal was to ensure that interns would be supervised, mentored, and trained by each participating library division at least once. This allowed each division to gain the support of the temporary intern staff for their daily operations and provide the interns with an opportunity to experience differing supervisory, communication, and training styles. The second goal was to promote teamwork among the interns by having them work in tandem each week on a variety of assignments. The final goal was to provide each intern with at least two to three consecutive days off each week to help prevent burnout during the summer.

Partner library staff members acted as weekly supervisors when the interns were working within their divisions. This included training the interns for their weekly tasks, plus teaching them skills and utilizing processes such as: putting data entry into an Excel spreadsheet, being familiar with the basics of integrated library systems, using the Xerox copier, learning the order and reasoning of the Dewey decimal system, following the chain of command, employing good telephone etiquette, describing preferred communication styles, and evaluating the interns on their work at the end of each week. The feedback they provided to Garcia and Monterrosa gave insights into helping the interns improve their work and communication skills before starting a new work week in a new division.

> **TEXTBOX 4.4 TEEN VANTAGE POINT**
>
> From my experience being an intern at the library, I have learned many valuable skills that I will be able to use for future jobs, such as being able to work with others, and feel comfortable working as part of a larger organization.
>
> The staff was very supportive and was eager to help with anything I had questions about. Everyone was very grateful whenever I helped with even the simplest thing, and that made me feel much appreciated.
>
> Morea Lee
> Rancho Cucamonga Public Library, California

Notes

1. Lee, Morea. September 29, 2020. Email message to author from Janet Monterrosa.

Each of the library divisions had a plan and a list of duties for the interns to follow and complete. The interns would check in with their division supervisor for the week and receive training and instruction on how to complete their weekly project list. For Teen and Tween Services, the interns planned and prepared for programs; used the digital single-lens reflex (DSLR) camera to photograph the programs in action; and processed items for the "library of things" collection, known as "RC Kits." For Children's Services, they did similar planning for, preparing for, and photographing programs. They assisted with the summer reading event table and made phone calls to over one hundred summer reading prize winners. In Technology Services, the interns inventoried technology for surplus; assisted with public technology courses; made copies of handouts and flyers; and did troubleshooting to identify technology updates and errors. As interns worked in Circulation Services, they shelved library materials; assisted with the check-in of returned library materials; and learned techniques so that they could repair books. And finally, at the Second Story and Beyond® area, the interns prepared for and helped run programs; created sample activity materials for program participants to use; disinfected program supplies and toys; and made copies of handouts and flyers.

Through their involvement in these activities and by taking on these tasks, Lee and Thompson gained new knowledge and developed many beneficial skills:

- By leading the children's summer reading registration and manning the weekly check-in tables, the interns learned to prioritize tasks, communicate and delegate assignments to other teen volunteers, and how to use Chromebooks with Google Drive.
- As the interns aided in implementing the summer reading programs, they learned about necessary preparation, shadowed library staff, assisted the presenters and performers, and ascertained the steps required to design an event for diverse demographics.
- The interns provided support and additional hands for large-scale events, including the summer reading kickoff and the finales, which allowed them to hone the skills necessary to communicate with large groups effectively and efficiently and manage crowds and lines of over five hundred people.

- Through collaborating with tween and teen services staff on programming, planning, ideas, and execution, the interns were taught how to and were able to use iPads, Windows computers, photo-editing software, and DSLR cameras.
- As they processed items for the "library of things" collection, the interns were instructed on using a P-Touch label machine, a small desk laminator, and the Xerox machine to copy and scan materials.
- The interns observed and learned about various communication, training, and supervisory approaches by being mentored and supervised by various library managers. They also learned about and applied, as applicable, library procedures and policies related to work schedules, tardiness, "sick phone line" call-in, and time cards.

Both interns were the recipients of $450 stipends, supplied by the grant, that were awarded upon satisfactory completion of their ten-week assignments. Interns were each asked to work an average of 19.75 hours a week. They were assigned projects that were significantly more dynamic and vital than the assignments given to the library's average teen volunteers. Typically, volunteers contribute no more than three hours a week and work on repetitive clerical tasks. Because of the more rigorous nature of the interns' work and schedules, their stipends were warranted. The total for both stipends was $900, with the remaining $100 from the grant award covering the expenses for office supplies used for intern training, such as name badges, planners, and photocopy fees.

The library's expected outcome was that the two interns would provide paraprofessional-level assistance during the library's busiest time. This outcome was achieved and surpassed expectations, so much so that library staff relished the teens' supplementary support. The outcome exceeded expectations due in no small part to the two high-performing interns' persistence and passion. Both requested an increase in their work schedules, which moved them from an average of twelve hours to 19.75 hours a week.

The interns' expected outcomes were increasing their employability by expanding their breadth of hard and soft skills. This was achieved through the program's curriculum and daily tasks, which were purposely designed to expose the interns to a variety of managers, teaching and communication styles, trainings, and experiential learning opportunities. The interns developed several hard skills, including, but not limited to, using Google Drive, Windows 7, Windows 10, DSLR cameras, and iOS 11. They also had many opportunities to develop their soft skills, including interpersonal interactions, manners, problem-solving, organizational, and communication skills.

The evaluation piece was a prominent feature throughout the internships. First, the program was evaluated by library staff before the internship commenced in terms of proposed schedules, projects, and outcomes. Each division made their needs apparent to the Teen Services staff regarding the intern schedules and which week(s) were best suited to their division's busy times. Schedules were drafted based on this need and intern availability. Once the interns began their weekly scheduled shifts, division supervisors provided informal evaluations to the Teen Services staff regarding the interns' punctuality, productivity, and communication. In addition, the Teen Services staff checked in with each intern at least once a week to see how they were doing and if they had any questions.

Furthermore, the interns were asked to "write a blog" about their experiences, which they shared with the Teen Services staff. In turn, the blogs were used as evaluation and feedback tools and were referred to during exit interview discussions. (Find out more about using blogs as evaluation tools in chapter 6.) Lastly, during the exit interviews, the interns were formally

FIGURE 4.8
A catchy and informative flyer promotes the Rancho Cucamonga Public Library's teen internship.
Credit: Rancho Cucamonga Public Library.

evaluated by the Teen Services staff, who put all the feedback received during the ten-week program to good use.

St. Louis County Library, St. Louis, Missouri

The Sidney Johnson Summer Internship was named as a memorial for a library clerk whose life was taken while still in high school. The internship's focus is to introduce library work to young people as a possible career path, emphasizing attracting diversity to the library field. The internship provides a broad overview of the St. Louis County Library's work and function. Because the internship was first awarded in 2019, the library has only hosted one Sidney Johnson intern so far. The second internship, scheduled for June 1 through August 7, 2020, was canceled due to the pandemic. The intention was for interns to spend time working at several library locations and possibly visit some other sites during outreach activities.

The St. Louis County Library Foundation funds internships. There is a salary of $10 per hour. The library's goal has been to attract qualified candidates for the internship and ensure a high level of commitment on the part of the chosen intern for completing the role and working diligently throughout the summer. To be considered, teens had to submit an application. Two staff members, Alaina Culbertson and Nicole Clawson, have partnered as coadvisors to review the submitted applications, select the most qualified finalists, and invite them to come in for interviews.

The library has created a general outline of the interns' learning opportunities and experiences. Each year, they plan to customize it to meet individual intern's particular interests. The coadvisors developed and will adapt a schedule and plan of activities with each selected intern's input. The Regional Branch Administrator coordinated the intern's experiences with other St. Louis County Library staff and provided day-to-day supervision and oversight of the intern, which will continue for future internship experiences.

By offering these opportunities, the library hopes that interns will develop a greater understanding of the library's complexity and an appreciation of the institution's value in general. The goal is that the interns might eventually consider employment with St. Louis County Library or think about pursuing a library career elsewhere. Furthermore, the internships allow teens to leave the experience with valuable skills and knowledge that can help them with academics in high school and college and help them envision what a professional working environment looks like so that they will be prepared for whatever career they eventually pursue.

Interns submit periodic reports throughout the summer. Feedback and coaching are provided to the interns throughout the experiences. They have a final wrap-up meeting to reflect on the overall results at the end of each internship term.[15]

West Custer County Library, Westcliffe, Colorado

Although the West Custer Library is located in a small, rural area, it reaches out to the broader world through an expanding network of advanced technology to accomplish its goals, to meet the growing needs of the public at large, and to enhance the quality of life for the community in Custer County. Its philosophy is to encourage lifelong learning; to provide resources to help people of all ages in their quest for knowledge, leisure, and problem-solving; and promote history, culture, and a free exchange of ideas among the diverse library users.[16]

To that end, the library has offered a Teen Summer Internship for several years. Applicants have been required to be thirteen to eighteen years old and to commit to approximately twenty-five hours of service. While the positions are unpaid, they are still a great opportunity to gain marketable job skills, job experience, and letters of recommendation for future jobs and college applications or scholarships.[17] An example of the internship job description can be found in appendix E.

In May 2016, between her eighth and ninth grade school years, Makynna Reiff served as the first teen intern at the West Custer Library. Her supervisor and mentor, Jessica Carter, the youth services librarian, had a full application and interview process that Reiff navigated before being offered the position.

Reiff knew and agreed that the only compensation she would get would be the learning experiences of organizing and running events. After going through orientation and an explanation of her duties, she began her internship by helping to prepare and run the Summer Reading Program for that summer. After the summer, the internship was extended, and she decided to stay on. Her job was to assist with the monthly children's program, Camp Happiness, throughout the 2016–2017 school year.

After the initial full year of being an intern until May 2017, Reiff volunteered as a shelver, summer reading program assistant, and Camp Happiness aide. During this period as a volunteer rather than as an intern, which lasted until September 2018, she went through an orientation for shelving and worked under Library Director Amy Moulton's supervision.

In August 2019, Reiff was again selected as a Teen Intern for her senior year to earn work-study credit for school. This time, her internship had a different tone. She worked on data management, analysis, and presentation. She also helped with event flyers, planning, and the occasional quick office task for both the circulation desk staff and the Youth Services Librarian, Angela McCaffrey. Again, she was given a full orientation for her new internship and received a document outlining her duties and responsibilities as a guideline.

For both of her actual internships, Reiff spent most of her time working independently. During her freshman year internship, after her orientation, she did this by designing, preparing, and leading the children's group events to which she was assigned, though she also joined in when there was a team-run activity. Two years after the conclusion of that first experience, in preparation for her senior year internship, new Library Director Sean Beharry required her to go through an additional orientation and watch instructional videos to ensure that Reiff knew how to do the different kinds of tasks she would be given. Reiff received emails from him, or one of the other librarians, with assignments on which she would work, and she followed through.

When Reiff graduated from high school in the spring of 2020, she was offered a paid job at the library as a substitute front desk assistant. She worked at that job over the summer and expects to continue filling in at the library during holidays when she is on college breaks.[18]

Reiff's story shows that even small, rural libraries can offer meaningful internship experiences for interested teens.

TEXTBOX 4.5 TEEN VANTAGE POINT

After my library internships and summer job, I am now in college and majoring in business intelligence and data analytics. I am also thinking about minoring in either international business or communication, but I haven't decided yet. Once I get into the rhythm of things, I hope to work at the college library while studying here.

My goals for the future are to work overseas and help people in different nations to improve their economic status. Once I get my master's, I hope to work with the United

Nations or similar-minded agencies. I plan to get my master's in statistics or economics. I am leaning toward both at the moment, but that can change by the time I get there.

I actually owe partial credit to my internship at the library for helping to decide my major. Because of the data analytics and demographic statistics that I did for my senior year internship, I realized that I enjoy that kind of work and can use it to help other people.

I am thankful that my internship was at a small library. I was able to be cross-trained in many different parts of the library, and that will give me an edge if I ever want or need a library job. Because it was a small library, I got a general knowledge of how libraries run as well as how specific programs are run. I may not have been able to get that much experience at a large library.

I would definitely encourage all libraries to have an internship program to get teens involved. If it weren't for my internship and volunteering, I probably would not have set aside time to do anything at my local library besides pick up and drop off books.[1]

Makynna Reiff
West Custer County Library, Westcliffe, Colorado

Note

1. Reiff, Makynna. August 25, 2020. Email message to author.

Notes

1. League of Volunteers. May/June 2018. "The Michael Gendreau Community Service Scholarship." LOV Notes, https://lov.org/wp-content/uploads/2018/06/May-June-LOV-Notes-2018.pdf.
2. Chavez, Yasmeen. August 21, 2020. Email message to author.
3. White, Anna, and Cody Brownson-Katz. August 25, 2020. Email message to author.
4. Brooklyn Public Library. 2019. "Librarians of Tomorrow." https://www.bklynlibrary.org/lot.
5. Osbourne, Megan. September 19, 2018. "Teen Library Intern Does More Than Shelve Books." I Love Libraries, courtesy of the *Herald Dispatch*, http://www.ilovelibraries.org/article/teen-library-intern-does-more-shelve-books.
6. Burson, Hayley. November 5, 2019. "2019 Teen Summer Intern Program: Teen Interns Contribute to Making a Community Library Brighter." YALSA Blog, http://yalsa.ala.org/blog/2019/11/05/2019-teen-summer-intern-program-teen-interns-contribute-to-making-a-community-library-brighter/.
7. Tudor, Nicole. October 1, 2019. "2019 Teen Summer Intern Program: Gadsden Public Library." YALSA Blog, http://yalsa.ala.org/blog/2019/10/01/2019-teen-summer-intern-program-gadsden-public-library/#more-39348. p 3.
8. VanArsdale, Patricia. February 21, 2020. Email message to author.
9. VanArsdale, email message.
10. VanArsdale, email message.
11. Williams, Natalie. February 13, 2020. Email message to author.
12. Perez-Gomez, Analiza. September 27, 2019. "Laredo Public Libraries Completes National Summer Internship Program." City of Laredo, Texas. Press release.
13. Perez-Gomez, Analiza. July 8, 2020. Email message to author.

14. Etheredge, Kate. August 13, 2018. "Teen Summer Internship." YALSA Teen Programming HQ, http://hq.yalsa.net/programs/4810/teen-summer-internship.

15. Button, Eric. March 3, 2020. Email message to author.

16. "About the Library." 2020. West Custer County Library, https://www.westcusterlibrary.org/about-the-library/.

17. West Custer County Library. 2020. "Teen Summer Internship," https://www.westcusterlibrary.org/teens/.

18. Reiff, Makynna. August 25, 2020. Email message to author.

5

Unique Internship Experiences at Schools, Universities, Public and Special Libraries, and through Partnerships

Algonquin Area Public Library District, Algonquin, Illinois

THE TEEN LIBRARY INTERNSHIP at the Algonquin Library was done in collaboration with Jacobs High School, which has an internship program that students can join. The program had primarily been done in tandem with one of the local businesses, but then a teen was interested in exploring library work. Maddy Lakeman was the first student to complete a school-related internship program at the library, with the internship taking place from August 2018 through June 2019—the entire school year. Since the internship was done for high school credit, no funding was required.

It all began when a teacher at the high school, Joy Fisher, who works with their special internship curriculum, approached teen services librarian Lindsey Tomsu to propose the possibility of partnering to provide the internship. Lakeman would take on either a one-semester internship, which would be for half a year, or a two-semester internship, to take place over the entire school year. Whichever extended period for the internship was chosen, it would allow Lakeman to get her wish for a real head start on exploring library careers.

Tomsu said, "She contacted me since I am the teen librarian. I told her all about the TAB Teen Internship program that I created at La Vista Public Library in Nebraska and shared with her a copy of the previous group's curriculum to see if it was something that would work. I was really excited about the prospect of offering my internship program again! I ended up meeting with Maddy Lakeman and signing some paperwork. We agreed to a year-long internship option in which I would actually extend the content of my ten-week version. We still followed the eight original units, but the units themselves lasted three to four weeks apiece instead of just one. Maddy was basically given early release two days a week to come to the library for two to three hours. The internship took place at the library. We met for 'classroom' time in the Teen Center, and Maddy used the public computers some days to work on her assignments."

Although Tomsu followed the same basic curriculum from La Vista Public Library, having held her last internship two years prior, she did a massive overhaul, updating the readings and some of the assignments based on her former interns' feedback. You can refer to chapter 3 to revisit her plan.

A significant improvement this time was that since they had three to four weeks to spend on a unit, they did not have to cram everything into one week. For each unit, Lakeman listened to lectures and shadowed people in the department about which she was currently learning. When Lakeman was shadowing, Tomsu noted that she came prepared with some major, in-depth questions to ask other staff members. If Tomsu was scheduled on the reference desk during Lakeman's scheduled time, the intern would work on her readings and assignments.

As the internship coordinator, Tomsu was responsible for sharing her knowledge and expertise. Because she has always believed in being honest with teens, she was straightforward with Lakeman about the potential difficulties of breaking into the library world, especially the reality of committing to a library master's degree, often for a lower-level part-time position to start. She also shared in-depth stories, experiences, and examples to supplement the actual internship curriculum that resembled what would be learned in a college-level library science class.

Tomsu was in charge of coordinating Lakeman's schedule, including her time spent with other staff members to job shadow and to ask specific questions about their responsibilities. Feedback indicated that everyone greatly enjoyed working with Lakeman. Tomsu appreciated being able to include this particular element that her La Vista teens did not experience because that library was much smaller than the Algonquin Library.

It was an essential requirement to keep tabs on Lakeman's hours and report them to her teacher. Monthly progress reports about Lakeman's participation were also required. The progress reports assured that the intern showed up when scheduled and that she was participating well and completing her work quickly. Tomsu felt that Lakeman deserved the regular glowing reviews she received.

Tomsu explained that her personal goal for the internship was, as it had been previously, to provide a college-level intensive course on librarianship. She believes that with this firsthand knowledge under their belts, teens would understand what can be achieved with a library degree and how to be prepared to face the harsh realities of breaking into the field. This knowledge base would help teens to make responsible choices if they ultimately decided to pursue librarianship as a career.[1]

TEXTBOX 5.1 LIBRARIAN VANTAGE POINT

According to Maddy and Mrs. Fisher, I definitely provided a much more detailed internship than what most of the other teens were involved in at a hospital or with police officers. Maddy said it was a lot of work, but it was never busywork or boring—it was fascinating. Most of her classmates said they were bored to death and not doing anything at their internships.

Maddy enjoyed her experience so much that she applied for and got a paid position when one opened shortly after her internship ended. Her new supervisor, in essence, said that Maddy just had to show up at the interview, and the job would be hers—because Maddy had shown such aptitude and professionalism in their encounters during the internship.

Lindsey Tomsu
Algonquin Area Public Library District, Illinois

Note

1. Tomsu, Lindsey. September 18, 2020. Email message to author.

Boulder Public Library, Boulder, Colorado

At the Boulder Public Library in Colorado, there is an assortment of inviting programs, activities, and exhibits for library users to enjoy. One of those appealing resources is BLDG 61, a free community workshop area that provides maker education and technology for all ages in a creative and inclusive environment. As an exemplary makerspace, it boasts a 3D printer; a large laser cutter and a vinyl cutter; sewing machines and sergers; an embroidery machine, looms, and spinning wheels; an electronics bench; soldering irons; an airbrush; woodshop tools; and several other machines and gadgets. The site even encourages expert makers from the public to submit proposals to run hands-on community projects. One of the projects was for users to sew masks during the pandemic.[2]

When funding has been available, a remarkable component of the makerspace has been the inclusion of teen interns and apprentices employed at the facility to create projects that can improve and even change their target audiences' lives. One such opportunity resulted from a partnership between the Boulder Public Library and the University of Colorado's "Build a Better Book" project funded in 2018 by the National Science Foundation to help create tactile books for those who have visual and print disabilities. The partnership provided an award-winning internship for underserved youth through which the hired teens were rewarded with gift cards. The teens' charge was to create projects to improve the lives of the visually impaired after the teens learned how to utilize the various technologies to do it.

The first teen intern for the project, and ultimately the second for which his younger sister joined him, was a seventeen-year-old who made a vibrant, raised board game to replicate the nearby river landscape. The game included its own vocabulary of textures, incorporated Braille, and included soundbites in English and Spanish.

During the second year of the teen internship, the brother and sister partnered to create a collaborative game that put all players on an even playing field. Blindfolds were included and were meant to be worn by sighted people during play. The game consisted of many laser-cut and 3D-printed, handmade pieces with the Braille typed by the interns. One of the teens commented that the goal of the game was for everyone of any race, gender, or other backgrounds to enjoy playing it. Many additional accessible games were a result of the second internship of the sibling partners.

The teen interns, neither of whom is visually impaired, met regularly with visually impaired mentors who helped them understand how those with seeing difficulties perceive the world. By consulting with the mentors, the teens received advice that enabled them to troubleshoot their games to assure that they were usable by the visually impaired community and to improve the game logistics. The teens said that they could add something more understandable and accessible every time they met with their mentors.

Following the internships, the older brother was recruited by the Build a Better Book project to mentor University of Colorado students and potentially devise an internship for the collegiate level. Both he and his sister agreed that consulting with their mentors was the most valuable part of their experiences, more important than the equipment they mastered. They also enjoyed getting feedback from game players who said that the games were fun, balanced, and promoted equality among differently abled players. As an ultimate consequence of partaking in the internship experiences, both teens were inspired to go into engineering in college and pursue publishing options for the games. The brother focuses on some aspect of physical engineering, while his sister aims to combine hands-on engineering with coding.

The Boulder Public Library and the University of Colorado demonstrated the benefits of such intensive internships where teens are encouraged to work independently. They discovered that teens could learn beyond expectations and become skilled at using advanced equipment. The internship program partnership motivated two teens to learn and grow to give them the tools to make a difference for others in their futures.[3]

Chicago Public Library, Chicago, Illinois

The City of Chicago has instituted Mayor Rahm Emanuel's One Summer Chicago (OSC) initiative, which has served over 31,000 youth ages fourteen to twenty-one each year. This youth employment program has connected government institutions, community-based organizations, and employers to provide subsidized employment and internship opportunities for this age group. The OSC is the overarching hub that has unified summer skill building throughout the city.

The initiative has united several partners representing the direct services jobs programs and other city partners. These have included the Chicago Department of Family and Support Services, the Chicago Housing Authority, Chicago Public Schools, Chicago Park District, the Forest Preserves of Cook County, Chicago Transit Authority, City Colleges of Chicago, and the Lincoln Park Zoo. Additional intrinsic parts of this partnership have been After School Matters and the Chicago Public Library.

Youth participants who were hired in any of these areas have earned "badges" relating to various essential work readiness indicators that comprise twenty-first-century skills, career preparation, goal planning, attendance, and financial responsibility. When youth have earned the OSC badges across the board, it has signaled their marketability and employment readiness to those who were hiring.

After School Matters has given Chicago teens and young adults who were currently enrolled in high school first-rate employment program opportunities during time out of school to explore and develop their talents as they gained vital skills for their futures. Teens had gotten hands-on, project-based apprenticeship and internship experiences in the arts, communications and leadership, sports, and STEM (science, technology, engineering, and math).

In coordinating with After School Matters, the Chicago Public Library has hosted teen interns at fifty-one library locations. There have been 150 positions available, and teens have been paid $10.50 per hour for sixteen hours a week from late June to early August. Applicants must have been sixteen years old or had a work permit and were interviewed after May 1.[4] Teens were hired as CyberTeens, Summer Learning Interns, and Junior CyberNavigators.

CyberTeen interns have assisted with an assortment of digital or other technological projects. These have included scanning documents and images, making photocopies, and completing inventories.

Summer Learning Interns have participated in behind-the-scenes library experiences to increase their knowledge of the everyday operations required for the summer engagement programs that have attracted and enlightened community children and teens. Interns and branch library staff members have collaborated in sustaining art and STEM activities and programming, branch tours, outreach, and co-designing and co-facilitating public programs.

Junior CyberNavigators have presented informational workshops and have aided library customers of all ages with a range of computer functions and applications, such as navigating email, evaluating and using apps and websites, applying for jobs online, and downloading ebooks. For youth to be considered for these positions, they must fit into the required age bracket of fourteen to twenty-one and have been currently enrolled in Chicago Public Schools.[5]

Despite the pandemic, the City of Chicago was determined to keep One Summer Chicago running in 2020 using virtual platforms. It appears that the city is planning to continue the program in the future.[6]

Howard County Library System Administration, Ellicott City, Maryland

In Ellicott City, Maryland, there are specialized high school curricular options through the Howard County Public School System's Career Academies. A Career Academy offers high school students with similar interests a unique opportunity to prepare for college and entry-level employment in specific career areas, such as aerospace engineering, construction, culinary science, finance, graphic design, and many more. Each Career Academy offers a recommended sequence of courses, internships, capstone projects, or research projects related to the individual student's career goals and the chance to earn college credit and industry certification while in high school. Career Academy programs are designed to prepare high school students to be college and career ready and meet twenty-first-century global economy demands.[7]

Since 2002, the Howard County Library System and the Howard County Public School System have worked together in a dual-system partnership to expand academic opportunities for all students. They have collaborated on multiple levels, including serving on joint committees. One eventual result of this partnership was the library system being asked to serve as an official internship site for the Career Academy's Graphic Design program with its home location at the Applications and Research Laboratory in Ellicott City.[8]

Starting in 2010, the Howard County Library System has hosted nine student interns from the Graphic Design course of study. Each intern has worked in the Communications Department at the library system's administration office doing design work. Every year, student interns began working at the library system in the fall and concluded in the spring.

The internship work time was part of the academic day for each student. There was no cost to the Howard County Library System. Since their work was part of the academic day and did not include financial compensation, students received grades for their time spent as interns. As an essential part of their overall internship experience, they were required to develop a portfolio of their work and interview prospective mentors at the internship sites. The anticipated outcome of being assigned internships following the interviews has been that all students in the program would produce professional-quality work in a business setting.

Students and mentors at each internship site for the Career Academies programs were matched and began work according to their individual internship plans. At the library system, library staff mentors assigned work and guided and assisted the students. Students who were library interns were expected to generate high-quality products seen and used by the library public. Through their library internships, students learned more about working in a business setting, learned a great deal about the behind-the-scenes of the library profession, creatively developed library publicity, and sharpened their skills. To monitor progress and follow up, mentors provided regular feedback and formal evaluations to the students in consultation with their Career Academy instructors.[9]

Ohio State University Libraries, Columbus, Ohio

The Ohio State University Libraries began a partnership with the Expanding Vision Foundation (EVF) in 2016 at the Thompson Library to host the nine-week EVF Career Institute for young adults. Students navigated modules on self-assessment; were taught how to apply for jobs; learned about using pre- and post-interview skills; created a professional resume; found out about credit responsibility; practiced business etiquette; and discovered how to thrive in the workplace.

The EVF is a nonprofit organization that serves the Columbus, Ohio community with career development and leadership services for both youth and adults. They are primarily focused upon building future leaders at an early age and in helping people to grow and succeed. Their programs are designed to prepare youth for potential careers and assist working adults with the tools needed to advance in theirs. In addition, they provide life skills instruction to program graduates to give them guidance and direction. Besides partnering with the university libraries, EVF has other community partners such as the Columbus Metropolitan Library, where they offer their high school program at several branches, and Columbus City Schools, where they offer middle school leadership and high school programs.[10]

At first, University Libraries provided a place for the Career Institute. During that time, they considered how they might help enhance the weekly learning sessions in the future. Attending the sessions and observing various workshops were university professor Nena Couch and associate professor Deidra Herring. They were impressed with the curriculum and could not imagine how University Libraries might improve upon the outstanding work the EVF was already doing. Despite this feedback, University Libraries still hoped to partner with EVF, and colleagues suggested that they focus upon the high school program. This was a workable solution, and after approval from the executive administrators, a new program was started to offer internships to some of the EVF high school program graduates.

Leading the creation of the paid internship program was program director for outreach and engagement, Quanetta Batts, in tandem with Couch and Herring. They devised a plan and served as liaisons for an EVF summer internship pilot program in 2017. Five high school interns were selected for this program, which proved quite successful.

Because of these positive results, the program continued with nine interns in 2018 and eight in 2019, and with Batts and Couch as the program coordinators and liaisons. A large part of the program's success had been the EVF partnership, through which the interns came well trained and ready to learn and grow through their experiences.

The teen interns have had well-rounded and enlightening summers. Interns were assigned part-time jobs in the libraries, where they had hands-on experience with administrative, clerical, and a variety of library-related tasks. Each Wednesday, they attended cohort meetings that lasted from an hour to an hour and a half to talk about college preparation, personal branding, and library careers. Field trips were also integrated into the internship programs. The students visited branch library locations that included the Billy Ireland Cartoon Library and Museum and University Archives, the Ohio Stadium, and the Ohio State University Planetarium. Another opportunity was participating in panel discussions that Ohio State University student employees led. Librarians or library staff members who served as mentors met their interns for lunch, had them shadow as they attended meetings, and otherwise interacted with them on an informal level.

According to Batts, University Libraries remains committed to improving and continuing the EVF high school internship program. This has been and will be accomplished by assuring that each program is carefully assessed at its conclusion. At the end of each summer, all parties are asked to complete a thorough evaluation to communicate the impact on staff, faculty, and the interns. All feedback has been thoughtfully considered, and program improvements reflect what has been learned.

Comments from internship program participants were especially appreciated. One supervisor particularly enjoyed the interns' enthusiasm and attitude as a great addition to the library. A mentor was very pleased with the opportunity to have lunch with her intern, to stroll around the campus in conversation, and to discuss his impressions and experiences in a relaxed atmosphere. And finally, another intern appreciated getting life and professional lessons at the same time through his internship.[11]

Princeton University Library, Princeton, New Jersey

In the summer of 2019, a pilot paid summer high school internship program at the Princeton University Library was offered in collaboration with the university's Office of Community and Regional Affairs and the summer youth employment programs in the cities of Princeton and Trenton, New Jersey. The library was thrilled to accept the prospect of connecting with the local community when the idea was proposed by the Office of Community and Regional Affairs. As a result, they hired three teenagers, two age sixteen and one age eighteen, for the positions that took place during seven to eight weeks from July to August.

The teen interns worked with their mentors' guidance on several tasks and projects. These included digital mapping, preparing course reserves for university faculty and staff, shelving, and assistance with cataloging. Along with these regular assignments and learning to search and scan materials and create bibliographies, each of the three interns had to complete a self-designed research project of their choice. They viewed all these experiences as positive elements that would help them with college-level research they knew they would encounter in the upcoming years.

The research projects varied greatly as they were based on particular intern interests. One intern examined art history after wars through the Marquand Library of Art and Archeology, especially how, following the American Revolutionary War, paintings became more patriotic and subject matter expanded from portraits to scenes. Another intern immersed herself in African American studies to learn more about her culture, background, and ancestors' accomplishments. The third intern enjoyed finding out about the history of the various library collections.

When anticipating the arrival of the interns, Anuradha Vedantham, the assistant university librarian for research services, said:

> Our interns will gain not only professional experience but also a stronger understanding of academic libraries, whether as a potential career path for them or as a partner in their future research. In turn, we gain insight into our rising student needs and interests, as well as the ways they might perceive our library—its buildings, its history, and its services. We can learn as much from the students as they learn from us.[12]

Teens were clued in about the existence of the internship opportunities through various means. One was informed through the Millhill Child and Family Development Center, which partners with the city of Trenton and the Princeton Regional Chamber of Commerce to foster job experience and workforce preparation by offering older teens summer employment with a local organization or city government. The other two teens learned about the internships through Princeton's Summer Youth Employment Program, which helps teens ages fourteen through eighteen who live in Princeton and attend Princeton High School to gain professional-level experience, job readiness, and career development training.

The director of the Office of Community and Regional Affairs, Kristin Appelget, gave feedback on her impressions of the internships:

> This is a superb opportunity for these youth to learn about Princeton University, working on a college campus, and in particular, the many interesting jobs and opportunities that are available in the area of library science. We are thankful for the Princeton University Library leadership and staff who are managing the student employees this summer in this pilot program. We hope to learn from the experience, and take feedback from participants in the program this summer, and to perhaps expand to other departments on campus in future years.[13]

Feedback was received via conversations with the interns, supervisors, and mentors and formal methods required by the nonprofit community partners. The interns said that they learned a great deal and gained insights into library careers, while supervisors and mentors were glad to have built a positive rapport with the interns. As the program develops, there is room for improvement based on the assessments. Some of the changes that will be made are better recognition of the time commitment needed, a better system to break large projects into more manageable smaller elements for interns to tackle independently, and further training to assist the interns both in and outside of work. Additionally, mentors and supervisors will be selected earlier to have time to identify internship projects in the spring. More attention will be paid to matching interns to locations and tasks, and intern cohorts will be encouraged to maintain connections with one another to increase the program's impact as it progresses.[14]

Although everyone has been enthused about the results of the pilot internship program, and it demonstrated a strong probability to continue, the pandemic prevented another round of internships in 2020. However, Vedantham indicates that Princeton University Library intends to make this opportunity available again, and it will potentially be extended to other departments as Appelget suggested.[15]

Sonoma County Library, Santa Rosa, California

You read about this internship program's publicity in chapter 3, and here are the further details. During the summer of 2019, the Sonoma County Library in California, which has fourteen locations, hosted a unique, paid teen library internship for a motivated, public-service-minded high school student. Candidates needed to be between the ages of sixteen and nineteen, going into junior or senior year of high school or freshman year of college, and to reflect the diversity of their community. Abilities sought in a teen intern were attention to detail, being able to prioritize tasks, a passion for helping others, and a willingness to learn and develop new skills. There was a preference for teens interested in history and culture—definitely a plus for this job. Teens applying for the internship, using a form available in English and Spanish, did so during May. Applicants could submit their form via a Google Forms link or through email with attachments. Of the fifty-six applications submitted for the one internship position, the list of applicants was winnowed down to nine students who were interviewed. Three people served on the interview panel: Kathy DeWeese, the youth services administrator, plus two librarian mentors, Joanna Kolosov and Zayda Delgado, who opted for a co-mentoring approach.

The position was funded by the Public Library Association's Inclusive Internship Initiative with the expectation of attendance of the selected intern and an assigned mentor at the kickoff and wrap-up events in the spring and the fall in Chicago and Washington, D.C., respectively, in addition to an agreement to adhere to the overall PLA internship requirements. The funding allowed the hired intern to earn $15 per hour for a maximum of 225 hours throughout the summer.

The teen who was chosen was Cortunay Minor, a recent Santa Rosa High School graduate at the time. Cortunay worked with her staff mentors at the Sonoma County History and Genealogy Library (SCH&G), the community resource that manages local history and genealogy collections, mentioned previously in chapter 3.

The library's extensive strategic plan guided the internship in addition to the PLA requirements. The internship experience was designed to cover a range of goals that supported professional exploration along with meaningful community service. To that end, Minor wrote about and otherwise shared her experience and also created a connected learning project with her mentors' guidance.

Mentor Joanna Kolosov's main focus at the library is preserving the web and protecting cultural heritage materials. Her fellow mentor, Zayda Delgado, enjoys drawing new audiences into local history.[16] Due to their co-mentoring approach, one of them traveled with Minor to the PLA launch event and the other to the wrap-up one. During the internship, they shared the responsibilities of oversight and guidance through day-to-day library operations and the development of Minor's connected learning project.

For her connected learning project, Minor built a website to collect and share the creative works of self-expression from teens of color, members of the LGBTQ+ community, and individuals of different abilities about identity and their challenges in Sonoma County. She called her project "By Our Own Hand" and crafted a project statement giving values to guide the contributors. She designed the project to allow for anonymous submissions and celebrate diverse voices for inclusion in the local historical archives.

Minor promoted the project through social media, targeted emails, attendance at local teen and open mic events, and by presenting during library staff meetings and to the Library Commission. She also included her own creative works on the site to encourage others to share their artistic expressions.

Kolosov and Delgado stated that they were pleased to have a local Spanish-speaker from a younger demographic than their typical SCH&G visitors. They also appreciated that Minor's passion, vision, and points of view helped them highlight their goals to document underrepresented communities, especially LGBTQ+ and people of color.[17]

Although there was no formal evaluation process, Kolosov and Delgado provided regular informal pointers through daily check-ins to set goals and review internship progress. In addition, they reviewed Minor's website content and suggested edits and additions. Other intern mentoring steps, input, and feedback that provided insights about the internship results included the following:

- Shadowing at library committee and community meetings by attending with her mentors
- Discussing social media strategies and highlights together
- Conferring with Minor about lessons that she learned
- Assigning readings for Minor on library/archives and discussing them, emphasizing works by Black, Indigenous, and People of Color (BIPOC) library workers

- Conducting informal conversations with Minor about the college experience, career paths, modeled workplace behavior, and library and archives best practices
- Encouraging Minor to relay her opinions about the mentors' communication[18]

Harry S. Truman Library and Museum, Independence, Missouri

The Truman Library and Museum has offered an unpaid High School Internship Program to teen volunteers aged sixteen or older each summer. The internships came about because teens specifically expressed curiosity about having such an opportunity, and the library obliged. There have been fifty-eight interns since the program started in 2004. Usually, there are two or three interns selected to work each June.[19]

The library initially planned to have the positions open and to invite teens to submit applications for the summer of 2020. Unfortunately, as with so many other libraries, the pandemic's unanticipated emergency caused the internships to be canceled. The facility hopes to offer them again in the future.

The internships were open to teens drawn to working in a place filled with historical information that does not sit dormant on a dusty shelf. At the Truman Library and Museum, history comes alive because it attracts people worldwide who come to explore its riches. Teens accepted for this internship get to experience history firsthand by working in the library archives facility, where plentiful historical documents relating to the Truman era are preserved and made available.

A required application packet must have been completed for teens to be considered for the internships, followed by an interview for applicants who met the program criteria. Besides the age requirement of sixteen or older, the internship program has sought teens with a 2.5 or higher grade point average; the ability to work independently while accepting supervision; an interest in history; good communication skills; and a track record of reliability, responsibility, and dependability. Additionally, computer skills have come in handy and have been appreciated.

Application submissions were due by May 1, along with an approximately five-page writing sample, two teacher references, and a current transcript. Successful candidates committed to 50 hours each for the length of their internships, and the library has been flexible about working around family vacations, summer jobs, and other possible conflicts. Interns have had a choice of working from 10:00 a.m. to 2:00 p.m. or from 11:00 a.m. to 3:00 p.m., Monday through Friday. Once teens were accepted into the program, appropriate training was provided.[20]

Each year, the projects created through the archives were determined by the archives staff and were based primarily on current needs at the time. The intern coordinator and other archives staff members supervised the interns. Each year, the teen interns got experience working in a professional environment, enhanced a variety of skills, could build their resumes with the internship credential, fulfilled community service hour obligations, and developed a reference source for future employment and higher education goals.

The expected outcomes have been that the interns would gain an understanding of how the archives work along with several levels of valuable work and life experience. As a rule, the evaluation process has consisted of informal conversations between the interns and the intern coordinator.[21]

University of Virginia Library, Charlottesville, Virginia

The University of Virginia Library is a vibrant place that offers the traditional elements of cataloging books and responding to reference questions, but, like many libraries today, they also do 3D printing, build websites and databases, digitize and preserve materials, maintain extensive archives of rare resources, teach classes on everything from research methods to geographic information systems (GIS), support media creation, and much more.

In this rich setting, two-week high school internships have been held in June each year since 2017 to allow local teens the opportunity to explore the vast array of library careers and services available (although, once again, the one scheduled for 2020 had to be canceled due to the corona virus). One primary purpose of the internships has been to attract students from populations usually underrepresented in the library field.

Applications have been due on March 1, and they required the inclusion of a reference letter from a school guidance counselor or teacher that would address a student's volunteer work, leadership roles, challenges that were overcome, outstanding qualities, and reasons that the student would be a good fit for working in the university library.

Finalists were interviewed via Skype or Google Meet. All candidates were notified of their status by May 1, with successful candidates and their parents or guardians contacted more directly soon after. As several library departments were providing internships, those teens who were selected were given details about each department for them to express their placement preferences.

During the three years the program has been held, interns who accepted the positions have committed to being present at work from 8:30 a.m. until 5:00 p.m. each day for the entire two-week period. In compensation, each intern received a stipend of $500.

Interns had mentors in the departments to which they were assigned. Mentors were attuned to the interns and offered them positive experiences. One intern said, "The most exciting thing I did today was probably when I got to go to a meeting with one of my mentors. It was really cool because they actively involved me and explained things so I would understand what they were talking about."

Other teens additionally praised the various things that they learned and got to do. They did this through a fairly unique way of giving feedback by being asked to make blog posts about their experiences and reactions each day.

For the first week, interns received prompts to inspire them to express what they hoped to get from the internship, say what surprised them the most, share the most exciting thing they learned, tell what was most interesting, and convey what they were most proud of accomplishing. You can find out more about this way of seeking input from teens in chapter 6, which centers on evaluations.[22]

University Libraries, University of Washington, Seattle, Washington

The University of Washington (UW) has offered a special high school internship program for several years at UW Seattle's Suzzallo and Allen Libraries. In 2017, its initial year, three students participated. In 2018, six students participated, and in 2019 ten students participated. In 2020, ten students would have been accommodated, but the program was canceled due to the pandemic. However, the UW Libraries is looking forward to hosting an internship program again.

The librarians in charge of the program, Geography and Global Studies Librarian Kian Flynn and English Studies and Research Commons Librarian Elliott Stevens, are reviewing their teaching materials and considering ways they might offer it as a hybrid or online program during the summer of 2021 if the health emergency still exists.[23] The good thing about preparing in this manner is that they would have a plan to keep the 2021 and future internships functioning whenever a situational urgency occurs.

The official name of the program is "The UW Libraries High School Internship." It has been a 30-hour, paid, project-based internship for young people particularly suited to teens who are first-generation college students or from groups that have been underrepresented in higher education and librarianship. This focus matches the targeted outcomes of the UW Libraries Strategic Plan to "Enhance Equitable Environments for Research, Learning, and Working." An interest in librarianship as a career has not been required, but if applicants happened to be thinking along those lines, it has been regarded as an advantage.

Students were hired through an application and interview process. When there have been ten spots open, about fifteen students were interviewed. Interviews have taken place at the closest public library to each teenager. Usually, the candidates would feel comfortable in these familiar spaces that they frequented. Flynn and Stevens have always been impressed by these interviews because the teens have often come well prepared and have asked good questions. They have found that it is important to interview more than ten students for ten spaces because, in the couple of weeks leading up to the internships, one or two students might choose an alternative experience. For instance, they may have decided to take a job for the entire summer, go on vacation, spend their time touring colleges, or accept other internships.

For the first three years, funding for the internship program came from internal UW Libraries with support from the Kenneth S. and Faye G. Allen Library Endowment. The program has also depended upon in-kind contributions such as the librarians' own work time and the use of the UW Libraries' spaces and facilities.

In 2020, the plan was to continue using UW Libraries' funds. Also, the Seattle Public Library was going to help by giving a significant amount of support through its Summer of Learning program funds. What an excellent partnership this would have been, and it is unfortunate that the program had to be canceled in 2020, like programs in libraries everywhere.

TEXTBOX 5.2 LIBRARIAN VANTAGE POINT

This is how the internships came about. Sometime in 2016, we were in a departmental meeting, and one person, Glenda Pearson, head of Government Publications, Maps, Microforms, and Newspapers, asked the group why we don't have internships for high school students in the UW Libraries. The staff seemed really interested in the question, and after that meeting, we started talking about it more because both of us have experience working with and teaching high-school students.

We did some initial research about paid internships for high school students in academic libraries and came back with nothing. Since, at that point, we couldn't find models at other academic libraries, we looked to the UW Career Center as well as the UW Dream Project, which is a center on campus that focuses on student disparities in higher education as well as how to connect such students with resources.

Through the Dream Project, we met Nancy Garrett, youth services librarian at the Lake City Public Library of the Seattle Public Library system, and she was initially instrumental—and continues to be a crucial partner—in finding young people who would like to participate in the internship. The Seattle Public Library has always been a strong collaborator, and this year of 2020, we were planning to strengthen that connection further in that they were going to fund stipends and dining cards for the students if only the program could have been held.[1]

Kian Flynn and Elliott Stevens
University of Washington Libraries, Seattle, Washington

Note

1. Stevens, Elliott. August 31, 2020. Email message to author.

The internships have been central to an enjoyable, project-based program for high school students considering enrolling in college after graduation. While the internships took place, the selected candidates also learned about available resources and got to know many people—other high school students, undergraduates, graduate students, faculty members, and librarians.

This had all come about during the two full weeks following the July 4th weekend. The timing had been convenient for both the librarians and the teenagers interested in participating. The internship schedule went from Monday through Thursday each week. In the first week, the internships ran four hours a day for a total of sixteen hours. In the second week, which totals fourteen hours, they ran four hours on Monday and Tuesday and three hours on Wednesday and Thursday.

Each student intern received a $500 stipend for completing the internship, and as noted, in 2020, the intention was to also provide lunches for them. The reasoning for paying the students was rooted in equity. The idea was that since students were working, they should have been paid for their work. Flynn and Stevens also said that it was important to pay students because, during the summer, their internship opportunities were competing with other paid internships and with summer jobs. Without pay, they realized that there would not be as many applicants.

There was a planned curriculum that interns followed, with wiggle room built into the plans to account for the artistic and creative processes associated with the special media projects included in their assignments. Over two weeks, in addition to completing information science activities, the students were asked to create two short visuals through digital storytelling and an interactive map using ESRI StoryMaps.[24] They then showcased at a presentation attended by twenty to thirty people. For the presentation, the interns talked about the work they did, screened their digital stories, and navigated attendees through their maps.[25] The digital storytelling ventures created through the internships were fascinating and can be found on YouTube.[26] The teens concluded their internship experiences by producing portfolios of finished projects, which have helped enhance their resumes or college applications.[27]

Student interns received assistance throughout the internship with mentors who comprised the Coaching Team. The Coaching Team usually consisted of Flynn and Stevens and a graduate student from the UW Information School. Their role has been to help define the parameters—physical, virtual, pedagogical, and emotional—of the internship and give it structure. But Flynn and Stevens believe that the roles of "teacher" or "student" were not fixed and instead shared. Students can teach, and teachers can be students. Their mindset on these roles is rooted in the writings, practice, and praxis of critical-pedagogy theorists like Paulo Freire, bell hooks, and Ira Shor. In effect, they continue to believe that empowering both students and teachers to learn together and independently and respectfully is key to effective learning.

By the end of the internship, Flynn and Stevens said that the expected outcomes were that the interns would have completed the two digital stories and an interactive map. But more so, they said that the aim was that students would have a better understanding of college and library resources and the experiences and accomplishments of faculty members, graduate students, and undergraduate students. Yet, they hoped that one outcome would be that, when the students were in college, they would grasp that the internship made things easier and gave them advantages.

Furthermore, Flynn and Stevens said that for the library workers and graduate students involved with the internships, an outcome should be that they all learned more about the needs and talents of students who have been historically excluded from higher education and librarianship. This learning should lead to action, which means putting resources toward the needs of students, especially those just starting as "new" adults.

Finally, when the internships concluded, Flynn and Stevens conducted a survey through which the students provided feedback. In 2019, they began doing a long-term assessment by sending out a short email to former interns, asking them about how the internship affected them afterward and during the onset of their college careers. They said that in 2019, they even had two former interns who shared reactions to their post-internship experiences with them during interviews and who returned to the university as mentors.[28]

As you can see from this example and those of the other three university libraries featured in this chapter, colleges and universities can play an important role in teaching, building self-esteem, and encouraging high school students through internships. At the same time, they bring the possibilities of a library career to light for them.

Waltham Public Library, Waltham, Massachusetts

At times, "internship" experiences can manifest as *internship-like* experiences. They provide independent leadership opportunities, teach teens about libraries and the myriad of opportunities they offer, are aided by astute adult guidance, and offer pay. Teens who participate in paid experiences like these are, in essence, getting the same experiential training as teens who take on more traditional internships. The way the opportunities unfold and the results they glean are very much the same, perhaps, in some instances, even more impactful.

This is true at the Waltham Public Library in Massachusetts, where teens have been encouraged to apply as Real Talk Conversation Forum leaders. A solo teen planner organized the inkling program in 2016. Due to its success, the program received grant funding in 2017 to pay stipends for four teen leaders. By 2018, the program and its financial support had expanded, and paying six teen leaders was affordable. Each teen-led event that they planned accommodated between ten and thirty teen attendees at a time.

To apply for the teen leader positions, those interested filled out an online Google Form application, usually in the spring. Some of the Real Talk participants signed up to be trainees with the leaders, and later, when they were ready, they could apply for actual teen leader positions.

The current teen leaders evaluated all of the applications, held interviews with the candidates, and then chose the ones who would become the next year's teen leaders. These new leaders have typically been announced at a Senior Toast event held at the end of the school year.

The Senior Toast has been held because, by the end of the high school year, all of those involved in Real Talk have had unique experiences together and have learned a lot about one another. Often, some of the teens would be graduating. Others, especially those who had been trainees, might have learned that they are the new teen leaders. To culminate the end of the Real Talk years, the Senior Toast events have reconnected everyone to the special conversations that have taken place, given the seniors a fond farewell, and welcomed the next group of teen leaders.

FIGURE 5.1
Haitian immigrant and Waltham High School graduate, Annie Jean-Baptiste, now attending Brandeis University, leads the discussion about immigration that she had developed as a paid teen Real Talk leader. Credit: Luke Kirkland.

Support costs have been funded by, and Real Talk leaders have been paid through, financial support from the Library Initiative for Teens and Tweens, distributed by the Rhyme and Reason Fund of the Boston Foundation. This monetary support has allowed the library to serve dinner to the teens at each event; to bring in professionals who sometimes led specialized workshops on the most challenging topics; to provide transportation for field trips; and to pay stipends to the teen leaders for building the discussion agendas, promoting the events, and facilitating the actual programs.

Teen specialist Luke Kirkland said, "Public libraries simply don't have the same leverage that schools or many other afterschool programs have. So we pay our teen leaders. This ensures that we're able to provide a reliable product for attendees. It means teens don't have to choose between having a job and leading Real Talk events, and it allows us to challenge our teens to reach for high standards." Teen leaders have been able to earn up to $50 for each event they piloted. Payment has been given in increments of $10 for each of two planning meetings, $10 for independent preparation work, and $20 for facilitating a complete two-hour event.

As a youth-founded and youth-led conversation forum, Real Talk has become the centerpiece programming at the library's Teen Room. Twice each month throughout the school year for the last three years, the six selected teen leaders have led and engaged their peers in carefully planned activities that promoted youth voice, encouraged social-emotional learning, and developed an awareness of social justice issues in the community. This amounts to eighteen themed conversations per year.

The programs were divided into two segments, the fall unit and the spring unit. Under the guidance of the adult facilitators, teens led pre-prepared events on eight topics that established a social-emotional foundation for the fall unit. Early events focused on the individual and then evolved outward to examine the world's larger spheres of influence. There have been several reasons for doing the Real Talk groundwork through these fall units. For teen attendees, these events have built trust in the group and helped establish a sense of individuality and interconnectedness. These events familiarized them with planning and organizing Real Talk events as a team for teen leaders, developing their activities, and leading and managing crowds. Finally, these events drew out valuable information about teens' personalities, backgrounds, and group dynamics for facilitators.

From the solid fall unit foundation, teen leaders and program attendees have been able to generate plans of their own in the spring. Using the format they have mastered, teen leaders came up with ten additional discussion events on the subjects they felt the group most needed or wanted. By now, the timing was right, and the leaders assumed full ownership of Real Talk by taking on challenging subjects in thought-provoking conversations.

It did not stop there, however, because teen leaders were also empowered to go further by showcasing their creativity, developing community service projects with peers, and building a network with educators and activists. One impressive example has been their lawn sign project, through which teens give some "real talk" to the whole community each year during election season about their thoughts and feelings on current issues of importance. The idea is to communicate to voters, candidates, and policymakers the hopes of Waltham teens for their lives, communities, country, and world. By the way, this has now become a national project, the For Freedoms Fifty State Initiative. You can read more about this and their other projects in the Real Talk Handbook.

In 2020, the Real Talk leaders faced the challenge of COVID-19. However, that did not stop their project! Although they could not create their signs in person with students in Waltham High School (WHS), they created an orientation video with Kirkland, visited sixteen virtual WHS classrooms, and met with nearly 350 teens to help them create hundreds of digital responses. Afterward, they re-created their digital signs as physical signs in the Teen Room, trying to represent best the most common and most vivid stories told by Waltham youth. You can view the nearly 240 responses displayed on the front lawn through Election Day online at YouTube.[29]

TEXTBOX 5.3 TEEN VANTAGE POINT

I helped start Real Talk because I believed this would have a huge impact on Waltham youth. It was a place to ask questions, sit and learn with friends, and have discussions about real-world topics that are never discussed in school. With that said, I would say it's important that Real Talk exists because it is a learning outlet that is not fashioned in a school setting. Students can learn from each other without worrying about being tested or quizzed afterward. It is important that Real Talk exists because you get to learn from different perspectives. Students of all races, identities, cultures, and backgrounds make their way to Real Talk, and it's truly amazing to hear what each person has to say on just one topic.[1]

Alia Touadjine
Waltham Public Library, Waltham, Massachusetts

Note

1. Touadjine, Alia. September 4, 2020. Email message to author from Luke Kirkland.

TEXTBOX 5.4 TEEN VANTAGE POINT

I started coming to Real Talk because it felt like it was the only place that I could have meaningful conversations about the things I cared about while still having fun and enjoying the atmosphere that was created. I joined as a trainee because I felt it was something I wanted to be a part of. I saw it as an amazing opportunity to educate people and help contribute to a space where both middle schoolers and high schoolers would want to come to hang out and learn.

Real Talk, to me, feels almost like a family. I've grown close to our team, and I've gotten to know the kids that come regularly fairly well. Real Talk has changed my perspective on what I find fulfilling in life. I've been reflecting a lot on what interests me and what I enjoy doing to better have an idea of what I'd like to do in the future. Honestly, Real Talk has shown me that educating and working with people is something I love doing and feel is fulfilling and important.

Being a teen leader for Real Talk has taught me that about myself and more. I've taken on more responsibility than I was previously used to, and I've learned how to collaborate with a team better. I feel it's important for both the teen leaders and the youth that come to events because it's a learning experience in such a safe, welcoming, and chill environment. It's important that we have that. In school, where we are used to going to be educated, not only are things being left out, but it's also a place that most kids feel is too structured and strict to enjoy. School causes many of us to grow to hate learning because we are told that that is what learning must be. Real Talk is proof it doesn't have to be like that. It's proof learning about real-world issues can be interactive, engaging, and fun.

It's important too that we learn how to interact with people that are different than us. While many of the kids that come have friends with them, they are still exposed to people that just aren't like them, and they are forced to learn to interact with them in a respectful way. For the leaders, like I said before, being a part of this means taking on responsibility and working with a team. It also means learning to set an example for others, something I admittedly still struggle with.

Iris Alvarenga
Waltham Public Library, Waltham, Massachusetts

Note

1. Alvarenga, Iris. September 4, 2020. Email message to author from Luke Kirkland.

The online Real Talk Handbook sustains the work of the teen founders and can be accessed by teens and librarians who are interested in emulating the program in their libraries. In the handbook, you can access the Real Talk curriculum, documents, units, guidelines for the programs, and descriptions of the special projects that teens can do. It is a carefully planned, highly recommended resource if you work with teenagers in libraries or elsewhere. If you are considering an internship or other opportunity for teens, whether for pay or not, the documents page is particularly useful in that it gives superb examples of an application form, teen contract, and evaluation form, along with other supporting materials.[30]

There are six primary goals for offering this program with paid teen leaders:

- To offer a forum for teens to discuss issues of importance in their lives
- To build life skills that help teens navigate tough times and difficult decisions
- To empower teens to have an impact in their lives and communities
- To foster a community of support and self-improvement
- To promote community resources related to the issues teens choose to discuss
- To reward the teen leaders in the community

In conjunction with these goals, the librarians who work with the Real Talk teen leaders have consistently anticipated the following results:

- Deeper relationships with the teen library users
- Increased teen engagement in academics, extracurricular activities, and employment
- Increased library use and teen involvement in teen services development
- Increased student voice in school policy decisions and community politics
- Stronger relationships with youth service providers
- Increased financial stability and established work history for the hired teen leaders

Statistics are kept on attendance to evaluate the Real Talk programs and leaders and to assure that the targeted outcomes are met. Also, as often as possible, evaluation forms are given to teens after events. There is an ongoing effort to obtain feedback from several perspectives, including teen leaders, program participants, and other youth workers. This information improves the programs and makes the series content highly productive.

One undisputable gauge has been the positive and significant reactions and behaviors of participants at and after the programs. When teens have regularly been drawn to come to them, it demonstrates that they enjoyed themselves as they were engaging in valuable conversations. Furthermore, there is evidence that they were then bringing what they had gleaned into their lives, homes, and schools. The Waltham Public Library librarians have realized that the programs have been filling an important niche for teens in the community. Likewise, when librarians have found that other community adults have noticed teens enthusiastically talking about the value in the programs, and those adults have asked for more details, that is also worthwhile feedback. Since they have created the Real Talk Handbook, they can readily share how it has been done.[31]

TEXTBOX 5.5 LIBRARIAN VANTAGE POINT

After nine years without a teen librarian, Waltham Public Library (WPL) added me as teen specialist. We began rebuilding services for middle and high schoolers in late 2015, rededicating the Teen Room as a "youth empowerment laboratory" that would be guided by the interests and input of young people.

The following summer, Waltham High School sophomore class president and Waltham Boys and Girls Club Youth of the Year, Rachel Cosgrove, approached me with a proposal for a group called Activism in Youth through Creativity. It immediately became the most successful of WPL's teen programs, drawing large crowds from diverse backgrounds for discussions about community policing, gun violence, healthy relationships, abortion, Black Lives Matter, and more. Based on first-year feedback, we doubled the number of events, emphasized socio-emotional skills, focused on teen issues rather than political debate, and rebranded the series "Real Talk."

There's a lot on this topic in the "Tips for Success" section in our Real Talk Handbook as far as supervising and mentoring. But essentially, I'm a hybrid of a teacher, secretary, mentor, commentator, and bouncer. I help train teens in what goes into being a Real Talk Teen Leader. I support teens in whatever way they need as they plan, create, execute, organize, and promote events. We create close relationships, so often we're talking a lot about what's going on in their lives and helping them achieve their goals. During actual events, I chime in to clarify information and opinions, ask questions, manage time and transitions between events, and give tips to teen leaders in different moments. And I do what's needed to help teen leaders manage the crowd.[1]

Luke Kirkland
Waltham Public Library, Waltham, Massachusetts

Note

1. Kirkland, Luke. September 2, 2020. Email message to author.

You may be wondering what the Waltham Public Library Real Talk teen leaders have done during the pandemic besides the For Freedoms video. The teens continued their programs virtually via Zoom and hosted several excellent ones during the summer. Three programs were attended by local school administrators whom the teen leaders invited—one program was with

FIGURE 5.2
Real Talk teen leaders Stevenson Youyoute, Alia Touadjine, and Rachel Cosgrove went to Washington, D.C., where they presented about Real Talk at the American Library Association annual conference in 2019. Credit: Luke Kirkland.

the English department head. One was with the History department head, and the third was with the incoming school superintendent. The teen leaders led the conversations as the adult guests responded to the observations and questions of teen participants who were visible online. All teens from the community were welcome with the teen leaders hosting, and turnout was good. One program even attracted thirty teens!

During the programs, the Real Teen leaders and program participants challenged the school leaders on issues surrounding curriculum development, equity, and school culture. The teen leaders said they were inspired to take some action around racial justice and understand why students learn what they learn in school and how they might influence curriculum development, so they decided to ask the folks in charge. The resulting series of programs was a big success.

Teen leaders have continued with their virtual presence. In January 2021, Real Talk teen leaders invited the entire Waltham community to join a youth-led conversation about race and belonging with Jennifer de Leon, the author of *Don't Ask Me Where I'm From*. Several teens participated in the conversation recorded from the Zoom program and posted on YouTube.[32]

In chapter 7, read more about teen leaders, volunteers, and interns from many libraries doing virtual/alternative programs following the pandemic and how teen library interns might emulate them.

Washington Latin Public Charter School Library, Washington, D.C.

Sereena Hamm, the school librarian at the Washington Latin Public Charter School, has been a great proponent of high school library internships or student worker programs. As a librarian working alone, she highly values the teen interns' contributions that have helped with general library functions such as shelving, assisting during busy times, and promoting innovative, teen-led avenues for developing programs, displays, and services.

She has aimed for one teen intern per school period (during normal times when school is in session) so that she would be able to focus on teaching when needed while knowing that during those times, the administrative and customer services elements of the library were being addressed by the interns. Hamm has been especially glad for the teens' dedication to the library, their enthusiasm for helping it function well, their enjoyment when encouraging its use to their peers, and seeing their pleasure in being responsible for it. She has delighted in their eagerness to help, and she has appreciated the adult-teen teamwork and strong relationships that grow from the teens' participation.

The high school interns have been scheduled in a unique way. Because the library has had a consistent flow of use, some students who might otherwise go to study hall have instead been assigned as library interns. Hamm has worked closely with the school's technology director because intern time has often been split between the technology office and the library. However, during training, all teens have learned how to work in both locations. The interns' typical breakdown has been fifteen students divided across seven periods, with up to four interns assigned per period and shared between both places.

Initially, there had been an informal application process, but in 2015, a formal application procedure was started. Since the school is a relatively small one, with around 350 students, all the teachers and staff get to know the students well. Supplemental information about applicants was easy to get, no matter the application format. Hamm says that they have not needed to do a great deal of active recruiting for applicants because the current corps of interns has regularly spread the word to their classmates and other student volunteers, instilling interest.

There have been a variety of responsibilities. Every intern has been accountable for managing the circulation desk and doing shelving. Hamm has maintained a list of continuing work choices in a task list that interns can select from during slow times. Besides these regular assignments, teens have been encouraged to devise individual projects independently. In this way, students have felt comfortable about customizing their internship experiences by choosing projects, activities, or roles that were of particular interest or for which they have special skills or expertise. Some of those choices for ongoing and individual contributions might be:

- Managing the circulation desk
- Shelving
- Creating displays
- Adding genre labels to help with a "genrifying" project
- Cleaning up the library
- Training subs and other students
- Labeling books for processing
- Entering books into the Destiny computer system
- Troubleshooting technology problems
- Helping with printing and copying
- Updating computer software with the support of the technology director

- Delivering laptop carts to classrooms
- Decorating library doors and windows
- Special library improvement projects, including creating original art pieces to decorate the library, writing book reviews, or learning how to present mini classes on library topics like using databases or NoodleTools

What are Hamm's main tips for offering a student intern program at a school library? She advises that no program is perfect and to be prepared for challenges. She has focused on getting the student interns to display initiative and work autonomously rather than expecting assignments to be delegated to them by her or the technology director. They have been considering the development of a checklist system for student interns to keep track of their assignments and what they have completed, in addition to simply looking through the task list.

Hamm further advises that, at times, school librarians should acknowledge that flexibility is important, because when a big project or test is coming up, students might temporarily need more time off internship duty to pay attention to those assignments instead. She has also noticed that detail-oriented tasks, such as shelving, have proved challenging for some interns, so she has designed a "shelving pop quiz" system for teens to master the skill. She added that librarians should be aware of what teens might find particularly hard to learn and do and help them master what they need to know to be successful.

Hamm has discovered that recruiting regular student volunteers during lunch, breaks, and a forty-five-minute tutorial time after school has been tricky. Because student volunteers have not received school credit for their work, they have not been as likely to follow through as students with internships because interns earn school credit. She knows that once interns have been placed on board, they have felt valued and rewarded, and despite the challenges, a library internship program can be meaningful. She encourages any library to design a teen internship program because the results greatly surpass the time it takes to manage the program.[33]

Notes

1. Tomsu, Lindsey. September 18, 2020. Email message to author.
2. "BLDG 61: Boulder Library Makerspace." 2020. Boulder Public Library, https://boulderlibrary.org/bldg61/.
3. Keasler, Christina. August 6, 2019. "Colorado Teens Use Makerspace to Create Accessible Board Games." *School Library Journal*, https://www.slj.com/?detailStory=colorado-teens-use-makerspace-to-create-accessible-board-games.
4. "Teens, Apply for Paid Internships at Chicago Public Library." April 6, 2020. Chicago Public Library, https://www.chipublib.org/news/teens-apply-for-paid-internships-at-chicago-public-library/.
5. "One Summer Chicago." 2020. City of Chicago, https://www.chicago.gov/city/en/depts/fss/provdrs/youth/svcs/youth-employment.html.
6. "One Summer Chicago."
7. "Focus on Your Future with the Career Academies." 2020. Howard County Public School System, https://www.hcpss.org/academies/.
8. "Graphic Design." 2020. Howard County Public School System, https://www.hcpss.org/academy/graphic-design/.
9. Lassen, Christie P. July 7, 2020. Email message to author.
10. "About Us." 2021. Expanding Visions Foundation, http://www.expandingvisions.net/aboutus.

11. Batts, Quanetta, Kian Flynn, Elliott Stevens, and Anuradha Vedantham. October 2020. "Starting Early: High School Students in Paid Internships at Academic Libraries." *College & Research Libraries News*, https://crln.acrl.org/index.php/crlnews/article/view/24645.

12. Ann Vedantham, as cited in Ramirez, Stephanie. July 26, 2019. "In Collaboration with Local Community, Princeton University Library Starts High School Summer Internship Program." Princeton University, https://www.princeton.edu/news/2019/07/26/collaboration-local-community-princeton-university-library-starts-high-school.

13. Kristin Appelget, as cited in Ramirez, "In Collaboration with Local Community."

14. Batts et al., "Starting Early."

15. Ramirez, "In Collaboration with Local Community."

16. "PLA Inclusive Internship Initiative." 2020. Sonoma County Library, https://sonomalibrary.org/iii.

17. Gore, Kat. October 2, 2019. "Sonoma County Library Completes National Summer Internship Program." Sonoma County Library, https://sonomalibrary.org/blogs/news/ma-county-library-completes-national-summer-internship-program.

18. DeWeese, Kathy. September 14, 2020. Email message to author.

19. Clark, David. March 4, 2020. Email message to author.

20. High School Internship Program." 2020. Harry S. Truman Library and Museum, https://www.trumanlibrary.gov/about/internships/high-school-internship-program.

21. Clark, email message.

22. "Paid High School Summer Internships." 2020. University of Virginia Library, https://www.library.virginia.edu/jobs/hs-internship/.

23. Stevens, Elliott. August 31, 2020. Email message to author.

24. "Arc/GIS StoryMaps." [n.d.]. ESRI, https://www.esri.com/en-us/arcgis/products/arcgis-storymaps/overview.

25. Flynn, Kian, and Elliott Stevens. September 9, 2020. Virtual meeting on Zoom.

26. "UW Libraries High School Internship." [n.d.]. YouTube, https://www.youtube.com/playlist?list=PLVQ3aPZNFf0FvV_kmwjHq95Xtq5o8ROmo.

27. "UW Libraries High School Internship." 2020. University Libraries University of Washington, https://www.lib.washington.edu/commons/programs/intern.

28. Stevens, email message.

29. "For Freedoms (2020) Physical Signs." 2020. Waltham Public Library, https://photos.google.com/share/AF1QipPCZnKv7m_Zf2awM8a2IOlJ_K89mUdZ3SHclWN68UhSGbiLeVn-XDOOcU_idzYwpQ?key=OFFNSnZmV1hGbDR5UkJWcE1neEZtZDJtSFczamt3.

30. Waltham Public Library. October 21-November 2, 2020."For Freedoms 2020 (Physical Signs)." Google Photos. https://photos.google.com/share/AF1QipPCZnKv7m_Zf2awM8a2IOlJ_K89mUdZ3SHclWN68UhSGbiLeVn-XDOOcU_idzYwpQ?key=OFFNSnZmV1hGbDR5UkJWcE1neEZtZDJtSFczamt3.

31. Kirkland, Luke. September 2, 2020. Email message to author.

32. "Real Talk Presents: Jennifer de Leon." 2021. YouTube, https://www.youtube.com/watch?v=whvuEhNNleg.

33. Hamm, Sereena. October 30, 2015. "Managing a Library Internship Program." Teen Services Underground, https://www.teenservicesunderground.com/managing-a-library-internship-program/.

6

The Importance of Feedback, Evaluations, and a Positive Internship Conclusion Process

As THE HOST AGENCY AND DESIGNER of your teen library internship program, you must provide interns with periodic and final performance evaluations. Since the defining characteristic of internships is learning about and developing experiences in library work while building knowledge and skills that teens can use as they go on to adulthood, offering reliable feedback is just as important an element, and perhaps a more important one, than the ones given to regular library staff members.

It is crucial to the learning process for interns to be aware of which areas of their performance meet or exceed library standards and in which areas they may need to work harder or adjust. Your teen interns can only grow and flourish from your program through your thoughtful and constructive feedback. No matter how you devise your evaluation process, it is important to carefully consider what works for you, your library, and within the context of your particular internship program.[1] Addressing this critical piece is the icing on the cake—the culmination of a satisfying work experience.

In this chapter, we'll be concentrating on the vital topic of evaluations and how to go about them. Typically, supervisors or mentors are expected to evaluate interns at a midpoint and the end of an internship. It is most important to review internship progress and accomplishments with interns before they leave. Evaluations are extremely helpful when determining interns' success in library settings and within the partner organizations at a time when interns will soon move on to other employment or educational opportunities.[2]

Considering Outcomes

Because with any job, including an internship, evaluations are essential, it helps to have a preplanned foundation comprised of projected outcomes. Think about what you would like the targeted internship outcomes to be and ask the interns if they agree to aim for them. This is a topic you may even want to discuss during interviews so that teens understand up-front what the expectations for the internships are before taking them on.

Even though the jobs will have set descriptions, you might ask interns if there are other outcomes they would like to add for when there is time. Perhaps there is a component of library work that interns have an interest in learning about and working on that does not directly fit the planned internship assignments. For instance, what if a teen is really curious about how books are ordered? Maybe you could show him the online ordering resources you use and explain how the process works. You might also give him a chance to try his hand at ordering a few books as you guide and observe.

Here's another example. If a teen is drawn to storytelling for children, even if the internship focuses on running computer classes for teens and adults, you might have her spend a little time with a member of the children's department to get an overview of how to develop this skill. Maybe the intern could be given a chance to observe an actual storytime and even tell or read a story or two during a program independently. Getting teens to contribute to the targeted outcomes makes the internship experience more meaningful.

Add any details needed to describe supplementary targeted outcomes based on unique teen interests when designing and completing individual development plans (IDPs) tailored to each job description, including short and long-term goals, objectives, and anticipated end results. When evalutating, use the IDPs as tools to track current skills and competencies, focusing on how they have been put into action and how teen interns have hopefully improved. Focus as well on additional skills teens indicate they want to master and any specific knowledge they want to gain on the job. Then the supervisors or mentors and teen interns can reflect on the IDPs when giving and responding to feedback during both the midpoint and the final evaluations that will be forthcoming.[3]

Why Do Intern Evaluations?

The essence of teen internships, like any employment position, is to evaluate outcomes so that both the library and the interns find the experience and work produced beneficial. Besides interviews, orientations, and on-the-job guidance, there should be evaluation procedures set in place, such as periodic performance reviews, final reviews, and an exit interview. If a teen has been expected to produce a portfolio or other culminating project, a review of that work would be included. More will be coming up about final projects toward the end of this chapter.

If teen interns are doing programs, conducting classes, providing tours, or otherwise interacting with the public, you might want to include an evaluation process for feedback from participants. Evaluation forms that are simple, carefully designed to give the most important reactions, and easy to fill out are best. Make them small and handy, and remember to provide pencils for quick completion.

Better yet, consider using a talkback board of some kind to gather results. Talkback boards present questions or prompts for people to answer, either by voting for possible choices with sticky dots or writing short responses on Post-it notes.[4] Find out more about creating and using them by visiting the Connected Learning Lab website.[5] You might take pictures of the boards when they are finished to save the comments.

Remember to take photos or videos, as permitted and appropriate, for further documenting. If your library requires any permission forms to do such recording, make sure to have them available. Participant evaluations and other documentation can be valuable when conducting performance evaluations and are especially useful later for any presentations that might culminate the internships.

Besides final overviews of a teen's work and accomplishments, it is helpful to first have mid-internship evaluations for several reasons. Midterm evaluations can be an opportunity to give needed advice to interns if they are struggling with something. You and the interns can make sure that they know what to do for the rest of their internships to make them as successful as they can be. It is also a good time to reflect on the supervision and management of interns to assure that these have been effective, and the teens are getting the best mentoring and guidance possible.[6] More about these points will be addressed in a moment.

Blogging and Responding to Prompts

Like the Rancho Cucamonga Public Library in California (chapter 4), the University of Virginia Library (chapter 5) has used a unique approach to getting feedback from teen interns that you might consider adapting. The interns were asked to blog every day during their time at the library. They were all also asked to respond to a specific set of questions the first week of their internship experience. The questions were:

- What do you hope to gain from your internship?
- What surprised you about your first day at the library and why?
- What was the most exciting thing you did or learned today, and why was it exciting?
- What are the most interesting jobs you have undertaken and the skills you have learned so far, and why were they interesting?
- What has been your proudest internship accomplishment so far?[7]

The answers from the six teen interns hired at the University of Virginia Library in 2019 were enthusiastic and inspiring. Responses to the first question included knowing more about how the library operates; learning about the many resources offered; becoming more open and outgoing; and finding out about writing, maps, history, art, and technology. Interns found that discovering special collections; dabbling in digital art; using 3D printers; testing a new library staff website; and sewing music sheets into folders were especially exciting, rewarding, and fascinating. Learning about how materials are cataloged and classified in the library caught one intern's attention!

It was evident that the interns were engaged in work that was a meaningful combination of connected learning, social-emotional learning, hands-on experience, and high interest. It was also evident that the teens greatly appreciated their dedicated, patient, and astute mentors.

Asking teens to write about their perspectives and experiences as they go is a first-rate way to find out what they are thinking and keep track of reactions and progress. Blogging, journaling, or even putting thoughts and feedback on a talkback board are positive, unique ways to approach or supplement the evaluation process. You might consider adapting and using this idea when you devise the evaluation process for your internships.

Midpoint Evaluations

It helps to sit down and talk midway through a teen internship. Both mentor or supervisor and intern get a chance to make sure that progress is being made and that the internship is going in the right direction. A midpoint evaluation can get a derailed experience back on track, or it can rechannel the internship in a different direction if necessary. Build time into your schedule, no matter how busy it might be, to include this helpful step.

At the Hussey-Mayfield Memorial Public Library, librarian Patricia VanArsdale had always planned a midpoint overview of the several internships the library offers for teens. When she meets with the teen interns, she says, "We are a little over halfway through the internship program. How has it been up to this point? Is it enjoyable or slow? Are there too many hours? What are your overall thoughts? Be honest—you are not hurting anyone's feelings. You are just letting us know how things are going for you."[8] Questions like these can kick-start a conversation that helps everyone to know where they stand as the internships move forward.

Incorporating inquiries such as these is a good place to start. In general, the topics that are important to cover during a midpoint evaluation fall in these areas:

- Reporting on the status of projects, activities, and tasks
- Reviewing how interns' work is contributing to the organization
- Conferring about both strengths and weaknesses and how to build upon the former and improve the latter
- Discussing areas that need growth and development, especially those teen interns are anxious to address
- Getting insights about the work that lies ahead[9]

Be sure when conducting midpoint evaluations with teen interns that they understand the purpose of such reviews is for give-and-take, and, in addition, that their thoughts, opinions, reactions, and needs—and yours—will be mutually respected.

SIDEBAR 6.1 TEEN VANTAGE POINT

The teen internship program was started by our librarian, Patricia VanArsdale. It is a way for teens themselves to promote and encourage other teens to enjoy and participate in the teen summer reading program. The interns do receive rewards, but that is not the sole motivation for the interns participating. The interns that do take part in this program usually do so because of their love for reading and the library.

There is an application and interview process and a set plan for the teens to follow. The adults that supervise the internship serve as a guide to help the teens understand what activities they need to complete each day to make the program succeed.

The expected outcomes for the interns are that they learn how to delegate and perform tasks themselves fairly. The library benefits from an increase of teen summer readers in the reading program.[1]

Jaishna Sivakumar
Hussey-Mayfield Memorial Public Library, Zionsville, Indiana

Note
1. Sivakumar, Jaishna. July 2, 2020. Email message to author.

Final Performance Reviews

Schedule the final performance reviews of your interns with enough time to comfortably go over the entire internship together. If you decide to ask your interns to complete self-evaluation forms, give them to the interns a few days ahead of time so that they get a chance to complete them thoroughly. Allow some time where they can work quietly alone on them. You will want to complete your supervisory form at the same time to review both at one meeting.

If your library has an open position for which your teen interns are qualified, the performance review would be a good time to let the teens know that you are encouraging them to apply if they would like. If there is interest, be prepared to share information about the job and what it entails. Even if interns decline, let them know that it is fine. Let them know how impressed you were with their work and that you wanted to extend the invitation at least. From earlier chapters in this book, you might remember that this very scenario of hiring an intern for a regular library position happened in a few different libraries whose internships were mentioned.

Teen Intern Self-Evaluation

It is helpful for teen interns to record the start and finish time they spend working at or for the library each workday. It is especially useful for teen interns to keep a "what I did today" record of their accomplishments and activities on the job. A companion or alternative plan might be to ask interns to keep a journal about their internship experiences or, as mentioned, to write a blog post. The Hussey-Mayfield Library asks interns to complete a daily shift summary sheet. As noted earlier in this book, a sample intern time sheet or task log is also included in appendix D. Whatever you decide works best—one of these methods or a combination of them—the completed records can provide a clear day-to-day picture of not only the number of hours worked but what was done during those hours.

These valuable documents can be paired with self-evaluation and feedback forms that interns can complete at the end of their jobs. It is essential to allow teen interns to do these self-evaluations and offer their feedback about the library, their mentors and supervisors, their coworkers, and their overall internship experiences. To get the best results, you will want to incorporate both aspects.

A self-evaluation doesn't need to be complicated. On the contrary, the more straightforward it is, the better. The same holds for an evaluation of the library and the internship experience taken as a whole. If you design it well, one form can cover both perspectives. It is a good idea to have checkboxes where teen interns can place rating scores and areas to write out their thoughts and reactions.

Again, sample templates for an hour/accomplishment form and a feedback and evaluation form that can be used with teen interns are included in the appendices. These forms give you a good place to start, and they can be adjusted and adapted as need be.

Supervisor, Advisor, and Mentor Evaluations

On the other side of the coin, it is helpful to have an additional form that you have designed or adapted for mentors and supervisors to use when evaluating teen interns. By completing such forms, you will have focal points for conducting evaluation meetings with your interns when they conclude their time spent working for you. You will also have helpful, stored records that will document the internship experiences. If you need to create follow-up reports for your administrators, grant-givers, or as reminders when you make recommendations for interns in the future, you will have the handy documents as a guide.

Like teen interns who might be keeping a tally of daily work hours and tasks, it can help if you keep notes during the entire internship period so that you can remember all the points you wish to make at the final review. In such notes, you can keep tabs on what your teen interns are assigned and what they have actually done, your personal perspectives on your own performance as a mentor, advisor, or supervisor, any notable details about library coworker reactions to and interactions with the teen interns, and any noteworthy customer impressions.

As with teen interns who are given prompts to get them inspired for blogging, it can be useful to have a few questions on hand if you want to do a self-evaluation of your performance as a supervisor, advisor, or mentor. Here are suggested questions you might consider to get you off and running:

- Did having an intern help me use my time and skills more effectively?
- Did my intern produce work that helped further our library's goals?
- Did I enhance and develop my managerial skills and supervisory skills by having an intern?
- Do I think our intern should be encouraged to apply for any open library positions? If so, why?
- Did our intern provide any insights that we would not have learned otherwise?[10]

If two or several library staff members guided the teen or teens, perhaps one serving as a mentor and another as a direct supervisor, it would help for them meet without the intern pres-

FIGURE 6.1
Mentor Holly Burrell and teen intern Cheyenne Jones from the Auburn Public Library in Georgia are shown attending the Public Library Association wrap-up meeting in Washington, D.C. The mentor-intern relationship and the final evaluation process they go through together are essential parts of any internship. Credit: Zach Miller.

ent before completing final evaluations. This offers a chance to discuss the internship privately before each teen's final evaluation meeting. It also allows a chance to converse as to whether it would be best to have both/all adults who worked with each teen in attendance for the evaluations or to have one person, representing all the adults involved, conducting exit interviews one-on-one.

TEXTBOX 6.1 LIBRARIAN VANTAGE POINT

When our intern, Emily Brooks, was asked what she would want other librarians to know about her intern experience, she said, "Tell them about that time I fell out of my chair at the circulation desk—that'll tell them all they need to know about me."

While that tidbit does provide just a glimpse of the humor and levity that Emily brought to our library, it doesn't tell the whole story. Emily brought so much value to our library. We are a small library, but we are insanely busy during the summer. Our circulation typically doubles, we have huge program attendance, and we added a free lunch program for the first time. Having the equivalent of another full-time employee who could jump in wherever needed was a game-changer. She was up for trying anything, and she did it all with a smile on her face. Even when she was at her least graceful, she was a huge asset to us, and our patrons adored her.[1]

Bel Outwater
Auburn Public Library, Georgia

Note

1. Outwater, Belinda. August 18, 2020. Email message to author.

Exit Interviews

Once you have gathered your teen evaluations and you have done your own, it is essential to conduct exit interviews before your teen interns depart from their jobs. It helps to consult a list of prewritten questions you have at hand as a reference point. Be sure to remain tactful, honest, yet objective about teens' work performance, and be ready to offer helpful advice and information that will be useful for the teens as they move on to other opportunities. Take brief notes if it can be done comfortably and without impacting the smooth flow of the conversation. Remember that you are aiming for a give and take conversation from which both mentors and supervisors and interns can learn. Add thanks and praise as appropriate during the interviews.

At Rancho Cucamonga Public Library in California, they have used the following questions for internship exit interviews:

- What did you find most valuable in the experience?
- Were there expectations that were met as well as ones that were not?
- What did you learn about Rancho Cucamonga Public Library? What did you learn about yourself?

> **TEXTBOX 6.2 TEEN VANTAGE POINT**
>
> It was enjoyable seeing the kids and even parents getting help from the volunteers and me.
>
> It sounds cheesy, but the most satisfying part of my internship is knowing that I have a place. I'm always doing something, even if it is something small. Every day during and after my shift is over, someone always says, "Thank you," or, "We appreciate your help." It's welcoming.[1]
>
> Nayana Thompson
> Rancho Cucamonga Public Library, California
>
> **Note**
>
> 1. Thompson, Nayana. September 29, 2020. Email message to author from Janet Monterrosa.

- What were the best and the worst job duties? Why?
- Did you have a favorite part of the internship? Why?
- What do you wish you were told before accepting this position that you feel was not communicated?
- What skills did you learn that you think you will apply in the future?
- Are there any projects that you did not complete that you wish you did?
- Looking back, are there any projects that you wish you could have done differently?
- Did you have a division or week that you enjoyed and in which you learned the most? What about the least?
- Was it better to have two interns working together rather than individually?[11]

Documenting Internships and Honoring Teen Interns

As mentioned before, you will want to document your teen internships in writing and other ways carefully. You might want to take pictures regularly and perhaps even some videos. Share details about the internships in library and community newsletters, social media, local media, and library or community blogs. You might even consider making a bulletin board with images of the highlights of the internships for everyone to see. The teen interns will be pleased to have their work publicly acknowledged, and they will get a further sense of accomplishment when they know their efforts are being noticed. Ensure you have any required library permissions for using intern names and images signed and sealed before you share or display them.

Remember that when you create your plans for your teen library internships, you will want to build in some kind of end-of-program way to thank and honor the teens. They have learned a great deal from the experience, but most likely, the library has also received important benefits from offering the internship positions. Whether it is a party or other gathering, be sure to have an event to show your appreciation and to give them a warm send-off.

Another way to honor teen interns is to ask them to keep in touch with you. You will enjoy seeing how they progress after they leave your library and move forward in their lives. Espe-

The Importance of Feedback, Evaluations, and a Positive Internship Conclusion Process 147

FIGURE 6.2
Interns can showcase their work in their community or library, at state events, and sometimes even nationally. The Public Library Association holds its closing event each year in the fall, where teen interns from around the country present their internship projects to a gathering of interns and mentors from around the United States. Credit: Zach Miller.

cially if some teen interns wind up working for the library after the end of their internships, you can keep in contact. By keeping connected, in the future, you might use your former teen interns as a good sounding board for ideas and questions for upcoming internships, or you might be able to have them mentor future interns. They might even be willing to serve on an advisory group for future internship programs, as mentioned at the end of chapter 2.

Culminating Presentations and Showcases

In addition to documenting teen internships in a variety of mediums, and as mentioned in some of the examples given in earlier chapters, at times, libraries oblige interns to create concluding presentations. This may be through featuring assigned work achievements or originally designed ventures that have been completed during internships, often to fulfill grant or high school capstone requirements. Frequently, interns showcase their accomplishments in a formal or informal public format—as an oral presentation, in an exhibit, in a printed work, or through another medium—as outlined in their internship program design. Having interns complete such requirements may become the crowning glory of their internship experience. It completes internship requirements and fills the role of a portfolio of sorts, especially when the interns leave the library with a lasting program or project that will go on after their internships are over. In whatever forums they are given, the presentations can be attended by any or all of those who were influential in supporting, providing, conducting, monitoring, and finalizing the internships—teachers, career counselors, mentors, supervisors, parents, peers, and guests.

During the presentations, interns provide evidence and documentation of their work and receive feedback from attendees. Mentors' expertise is crucial to this process as they provide unique skills and insights into the quality of work and accomplishments expected for the internships. Besides demonstrating interns' achievements, the presentations offer an opportunity to showcase the internship program and encourage future interns to apply if the internship program is ongoing.[12]

If final internship presentations are required, be sure to begin planning for them before the internships begin. Teens need to know ahead of time that this will eventually be taking place, in whatever format the presentations will take, whether at a national Public Library Association gathering or in the library's large meeting room with local guests. If arranged locally, reserve and confirm a room for the event in advance on the library calendar or through another medium and begin making a list of those who will need to be invited.

FIGURE 6.3
Teen Leaders Stevenson Youyoute, Alia Touadjine, and Rachel Cosgrove from the Waltham Public Library presented their Real Talk paid teen leaders' programs at the Massachusetts Library Association Conference in 2019. Credit: Luke Kirkland.

When an Intern Requires Counsel, Reassignment, Reprimand, or Dismissal

Up to this point, I've discussed the procedures to follow or consider if internships are running soundly. However, it is also essential to think about times when things may not be turning out as well as you might have hoped and planned.

One of the central aspects of internships is assuring that interpersonal relationships run smoothly. These relationships may be between interns, mentors or supervisors, teen peers, library staff members, administrators, library customers, and anyone representing a partner organization. Ongoing, honest check-ins by advisors with their interns, while establishing and maintaining supportive, respectful environments, can be surefire ways to deflect difficulties and conflicts. These practices also lead to creating an open dialogue with interns.

Nevertheless, despite diligent efforts to build solid relationships, and no matter how well-matched interns seem for particular library or partnership settings, you may still face the prospects of counseling, reprimanding, reassigning, or even dismissing interns. As unsavory and stressful as such situations might seem, they are best resolved by confronting them objectively with good documentation and head-on. Avoidance by rationalizing to make concerns seem less burdensome only intensifies the problems. This is unfair to all parties who comprise the interpersonal relationships surrounding and involving the interns, especially the interns themselves.

Well, then, what do you do when you are faced with such uncomfortable challenges? The first step is to calmly revisit the mutually agreed-upon expectations, goals, and objectives with interns. Bring documented inconsistencies to light and determine if interns understand your concerns and are still committed to the principles and practices upon which you both had agreed. After carefully talking things over, you may need to assess internship goals to find jointly acceptable alternatives that satisfactorily cover what needs to be done and what the interns can do. As an example, you may want to revisit the story of the teen who finally found his rewarding internship niche at the Gadsden Public Library in chapter 4 after he was reassigned to quiet duties at the library instead of those in noisy areas.

With this example in mind, realize that the interns might express concerns of their own when presented with your concerns. They may also approach you with their concerns first. You may need to discuss a lack of support or instruction, insufficiently challenging or overwhelming work, unrealistic deadlines, misinformation leading to missteps when dealing with other staff, or other issues directly connected to how they are supported or prepared for their tasks. When these things occur, listen considerately, offer suggestions for resolutions, and stand by and stand up for your interns' needs and viewpoints.[13]

Despite your best intentions and those of your interns, there may come times when counseling is not the final answer. You may encounter more serious issues or find that your interns are truly not following through. In these cases, you may need to formally reprimand your interns or resort to dismissal in the worst-case scenario. These are very challenging and taxing circumstances in any work environment, but when dealing with interns, they can be more traumatic. Still, when you handle them with forthrightness and impartiality, you will be doing what is best for the library, for those who have been in working relationships with the interns, and hopefully for the interns themselves. When handled with aplomb, interns may learn important life lessons from encountering such consequences.

Attendance and Performance Requirements Are Essential

When orienting interns to their new jobs, addressing the importance of good attendance is fundamental. Most teen interns will take prompt and regular attendance requirements seriously, though sometimes you may encounter teens who are often late, do not show up for inappropriate reasons, are no-shows at times, or miss work too frequently. You may be able to deflect most of these kinds of absences by discussing the importance of good attendance prior to internship start dates.

Remember to approach conversations about attendance with concern and clear information. A national survey of youth showed that connecting absences with consequences motivates them to go to school, but it can also motivate them to take their jobs seriously in the present and futures. A job applicant who builds a strong attendance record has a better chance of getting and keeping a position later. Documenting a positive work attendance record for an intern in good standing can enhance job and other applications.

Express authentic concern about interns' attendance performance because you genuinely want them to learn responsibility and succeed. Missing work causes problems for the employer and can set back assignments and tasks from being completed effectively and on schedule. Explain that you will be keeping track of interns' attendance, including reporting on time, leaving on time, and coming to work on the days expected. Be sure that interns understand that if they indeed are sick, if there is a family or other emergency, if there is a transportation issue out of their control, or another serious incident that you will, with appropriate notice, accept such special circumstances as good reasons for missing or being late for work. If you have an agreement that you will accept schedule rearrangements for a family event or vacation, make sure teens understand that they must clear the dates in advance. When any of these things occur, decipher and agree upon how interns will compensate for missed time. Stress that absences and lateness must be the exceptions and cannot be the norm. Teens who are given this information with care and a positive attitude will usually respond by following through as anticipated.[14]

If you have presented teen interns up-front with your attendance policies and discover that they are not following through with good attendance, you will need to take steps to remedy the situation—likewise with performance and behavior policies. You may want to set up a warning plan to document unacceptable absences, tardiness, or behavior issues. Perhaps a "three strikes and you are out" policy would be sufficient. It is helpful and comforting to have this policy, related procedures, and any forms prepared, agreed to, and on hand ahead of time, just in case they are needed at some point. In those circumstances, the more ready you are to confront the problems, the better.

TEXTBOX 6.3 SAMPLE INTERNSHIP PROBATIONARY FORM CONTENT

Name of Intern:
Date of Notification:
Name(s) of Mentor(s)/Supervisor(s):
Name of Library or Other Work Site:
NOTICE OF PROBATION AND PLAN FOR IMPROVEMENT

Rationale
During the internship, interns are given a safe place to learn job skills while learning from missteps that may be part of the experience. Interns are expected to pay attention, follow directions, and display respectful behavior. While doing this, they need to accept instructions and not be cavalier about mistakes so that they can incorporate what those mistakes have taught them and use that knowledge to improve and foster progress. Plac-

ing an intern on probation presents an ideal way to advance good behavior before the necessity of terminating the internship comes to pass.

Reason for Probation
It has become evident that a pattern of behavior has developed that may be detrimental to your continued participation in the internship program. Here is what has been noticed:

On [date(s)], you were warned regarding your [poor performance of duty; absenteeism; tardiness, etc.]. NOTE: Be sure you have carefully and objectively documented this/these occurrence(s).

Opportunity for Improvement and Potential Consequences
Your conduct constitutes adequate grounds for terminating your internship; however, we wish to offer a final opportunity to prove your desire to learn and grow through the experience. Without complying with these conditions for improvement and failure to follow through, there will be no choice but to set your termination process in motion. Here are the steps you need to address:

- Complete the intern self-assessment section of this probation notice
- First condition [describe it here]
- Second condition [describe it here]

Intern Self-Assessment

- Please describe and explain the factors that are contributing to your difficulties in your own words.
- Using this checklist, mark all the issues that have been challenging you recently:
  - Home and family problems
  - Socially related issues
  - Uncertainty of work goals
  - Unsure of interests, skills, or abilities
  - Problems with peers, customers, or others
  - Balancing work and other obligations
  - Having trouble concentrating at work
  - Stress, sadness, or loneliness
  - Illness or other health issues
  - Difficulty managing time
  - Other
- Despite the difficulties you are experiencing, please describe some personal or academic successes over the last few months of which you are proud.
- What people and resources are available to help you as you move forward?
- Name at least two goals to help you succeed as you proceed.

NOTE TO INTERN: Your signature confirms that you have discussed this notice with your mentor/supervisor, even if you do not agree with the probation.

Intern Signature: Date:

Mentor Signature: Date:

[Duplicate copies of this form should be given to the intern, mentor/supervisor, library administration, or any others required to have it.][1]

Note

1. Kyler, *Internship Guide*.

Dismissal or Resignation of an Intern

If you find yourself in the unfortunate situation where a teen intern on probation does not improve, you will need to confront intern termination. Another way you may lose a teen intern is if the teen gives *you* notice of resignation. Either situation may be uncomfortable, depending on the circumstances. But again, if you are prepared, you can help the finalization go easier on both you and the intern.

With a termination resulting from an unsuccessful probationary period, you will need to follow the process you set in motion at the probation meeting unless there is an incident that warrants immediate action and no probation is offered. Document the unacceptable performance or conduct and use that documentation to objectively explain to the intern that their employment is ending in light of it.

You can also do this with unpaid interns when the situation calls for it. Keep records and follow procedures just as if the teen intern was being paid. Try to say something positive about the intern's performance that you may have noticed, despite the negative comments you are obligated to make. Present the latter comments in a straightforward, tactful manner. The intern may learn a memorable lesson from the experience, even an unpaid intern, as long as you keep your interactions during the termination process on a professional, considerate, and objective level.

Although the example I will relay now is from a volunteer and supervisor perspective—not an internship—from my former library in Arizona many years ago, I want to share it because I think it will clarify my point about dismissal procedures being potentially positive and helpful. We had a teen volunteer who was actively assisting us in running our summer reading program. He was a regular teen user of the young adult room and seemed to be a dependable worker we could trust. However, we had a stack of tickets to Arizona Diamondbacks games donated as summer reading prizes that went missing. The teen volunteer's mother found them in his room and reported her finding them to us. We had no choice but to dismiss the volunteer. Years later, as an adult, the teen found himself as an employee of the aforementioned baseball team. He brought a stack of donated tickets to the library, said we had taught him an important lesson as a teenager, and hoped the donation would make up for his terrible mistake as a volunteer. When you need to dismiss an intern and do it sensitively and with concern, you may be providing a similar service for that teen.

When a teen intern must resign, it is usually a different story. It could be that the teen has personal reasons for leaving or a realization that the library environment is not a good fit. Before breaking ties, you will want to talk carefully with the intern and determine if there is anything you can do to remedy the situation. Perhaps switching the intern to a different library

---

TEXTBOX 6.4 SAMPLE TERMINATION NOTICE CONTENT

Name of Intern:
Date of Notification:
Effective Date of Termination:
Name(s) of Mentor(s)/Supervisor(s):
Name of Library or Other Work Site:
Reason for Termination (check all that apply)

- Intern request
- Parental request
- Mentor/supervisor request
- Excessive absences or tardiness
- Failure to complete assigned tasks or projects
- Failure to complete and submit assigned reports, forms, documents, or evaluations
- Unprofessional responses to or actions toward mentor/supervisor or coworkers
- Unprofessional behavior toward library customers
- Not complying with the rules, policies, and regulations of the library and the internship program, including breach of confidentiality and nonadherence to the dress code
- Other (describe)

Was a probationary period offered to the intern? If so, what were the terms of the probation, and how were those terms not met?
Other comments:

NOTE TO INTERN: Your signature confirms that you have discussed this notice with your mentor/supervisor, even if you do not agree with the termination.

Intern Signature: Date:

Mentor Signature: Date:

[Duplicate copies of this form should be given to the intern, mentor/supervisor, library administration, or any others required to have it.][1]

Note

1. Kyler, *Internship Guide*.

branch will alleviate transportation problems that have materialized. Maybe transferring the intern to a different department or office might do the trick. However, if no other options are suitable, or if the teen truly does not find the work satisfying, you will need to accept a tendered resignation.

Hopefully, you will never encounter such issues even if you have planned for them. However, remember that if you do, no matter how difficult it may be to have interns leave before their time is up, you will want to keep the experiences as cordial and constructive as possible. Wish the interns well. Encourage them to visit the library and let you know how they are doing. Make the situations into learning opportunities if you possibly can. You still want the teens to feel welcome and move forward in positive directions.

Notes

1. Siegel, Ben. January 3, 2020. "Tips for Conducting Intern Evaluations." Scholars, Inc., https://hirescholars.com/2020/01/tips-for-conducting-intern-evaluations/.

2. "Employer Guide to Organizing a Successful Internship Program." [n.d.]. Richmond Community College, https://richmondcc.edu/sites/default/files/employer_guide_to_internship_program.pdf.

3. "YouthMade Toolkit: How to Develop a Local Manufacturing Youth Internship Program." [n.d.]. SF Made, http://sfmade.org/wp-content/uploads/YouthMade-Toolkit.pdf.

4. Capturing Connected Learning in Libraries Team and Partners. [n.d.]. "Talkback Board Repository." Connected Learning, https://connectedlearning.uci.edu/wp-content/uploads/2020/12/Talkback-Board-Repository.pdf.

5. "Capturing Connected Learning in Libraries." [n.d.]. Connected Learning Lab, https://connectedlearning.uci.edu/project/capturing-connected-learning-in-libraries/.

6. "Internship Plan Handbook." 2019. Parker Dewey, http://info.parkerdewey.com/internship-handbook?hsCtaTracking=570d2f87-3e56-41ec-b4b6-79c615045c58%7Cc7f34a38-c109-46f6-96bd-c19937726e29#to-go.

7. "News, Announcements, Updates, and Happenings at the UVA Library." 2020. University of Virginia Library, https://news.library.virginia.edu/tag/hsinternship/.

8. VanArsdale, Patricia. September 29, 2020. Email message to author.

9. "Employer Guide to Organizing."

10. "Internship Plan Handbook."

11. Monterrosa, Janet. September 29, 2020. Email message to author.

12. Kyler, Nina J. [n.d.] *Internship Guide: A Resource Toolkit*. Regional Office of Education # 17, DeWitt, Livingston, Logan, McLean Counties of Illinois. Contact https://roe17.org/contact-us or Regional Office of Education #17, 201 E. Grove Street, Suite 300, Bloomington, IL 61701, to obtain a copy.

13. Kyler, *Internship Guide*.

14. "Sending the Right Message about Attendance to Teens." 2017. Attendance Works, https://www.attendanceworks.org/wp-content/uploads/2017/09/SendingTheRightMessageAboutAttendanceToTeens_3-1.pdf.

7

Dealing with Teen Library Internships When the Library Must Be Closed

IN MARCH 2020, EDUCATORS, parents, administrators, and nonprofits that serve youth, including libraries, had to adjust to the sudden reality that "out-of-school-time-is-all-the-time." Since then, leaders responsible for directing work with youth found themselves in countless hours of virtual meetings to shift their sights on working with and serving youth from days to weeks to months to years. Often, meetings within the individual agencies were not collaborative and focused on reenvisioning together. However, dealing with the pandemic taught an important lesson about building back better, more broadly, and together.[1] As part of this picture of addressing youth needs, libraries have been an essential facet in keeping teens moving forward in their lives, despite the incredible challenges everyone in the entire world was confronting.

Teen Social-Emotional Development during Taxing Times

In a webinar provided in August 2020 by the Collaborative for Academic, Social, and Emotional Learning (CASEL), Daniel Siegel, MD, the author of a well-known book about the maturation process of the teen brain, shared his knowledge and perspectives about building teen strengths and promoting social-emotional learning during the challenging times being faced due to the COVID-19 pandemic. He carefully explained how adolescence, when the brain is still gradually developing, takes time—from about age eleven until the mid-twenties—and caring adults can encourage teens to assert independence as they go through this phase with the guidance of adult authority. In school and other places in their world, teens can successfully navigate the challenges they face when adults are truthful and understand that teens have matured enough to comprehend the reality that life is uncertain.[2] However, when the world is turned upside down, what can adults do to keep teens on an even keel?

First, parents, educators, and other adults in teens' lives must acknowledge how especially difficult it is for people in their age group to deal with challenging times like a pandemic, an evacuation, or other emergencies. Children who have not yet approached adolescence might be thrilled to receive extra attention at home from the adults in their families, but teenagers usually feel differently. They are isolated, cut off from their friends, missing graduations, proms, extracurricular involvement, college visits, and additional long-anticipated activities. When adults carefully advise and level with teens, it helps them tremendously.

Parents, grandparents, and guardians can communicate with teens and offer advice, necessary rules, and guidelines. This includes helping teens to stick to schedules that most closely reflect regular days; reinforcing routine meal and sleep times; building in discussion times with a focus on gratitude; talking about new responsibilities, like assisting with younger siblings; and allowing personal time for privacy, virtually meeting with friends, reading, exercise, hobbies, and games. It also means that teens receive honest and straightforward information, particularly in the event of a pandemic. They need to know the current health and safety recommendations and regulations, such as mask-wearing, hand-washing, social distancing, or whatever might be appropriate for the circumstances, and that there is a "no cheating" policy about them. It is also important to check in regularly with teens to assure that they are feeling okay or to see if they need more support.

Another important element in dealing with a health or other emergency is keeping teens feeling like they are accomplishing meaningful things and contributing to their home and outside communities. Showing understanding by validating their disappointments, integrating mindfulness,[3] and instilling positive behaviors can help deflect anxiety and depression. At home, teens might be encouraged to teach older family members how to be in touch virtually, plan virtual gatherings for the family, assist with the educational instruction of younger siblings, reduce clutter in the garage, or prepare items for donation to charities. Likewise, teens might still contribute as volunteers in their communities when local health requirements are incorporated. It is beneficial and highly encouraged for them to do so.[4]

Here is where libraries and other community institutions come into play. If teen library volunteering and internship opportunities can be transitioned to virtual or other formats that follow guidelines for well-being, teen volunteers and interns can still have positive participatory and work experiences that enhance their skills and growth processes toward adulthood. They can still get the chance to do meaningful things that will hardwire their brains for the good.

Ultimately, as CASEL has pointed out, "When physical distancing is deemed necessary, social and emotional connectedness is even more critical." Libraries are certainly part of this connectedness, or can be. Further:

> As the country and the world absorb[ed] the impact of the coronavirus, our interconnectedness has never been more clearly on display. Social-emotional learning offers a powerful means to support one another—children and adults— during this challenging time. Now, more than ever, we understand how important it is to demonstrate empathy and resilience, build relationships across distance, and call upon our collective resolve to strengthen our schools and our communities.[5]

The bottom line is that finding channels to continue outstanding programs, services, and opportunities for teenagers through libraries during challenging times is fundamental for our communities' well-being.

Circumventing the "Learning Slide"

The concept of "summer learning loss" or "summer slide" was first documented in 1996 and continues to be studied by experts in education. It refers to the consequence of young people being out of school for several months before resuming normal academic and other activities each fall. Research has shown that they can regress in what they learned during the previous school year unless their summer learning experiences are positively enhanced. Younger children are affected academically more than teens, but generally, teens are also impacted, as are all young people from low-income backgrounds.[6] The evidence is clear that even though losses do occur for all ages, when students are encouraged to stay engaged in learning during their breaks from school, they may not only maintain but also improve their knowledge.[7]

During emergencies and other unusual conditions, like a pandemic, the definition of the concept can be expanded to apply to other situations. In some circles, "summer slide" is now being called the "COVID slide" because, despite virtual learning that was put into place quickly, parents have struggled to maintain a top-notch learning environment at home and keep themselves and their offspring engaged. Youth and parents were not prepared for the drastic changes and challenges that remote learning would entail, and often it has been difficult for children and teens to concentrate and stick to their work. Navigating these complicated times has been a learning process for youth, parents, and educators alike.

Traditionally, libraries have played an essential role in encouraging young people to read and learn over the summer months, and this is, naturally, the basis for many libraries changing the names of their summer reading programs to summer "learning" programs or summer "challenges." Libraries have also evolved into places that can alter the effects of "summer slide" by providing fun, enlightening, appealing, and pertinent learning experiences in addition to reading programs. Libraries have also added special learning and exploring opportunities during other times when school has been out of session, such as for spring breaks. For most libraries, these opportunities had been going swimmingly for many years, with progressive adjustments being made over time to improve them. These opportunities have included volunteer and other meaningful participatory experiences, plus the new trend of adding teen library internships when opportune.

During the pandemic and other emergency times, the basic precepts that zero in on how adults relate to teens and promote their growth and development have become key. As already noted, it is unmistakable that no matter what is happening, teens are still working their way through adolescence, and they need the reassurance, wisdom, and guidance of the adults in their lives to help them to continue progressing positively. They still need to be exposed to and expand soft skills and increase their knowledge as they approach and reach adulthood. At the same time, they continually need to widen their social-emotional and connected learning proficiency. As you have seen in the other chapters of this book, providing teen library internships and similar opportunities is an important way to help teens meet these learning and developmental needs. When challenging times encroach, the things that teens need to succeed are still crucial to their lives. Their growth is not put on hold. All significant adults in teens' lives must work together to make sure that effective workarounds are created, so that experiences that help them gain knowledge, skills, and information remain in place, even if shaped differently.

As Forum for Youth Investment experts stated about the essential role of community partnerships in providing these experiences for teens beyond academia at the time of the pandemic:

> Learning for life is a progression from simple to increasingly complex adaptive skills. Motivation, meaning making, and identity development are key to learning, especially for adolescents. Community organizations and nonprofit partners play important direct and complementary roles across all dimensions of learning. In particular, because participation is usually voluntary and interest-

driven, adults in these settings create relational experiences that activate motivation, skill development, and identity formation and provide real-life opportunities to plan, fail, and contribute that build confidence and agency.[8]

Those advocates who provide inspiration to and plan meaningful participation for teens will find it helpful to take these comments to heart. By paying attention to teen needs despite challenging circumstances, we not only give them opportunities to learn and mature, but we show them that it is possible to persevere, to manage life as it comes, and to move forward no matter what.

Managing Teen Internships When Libraries and Other Agencies Must Be Closed

When the year 2020 began with the fears and realities of a widely spreading global pandemic, the world environment was quickly transformed by a monumentally challenging phase in modern history. The pandemic spread far and wide and disrupted human life and social interactions. The upheaval significantly impacted businesses, organizations, agencies, schools, and, yes, libraries. Library youth services, other community youth-serving programs, and school clubs and sports teams canceled or postponed planned opportunities for teens to be dynamically involved and engaged in any number of ways. Teens were on a seesaw of openings and closings as adults tried to get opportunities restarted only to find themselves having to close things down again. One of the many ways teens were impacted was by having most teen internship opportunities canceled, postponed, or delayed indefinitely.

Despite all of the sudden changes that affected teen internships, some efforts were made to keep teens involved. For example, adult leaders of the Teens in Public Service (TIPS) program in the Puget Sound area of Washington State were uncertain how to approach their upcoming teen internship program. Should they cancel it? Postpone it? Delay it? Those were the same questions that needed answers and solutions at youth-serving agencies and libraries everywhere.

Wondering if they would be able to have internships at all, the TIPS directors decided to seek and heed the advice of their recently formed Youth Advisory Committee, comprised of past teen interns from their program and mentioned earlier in this book. You will recall that this group's formation and purpose were explained while encouraging libraries to consider emulating them in chapter 2.

From their still youthful perspectives, the committee members focused upon the need to continue fulfilling the TIPS mission. They urged the directors to figure out ways to keep internships going in other formats. Just like Dr. Siegel stressed, they knew as young adults themselves how urgent it was for teens to continue developing their skills, knowledge, expertise, and positive contributions. As a result of respecting and taking their advice, the directors sent out a message explaining that the internships would continue in different formats. Part of the message said:

> Safety is our number one priority. Teens In Public Service is making adjustments to our program activities to ensure the safety of our staff, interns, and volunteers. The TIPS office is closed, and our staff is working remotely to ensure we can still provide meaningful internship experiences to teens this summer.[9]

They went on to say that they still intended to run a scaled-down summer program with a smaller intern cohort and a delayed start date. This was done to ensure that any teen placements were carried out safely. Internships that were still offered allowed the teens to support their communities through office-based or remote digital work opportunities, held online and adjusted for the pandemic environment. TIPS further stated:

> We remain committed to carrying out our mission. Given Covid-19's impact on the Seattle nonprofit sector, developing teens into dedicated, empathetic community leaders is more relevant than ever. We know there is still a need for organizations to receive the support of paid service interns, and we will work to provide safe, meaningful internships that meet the changing needs of our community.[10]

Ways Libraries Can Keep Teens Hired and Engaged During Tough Times

As with TIPS, whether teens are selected for internships that compensate them with school credit or other non-monetary rewards or are hired for stipends or paychecks, there are various ways that teens can still experience library internships despite hard times that prohibit in-person contact. In addition, teen volunteers and teen council members can sometimes find ways to continue their active library involvement while distancing. For example, teens can plan and run virtual programs for their peers, create flyers and documents that can be shared with the public, review and promote books and other materials, or make videos of storytimes. Many libraries have had to experiment quickly with alternative opportunities as the pandemic worsened, and many of them learned a great deal through doing it.

When using imagination, the list of possibilities can go on and on. You can incorporate many ideas so that teens can still have a rich encounter with library work and activities through a remote internship. For the future, the ticket is in preplanning for situations when such ideas need to be put into action.

One of the best ways to solicit ideas for virtual internships is by asking teens themselves. You might consider consulting with your teen leadership council or another teen-oriented library group to imagine ways to develop meaningful programs, tasks, and activities that would allow them to contribute to the library environment as challenging times dictate. Another approach might be to form a teen focus group to brainstorm potential virtual programming concepts. If you have already had or plan to have teen interns on board, you might ask them if they have ideas about a virtual internship. You might be surprised at the unique ideas that teens can have!

Remote Internships

If you decide to implement a remote or virtual internship, either due to unforeseen conditions or as the way you design an internship, even in normal times, there are important considerations. The most important one is that virtual internships should incorporate the basic elements that give your internships value to the teenagers hired to take them on. As you would with an in-person internship, be sure that you assign projects and tasks that fit your library's mission and goals. You will also want to find a way to immerse the virtual interns into your library's culture and, if there are several interns, to give them opportunities to build community with intern peers.

Be sure to get the go-ahead from your administrators and human resource specialists for transitioning to a virtual internship format. You might even choose to have a plan ready in the wings. Contemplating the challenges that could arise during an emergency and thinking in advance about how important continuing teen internships would still be in those circumstances will help you figure out what to do on an as-needed basis. By looking ahead and having an approved plan in place for any times alternatives must be put into place, you will be one step ahead of the game.

To create a plan, include anyone who would be working with interns in a virtual environment, such as supervisors, mentors, and technology staff. Together, revamp internship job descriptions to transition them to the new assignments and procedures. Your library probably has an arrangement in place in case of flood, fire, or another emergency that can be activated in a flash. Your alternate internship plan would operate similarly.

There are several things to cover in your optional plan. One is assuring that teen interns have the appropriate technology handy to work on virtual tasks. If they do not have access to Wi-Fi or a laptop, they might not complete their assignments. You may need to set up special access and equipment for teens under these circumstances. Also, keep in mind that interns would most likely be working from home, where they may be dealing with a lack of personal space, background noise, family expectations, and other distractions. Giving schedules and deadlines for virtual assignments, as you would with in-person work, is a good way to give an online internship structure. However, refrain from making them static or rigid, and be flexible with requirements.

Because virtual internships have an element of disconnect built in, library mentors and supervisors need to keep in good contact. Be certain that assignments are purposeful and relevant to your library and contribute to library goals, and that teens receive regular input and feedback. Arrange regular check-ins with interns as part of the virtual internship process and incorporate evaluations into your plans.

If you have more than one teen intern, figure out ways for them to communicate and correspond with one another. When possible, provide the means for the teens to work in teams, connect socially, and have regular interactions. Virtual interfaces can come in handy in these instances, similar to the ways libraries have been providing virtual teen programming.[11]

TEXTBOX 7.1

Essential points to remember when arranging virtual teen internships:

- Ensure that your interns have the proper equipment at home to take on virtual internships. If not, have an arrangement to supply what is needed.
- Have a plan in place to provide virtual training for your interns.
- Create an internship handbook that teen interns can access online.
- Make sure you know how to contact your interns, including parent or guardian contacts.
- Be sure that your interns know to whom they are to report regularly and to whom they can address problems, concerns, or new ideas.
- Give your interns a backup person's contact information for when their direct mentor or supervisor cannot be reached.

- Even with remote internships, schedule check-in dates and times with your interns to ensure that everyone stays informed and up to date on projects and assignments.[1]

Note

1. "Internship Plan Handbook." 2019. Parker Dewey, http://info.parkerdewey.com/internship-handbook.

Ideas That Have Worked or Could Work

Several libraries have designed alternative ways that teens can make meaningful contributions. These ideas could be employed for internships, volunteering, teen councils, teen focus groups, teen tutors, or any other way that teens are involved in participatory library efforts. The following ideas are ones some libraries have already put or are putting.

- Teen services librarian Nicole Burchfield from the Poudre River Public Library District in Fort Collins, Colorado, organized a virtual meeting of Colorado librarians serving teens and tweens to talk about their pandemic programming—how the programs are going, what is working and what is not, and to discuss new ideas. They began meeting via Zoom in December 2020, had another meeting set for March, and plan to continue these meetings as long as they are needed. Through this cooperative effort to share information, several great programs have begun at the libraries involved, and the group is anticipating that more programs will be starting. Programs for teens that have been put in place at the Poudre River Library are:
    - A virtual D&D program that has been a huge hit. Although teens do not run it in this instance, they actively move the story along independently. For a teen intern drawn to fantasy role-playing games, starting and running a similar virtual program would be an exciting project.
    - The library teen council is planning a spring virtual murder mystery. A group of teen interns could design, prepare, and run a program like this one.[12]
- At the Greenburgh Public Library in Elmsford, New York, they offer teen internships and a teen volunteer program called VolunTeens. They also created a group called Virtual VolunTeens. For the virtual program, teens can choose from a variety of projects. These are appropriate for teens who need to earn volunteer service hours, but perhaps they could be adapted to provide assignments for virtual internships:
    - Write reviews or make videos on books or book series in any format, movies, or video games, and include a rating of one to five (with five being the best).
    - Subscribe to the library's Poetry Jam YouTube channel and make videos to be considered for posting on the channel.
    - Create ten-item lists or make one-minute videos recommending similar titles for favorite library materials.
    - Create a "how-to" or tip guides for selected library electronic mediums or materials either in writing or in a video design.
    - Be virtual teen tutors on various subjects, homework, or test preparation.

- Contribute to the library's virtual COVID-19 memory project.
- Devise projects of teens' own choices. This requires a submission form for consideration.[13]
- When the Pima County Library in Tucson, Arizona, heard from teens who asked how they could still be involved at the library during the pandemic, the Library Virtual Volunteer Program was formed. It has allowed teens to continue developing the skills they need to enter adulthood while earning volunteer hours. Projects that have been done and ones that are planned include:
  - Contribute to the Pima Love Notes Project through which teens write notes to elders in assisted living and long-term care homes, whether on their own or in a library-organized Zoom meeting to create cards with other teens. Materials have been provided for teens who needed them.
  - Be taught about voting and the census to teach others what they learn.
  - Write book reviews.
  - Host or cohost virtual programs.
  - Illustrate stories contributed by children and teens for the library's Story Sketches project, part of its summer learning program.
  - Design a project or program of their choice.[14]
- At the Berwyn Public Library in Berwyn, Illinois, they have had an ongoing volunteer program for those in grades nine through twelve. During the pandemic, teens were invited to choose from a menu of six choices for remote projects and activities in lieu of in-person opportunities. Those choices were to:
  - Make toys for animals in local shelters using kits provided by the library.
  - Create a piece of artwork for the library's gallery, which could be in the form of a drawing, 3D sculpture, or even an artistic food picture.
  - Write reviews on books, movies, or video games to be posted on the Teen Blog.
  - Submit a personal work to the #WeWereHere Project, a repository for teen voices and stories during the COVID-19 pandemic.
  - Investigate race and antiracism by reading or watching suggested titles from a list called Fighting Racism, then writing reviews.
  - Contact local representatives by letter or phone to express opinions on topics of concern. A list of contact information and ideas for current issues to address was provided.[15]
- The New Providence Memorial Library in New Providence, New Jersey, has an active teen volunteer program, and they provided alternatives to their regular volunteer opportunities during the pandemic. Some of the options they offered were to:
  - Serve as book review bloggers.
  - Create video programs for the library's YouTube channel that presented useful lessons to others, such as teaching younger children STEM-oriented experiments, teaching older people technology skills, or developing another educational program of a teen's choosing.
  - Deliver summer reading prizes.[16]
- At the Charlotte Mecklenburg Library in Charlotte, North Carolina, they offered plenty of virtual opportunities for teens at their digital library and also through community partnerships. These opportunities gave teens a chance to:
  - Write reviews or make review videos on library books and other resources. With parental permission, selected reviews were posted.

- Create short, informative videos about nature that people would enjoy from home for a local partner, Anne Springs Close Gateway.
- Assemble kits, make supplies such as masks, and write notes of encouragement that were dropped off for students and teachers at Charlotte-Mecklenburg Schools.
- Investigate and choose from an assortment of other listed opportunities to support the community.[17]

• The Boston Public Library not only moved their teen volunteer program to a virtual environment in 2020 but also completely revamped the adult internships they offered for graduate library master's program students from Simmons University into a virtual format. One intern, Kerri MacLaury, has many reasons to feel that the virtual internship experience was extremely valuable for her while embarking on her librarian career.[18] As part of what she learned and explored, she was impressed with the aforementioned teen volunteer program, which held online interviews for participation and offered opportunities to:

- Read books and write or record book reviews.
- Create lists of ebooks or audiobooks with specific topics.
- Write or record game reviews.
- Write instructions or record videos demonstrating fun at-home activities for other teens on such subjects as making crafts, cooking, or whatever else might reflect their knowledge and interest.
- Assist with the Twitch online gaming channel.
- Take part in thirty minutes of weekly meetings led by the volunteers.[19]

Remember also that at the Waltham Public Library in Massachusetts, the paid teen leaders altered their Real Talk program to a virtual format due to the pandemic. As relayed in chapter 5, they planned and ran a Zoom program with local school administrators, helped to create a promotional video for their For Freedoms project, which they posted on YouTube, and hosted an online author interview, which they also posted on YouTube.[20]

Hopefully, all the examples given here will inspire you to plan future or imminent virtual teen internship activities and projects. You might also use these ideas as starting points to aid teens who help you develop solutions. But in case you would like more, here are some other ideas to consider:

- For teens who have solid writing skills, other writing projects besides blogging or doing book reviews could be assigned. Perhaps teens could write copy for upcoming programs or activities, write newsletter articles, or transcribe interviews with local people of interest. Be imaginative and ask teen interns what they might like to write.
- Teen interns who excel at drawing might design posters, create logos, design T-shirts, or delve into any other artistic tasks that need to be addressed. Again, ask teens what would catch their interest.
- If a library needs to conduct surveys of patron reactions or usage, trained teen interns with good communication skills could handle this task.
- Teen interns could take on data entry, compile surveys, proofread and edit written content, test a website's functionality, or produce unique reader advisory tools.
- Managing social media or website content for a teen page or other library area could be an assignment a teen intern would relish.[21]

- Ask interns to create "make and take" packets with materials for crafts or other activities to be done at home. Although this is not a virtual activity, it is something that interns could do at home and turn in to the library when prepared for the public. Library customers who would like the packets can then stop by and safely pick them up in a designated area.[22]
- Once more, check in with teen interns and other library teen volunteers for their suggestions.

Here is one last idea that could be adapted to a library or school environment. This example comes from teenage volunteers at Delphi High School in California. A group of eighty or so students have an ongoing club called the Helping Hawks. They perform service work, such as spending lunchtime with special needs students, running coat drives for needy younger children, or cleaning the stadium after football games. The group was formed by students and became a symbol of outstanding community volunteerism.

When the pandemic struck, the group could not do any regular helping activities. One student, Matthew Ward, came up with an idea to create an offshoot group called the Reading Hawks. The school principal gave his blessing on this wonderful idea, teachers and other adults helped spread the word about it, and now the teens meet regularly online to share stories, insights, and encouragement. Through the Reading Hawks, the teenagers read to younger children online, and participation keeps growing.

Matthew said, "As I watch my club members engage in service, there is light in their eyes while they connect and read to these young children. These young kids smile, converse and have a similar light as they receive the generosity extended to them. While we are still distant from each other, the connection is real, and the closeness is evident. This is not only a service club these students are running but also a modified reading program. They get all the credit. They have risen to meet the needs of others and, in turn, have seen their own need and their inner drive to serve be met. They talk about the day they will be able to meet their young friends face to face."[23]

If you have teen library interns, especially in a school library but not limited to that setting, this could be another way for them to continue working when the library must be closed. Maybe you could set up a schedule for them to spend time reading with children from the community or individual classes online or develop other reading activities they can share virtually. Like Matthew thinking up this idea and having everyone buy in, it would most likely be beneficial to have the interns develop their version of a program akin to this one with adult guidance.

Many libraries and other agencies find purposeful ways for teens to work, learn, and grow through remote volunteering, adapted to interning. Hopefully, this information will help you consider including plans for these kinds of experiences when you design and conduct teen library internships, now or in years to come.

Andrew Crain from the University of Georgia said at the time of COVID-19, but it could be applied to any exceptional circumstances:

> All in all, a great deal of the typical internship experience can be adapted to virtual settings with a little ingenuity and pre-planning. While some aspects of the internship experience will inevitably be lost in a virtual setting, it is possible that many students may actually thrive in a remote work environment. When in doubt, just remember—we are in the midst of a pandemic and facing unprecedented challenges to our work and our lives. Be gracious, be flexible, and be creative. Students are certainly appreciative of organizations that are committed to providing them with an experi-

ential learning opportunity during this chaotic time, and we all may learn some interesting lessons along the way.[24]

When you adapt to virtual experiences and offer them for teen interns, whether due to an emergency or simply to provide an alternative to more traditional, in-person internships, remember that with useful insights, careful planning, and thoughtful follow-up, the experiences can still be significant learning ones on many levels for the participating teens.

With that thought in mind, it brings us to a fitting conclusion to this book. Whether you offer teen library internships, internship-like experiences, in-person or virtual, in the library or working behind the scenes, or doing outreach or collaborating with a partner organization, I think you will discover that it will be extremely rewarding for your library and the teens.

As a final point to sum up the myriad of information I have offered you throughout this book, please enjoy the inspiring words of one of the many teen interns who shared their perspectives with me for a culminating Teen Vantage Point.

TEXTBOX 7.2 TEEN VANTAGE POINT

I am so honored to have been able to complete Lindsey's internship and be the only intern so far to do it as a year-long course and not just ten weeks. I am amazed at the work Lindsey [Tomsu] did. When I first called the library and spoke to someone, they were not responsive toward the idea of a high schooler doing an internship, but then my teacher, Mrs. Fisher, called and spoke directly to Lindsey.

After that, I Googled her and was amazed at the fact of all she accomplished and that she wanted to spend part of her day with me for a whole year doing something that technically wasn't a requirement of her job. I was so excited to work with her—it's like she's a librarian celebrity. She mentored me, then she helped me get hired by the library, and I am happy to call her a friend now.

I hope more teens take advantage of her internship program in the future. It's hard work, but it was never boring. It was exciting and gave me an even greater appreciation for librarians and what they do. If anything, Lindsey needs to be a library science professor because she was one of the best teachers I ever had, and I'd gladly do it all over again![1]

Maddy Lakeman
Algonquin Area Public Library, Illinois

Note

1. Lakeman, Maddy. September 18, 2020. Email message to author from Lindsey Tomsu.

Notes

1. Pittman, Karen. May 29, 2020. "Summer. Learning. Loss. Leadership." Forum for Youth Investment, https://forumfyi.org/blog/summer-learning-loss-leadership/.

2. Farmbry, Deidre, et al. August 7, 2020. "Brainstorm: How We Can Best Support the Power and the Purpose of the Teenage Brain." Webinar. Collaborative for Academic, Social, and Emotional Learning, https://casel.org/wp-content/uploads/2020/08/CASEL-CARES-Aug-7-Teenage-Brain.pdf.

3. Miller, Caroline. 2020. "Supporting Teenagers and Young Adults during the Coronavirus Crisis." Child Mind Institute, https://childmind.org/article/supporting-teenagers-and-young-adults-during-the-coronavirus-crisis/.

4. American Academy of Pediatrics. June 5, 2020. "Teens & COVID-19: Challenges and Opportunities during the Outbreak." HealthyChildren.org, https://www.healthychildren.org/English/health-issues/conditions/COVID-19/Pages/Teens-and-COVID-19.aspx.

5. Niemi, Karen. 2020. "CASEL Cares Initiative: Connecting the SEL Community." Collaborative for Academic, Social, and Emotional Learning, https://casel.org/covid-resources/.

6. Austrew, Ashley. June 5, 2019. "How to Prevent Your Kids from Losing What They Learned in School during Summer Vacation." Scholastic Parents Blog, https://www.scholastic.com/parents/books-and-reading/raise-a-reader-blog/summer-slide.html.

7. Cornell University, Bronfenbrenner Center for Translational Research. July 6, 2020. "What We Know about Summer Learning Loss: An Update." *Psychology Today*, https://www.psychologytoday.com/us/blog/evidence-based-living/202007/what-we-know-about-summer-learning-loss-update.

8. Pittman, "Summer. Learning. Loss. Leadership."

9. TIPS Board of Directors. April 15, 2020. "Covid-19 Update: A Message from TIPS Board of Directors." Teens in Public Service, https://teensinpublicservice.org/tips-blog/2020/tips-covid19-response.

10. TIPS Board of Directors, "Covid-19 Update."

11. NACE Staff. May 1, 2020. "Best Practices for Virtual Internships." National Association of Colleges and Employers, https://www.naceweb.org/talent-acquisition/internships/best-practices-for-virtual-internships/.

12. Burchfield, Nicole. January 31, 2021. Email message to author.

13. "Virtual VolunTeens @ GPL." 2020. Greenburgh Public Library, https://greenburghlibrary.org/Teen/volunteen.

14. Cruz, Veronica M. September 18, 2020. "Pima County Library's New Virtual Program Filling Pandemic Volunteer Void for Teens." This Is Tucson, https://thisistucson.com/tucsonlife/pima-county-librarys-new-virtual-program-filling-pandemic-volunteer-void-for-teens/article_a7ca6102-e710-11ea-b321-679d9ad63ae0.html.

15. "High School Volunteer Program." 2020. Berwyn Public Library, https://berwynlibrary.org/high-school-volunteer-program/.

16. "For Teens." 2020. New Providence Memorial Library, https://www.newprovidencelibrary.org/services/teen-services?view=article&id=209:teen-volunteers&catid=2:uncategorised.

17. "Teen Programs." 2020. Charlotte-Mecklenburg Library Digital Branch, https://digitalbranch.cmlibrary.org/online-programming/teen-programs/.

18. MacLaury, Kerri. January 8, 2021. "Virtual Internships: Fun, Valuable, and Worth Going For!" Simmons University Student Snippets, https://slis-students.simmons.edu/2021/01/08/virtual-internships-fun-valuable-and-worth-going-for.

19. "Teen Volunteer Program." 2020. Boston Public Library, https://bpl.bibliocommons.com/events/5eb568b697bfe62f00074765.

20. Kirkland, Luke. February 2, 2021. Email message to author.

21. "Online Jobs for Teenagers." 2020. Hire Teen, https://www.hireteen.com/online-jobs/.

22. Burchfield, email message.

23. Ward, Matthew. December 9, 2020. "How I Helped My High School Service Club Find a Way to Keep Helping." Youth Today, https://youthtoday.org/2020/12/how-i-helped-my-high-school-service-club-find-a-way-to-keep-helping/.

24. Crain, Andrew. June 15, 2020. "Hosting Virtual Interns: A Primer for the Summer of COVID-19." National Association of Colleges and Employers, https://www.naceweb.org/talent-acquisition/internships/hosting-virtual-interns-a-primer-for-the-summer-of-covid-19/.

Appendix A

Rancho Cucamonga Public Library—Summer Teen Volunteer Internship Information and Application Form

Appendix A

RANCHO CUCAMONGA PUBLIC LIBRARY

SUMMER TEEN VOLUNTEER INTERNSHIP 2019

Applications open: April 15 - May 1
Interviews: Early May
10 week internship; May 20 - August 3
Internship at both locations: Archibald and Paul A. Biane Library
$450 stipend upon successful completion of internship

INTERNS DUTIES:
- Shelve and maintain neatness of the collections
- Assist with the Summer Reading Program registrations, check ins, and programs
- Learn the basics of each Library Division through mentoring and training
- Collaborate with staff on program planning and provide program assistance
- Work with Teen Services staff on grant-funded programs

REQUIREMENTS OF THE POSITION:
- Must be available to intern weekly shifts between May 20 - August 3
- Must be available to intern at the Archibald and Paul A. Biane Library
- Must be available to intern the following dates: May 25, July 19, and July 27
- Must be available for interviews

Rancho Cucamonga Public Library does not and shall not discriminate on the basis of race, color, religion (creed), gender, gender expression, age, national origin (ancestry), disability, marital status, sexual orientation, or military status, in any of its activities or operations.

Summer Teen Volunteer Intern Application 2019

This application is how we decide who to interview, so tell us how awesome you are! Please fill out completely. You may attach additional information...or anything else to show us why you're the best candidate!

Name:	Age:	Date of Birth:	Phone #:
Mailing Address:		Email:	
School & Grade:		Do you need community service hours?	

How do you currently use the library? Have you ever attended a teen program?

What are your hobbies and interests? What are you passionate about?

Describe yourself using only 5 words.

Why are you interested in this internship? What do you hope to gain from it?

Have you had a job or volunteer anywhere before? If so, briefly explain your responsibilities?

	Monday	Tuesday	Wednesday	Thursday	Friday	Saturday	Sunday
Times you are available during the summer?							

List any specific availability details. (Including day/times you can never intern, vacation, etc.)

Signature	Date:

Parent/Guardian Information

Name:	Relationship to Teen:
Mailing Address:	Phone #:
Signature	Date:

Summer Teen Volunteer Intern Application 2019

Please fill out the information for your personal or professional reference for this position. Your reference should be an adult who knows you and is willing to be contacted by the Library to discuss your character and recommend you for this possition.

Reference's Full Name:

Position:

Email:

Phone Number:

How do you know this reference? How long? From where?

Are you still in contact with this reference? If so, when was the last time you spoke to them?

Summer Teen Volunteer Intern Application 2019

For this portion of the application, please include any information you believe is relevant for this position or that you would like the Library to know about in the space below or on the back.

For questions about this application, please contact 909-774-3965 or 909-774-3932

Please return this internship application to the Library's Information Desk when completed.

Rancho Cucamonga Public Library does not and shall not discriminate on the basis of race, color, religion (creed), gender, gender expression, age, national origin (ancestry), disability, marital status, sexual orientation, or military status, in any of its activities or operations.

This is not an offer of employment.

Appendix B

Sonoma County Library
PLA Inclusive Internship Initiative Application

Application: PLA Inclusive Internship Initiative Program

Complete and submit the following information to apply for the 2019 Inclusive Internship Initiative at Sonoma County Library. Submit the completed form via email to Kathy Deweese, kdeweese@sonomalibrary.org.

Deadline to submit application materials **is Tuesday, May 7, 2019.**

For more information about the Inclusive Internship Initiative, go to: https://sonomalibrary.org/iii.

Name: _____ Date: _____

Email: _____ Phone Number: _____

Age: _____ School Name: _____

Most recently completed grade: _____

Desired start date: _____ Desired end date: _____

Internship availability (times/days of week):
_____

Have you worked in the library previously? If yes, please describe.

Describe a time when you overcame a barrier to be included:

Short Essay:

Please tell us about your skills and interests. How will working in the library build your skills and interests? What area(s) of the library are you most interested in working with and why?
(Attach a separate sheet if necessary)

Appendix C
Template—Teen Library Intern Feedback Form

Teen Library Intern Feedback Form

Name_____

Supervisor/Mentor(s)_____

Library Branch Location_____

Put a check mark in the appropriate box that reflects your opinion:

#	Evaluation topic	Excellent	Very good	Good	Just okay	Not okay
1	I received helpful training and instruction.					
2	I learned a lot about libraries.					
3	I learned valuable work and personal skills.					
4	My ideas were appreciated and used.					
5	I got to work as a team member.					
6	I had chances to work independently.					
7	I had helpful feedback and advice from my mentor.					
8	I would recommend this internship to other teens.					

Please answer the following questions:

1. What did you like best about your internship experience? Describe.

2. Was there anything you did not like and which you think could be improved? Describe.

3. Are you more interested or less interested in a future job or career in a library since completing your internship? Why?

4. On a scale of 1-10, with 10 being the highest and 1 the lowest, what rating would you give your internship overall? _____

Please sign this form after you have had a chance to discuss it with your supervisor/mentor.

Signature of teen intern _____

Date _____

Signature of supervisor/mentor _____

Date _____

Appendix D

Template—Teen Library Intern Time Sheet and Task Record

Teen Library Intern Timesheet and Task Record

Intern Name _____

Mentor/Supervisor_____

Intern: Fill out your hours each day. Record what work you did and what you learned.

Date	Start	End	Total	What I did and what I learned

Appendix E

West Custer County Library
Teen Summer Internship Job Description

Teen Summer Internship Job Description

The West Custer County Teen Summer Internship is an opportunity to receive marketable job skills (you can tell employers about all the stuff you did and experience you gained while being intern when you apply and interview for other paying jobs). The following is a description of what you will be doing as a library intern. In exchange for doing your best work, the library will provide you with a letter of recommendation and a statement of how many volunteer hours you served.

The Teen Summer Internship is an unpaid, temporary position. The internship constitutes a commitment of approximately **25 hours** during the library's Summer Reading Program from **May 30 - June 29**, which includes helping with **weekly event set up, execution and clean up**. You will work under the supervision of the Youth Services Librarian, Jessica Carter.

One part of this internship will involve assisting with Summer Reading events. This will require working with children of all ages. Good judgement, listening skills and problem solving skills are imperative.

You may be required to help or supervise other volunteers both teen and adult. You will need to use good communication, appropriate humor and cooperation in dealing with team work assignments and with overseeing volunteers.

As a member of the library team, you will be representing the library to the community. The position requires the ability to understand and follow moderately complex directions. Interns are expected to be able to work independently and give attention to detail. You must be courteous and cooperative with your supervisor, other volunteers, children and parents. Interns are expected to show up at the right time, in the right place, with the right attitude and work their full shift, which will vary in start and end times.

Please consider carefully whether this opportunity is the right one for you.

Thank you for your interest!

Selected Bibliography and Webliography

Bibliography

Boland, Becca. 2020. *Making the Most of Teen Library Volunteers: Energizing and Engaging Community*. Santa Barbara, CA: Libraries Unlimited.

Braun, Linda W., and Shannon Peterson (Eds.). 2017. *Putting Teens First in Library Services: A Road Map*. Chicago: Young Adult Library Services Association.

Natterson-Horowitz, Barbara, and Kathryn Bowers. 2019. *Wildhood: The Astounding Connections between Human and Animal Adolescents*. New York: Scribner.

Philibert, Carla Tantillo. 2017. *Everyday SEL in High School*. Milton Park, Abingdon, UK: Routledge.

Smallwood, Carol, and Lura Sanborn (Eds.). 2016. *Library Volunteers Welcome!: Strategies for Attracting, Retaining and Making the Most of Willing Helpers*. Jefferson, NC: McFarland.

Stegel, Daniel J. 2014. *Brainstorm: The Power and the Purpose of the Teenage Brain*. New York: TarcherPerigee.

Steinberg, Laurence. 2015. *Age of Opportunity: Lessons from the New Science of Adolescence*. New York: Eamon Dolan/Mariner Books.

Tuccillo, Diane P. 2020. *Totally Tweens & Teens: Youth-Created and Youth-Led Library Programs*. Lanham, MD: Rowman & Littlefield.

Wycoff, Amy, and Marie Harris. 2019. *Career Programming for Today's Teens*. Chicago: ALA Editions.

Webliography

"The After-School Apprenticeship Program Toolkit." 2010. Collaborative for Building After-School Systems, https://education.ohio.gov/getattachment/Topics/Career-Tech/Apprenticeships-and-Internships/Apprenticeship-After-School-Toolkit-cbass_asap_toolkit.pdf.aspx.

"CASEL." 2020. Collaborative for Academic, Social, and Emotional Learning, https://casel.org/.

"Connected Learning in Libraries." [n.d.]. Connected Learning Alliance, https://clalliance.org/connected-learning-libraries/.

Connecting Youth & Business: A Toolkit for Employers. 2014. Opportunity Nation, https://opportunitynation.org/wp-content/uploads/2014/06/ON_Youth_Business_Toolkit.pdf.

"Employer Guide to Structuring a Successful Internship Program." [n.d.]. Bridge—Connecting Academia, Business, and Community, https://career.bryant.edu/resources/files/RI%20Employer%20Guide%20Good%20Internships%20are%20Good%20Business2%20(3).pdf.

Exploring US Department of Education Career Clusters Archive. 2019. Learning for Life Corporation, https://www.exploring.org/activity-library-category/us-department-of-education-career-clusters/#.

Funders' Guide to Quality Out-of-School Time. 2016. Grantmakers for Education, https://edfunders.org/sites/default/files/OST_Funders_Guide_2016_final.pdf.

Klein, Rachel. 2018. *Job Readiness Skills for Youth: A Clear and Actionable Definition*. City of Seattle, Washington State's King County, and the Seattle Regional Partnership, bit.ly/job_career_report.

Office of Youth Programs. 2020. *Mayor Marion S. Barry's Summer Youth Employment Program 2020 Supervisor Handbook*. District of Columbia Department of Employment Services, https://does.dc.gov/sites/default/files/dc/sites/does/page_content/attachments/2020_MBSYEP_Supervisor_handbook.pdf.

Real Talk Handbook. 2019. Waltham Public Library Teen Room, https://sites.google.com/minlib.net/real-talk-teens/home.

Search Institute. 2020. *The Intersection of Developmental Relationships, Equitable Environments, and SEL*, https://www.search-institute.org/wp-content/uploads/2020/10/Insights-Evidence-DRs-DEI.SEL-FINAL.pdf.

South Dakota Department of Education. [n.d.]. *Youth Internship Program Framework*. Pierre: SD Office of Career and Technical Education, https://doe.sd.gov/cte/documents/YI_Manual.pdf.

Summer Reading Teen Intern Toolkit. [n.d.]. Young Adult Library Services Association, http://www.ala.org/yalsa/sites/ala.org.yalsa/files/content/Intern%20Toolkit_Final_0.pdf.

Teen Intern Toolkit. 2020. Young Adult Library Services Association, http://www.ala.org/yalsa/sites/ala.org.yalsa/files/content/YALSA-Teen-Intern-Toolkit_FINAL.pdf.

United States Equal Employment Opportunity Commission. 2020. *Youth at Work*, https://www.eeoc.gov/youth//.

Young Adult Library Services Association. Spring 2020. "Teen-Driven Services" issue. Young Adult Library Services, http://yalsjournal.ala.org/publication/?m=53337&i=671334&p=0.

Index

Photographs are indicated by page numbers in *italics*.

Adler Planetarium, Chicago, 40
Adult 101 Life Skills for Teens Mental Health program, *46*
Adult 101 Life Skills for Teens Time and Stress Management program, *12*
advisor and mentor evaluations, 143–45
After School Matters (ASM), 40, 118
Alameda County Library, California, 32, 34, *45*, 83–85
Algonquin Area Public Library District, Illinois, 115–16, 119
Allen, Ty, 99
Alvarenga, Iris, 131–32
American Library Association (ALA). *See* Young Adult Library Services Association (YALSA) grants
Anne M. Jeans Elementary School, Willowbrook Corner, Illinois, 100–101
Anne Springs Close Gateway, 163
Appelget, Kristin, 122
applications, 55–59. *See also* application procedures for specific libraries
Applications and Research Laboratory, Ellicott City, Maryland, 119
apprenticeships, 17–18, 38
Archibald Library, Rancho Cucamonga, California, 106
Armstrong, Thomas, 7
Assurances and Certifications, 42
at-risk behaviors, 9–10

attendance and performance requirements, 149–52
Auburn Public Library, Georgia, *24*, 31, 85–89, 145
Austin Public Library, Texas, 39

Bahlmann, Scott, 55
Bailey, Raishara, 33
Baltimore County Public Library, *13*, 31–32, 36, 89–92
Baltimore County Schools, 36
Baright Public Library, Ralston, Nebraska, 80
Batts, Quanetta, 120
Beharry, Sean, 111
Bellevue Public Library, Nebraska, 80–81
Bennett, Marcus, *73*
Berwyn Public Library, Illinois, 162
Billy Ireland Cartoon Library & Museum, 120
BLDG 61, Boulder Public Library, Colorado, 39, 117
blogging and responding to prompts, 141
Boston Public Library, Massachusetts, 163
Boulder Public Library, Colorado, 39, 117–18
Bowen, Breana, 93
Brannen, Betsey, 65–66
Braun, Linda W., 35
Brooklyn Public Library, New York, 92–93
Brooks, Emily (Friel), 85–86, *86*, 145
Brownson-Katz, Cody, *13*, 89
"Build a Better Book" project, 117

Burchfield, Nicole, 161
Burrell, Holly, 88, *144*
Burson, Hayley, 94

Cabell County Public Library, Huntington, West Virginia, 93
capstone/project-based learning, 24
Career Academies, 119
career clusters, 16–17, 37
career planning workshops, 36–38
Carnegie, Maggie, 92
Carrillo, Ricardo, 101
Carter, Jessica, 111
CASEL (Collaborative for Academic, Social, and Emotional Learning), 155
"catch and hold" process, 16
C. Blythe Andrews, Jr. Public Library, Tampa, Florida, 32
Charlotte Mecklenburg Library System, Charlotte Mecklenburg Counties, North Carolina, 93–94, 162–63
Chavez, Yasmeen, *34, 45*, 83–85
Chicago Public Library, Illinois, 40, 118–19
child labor laws, 23
civic engagement, 24
CL (connected learning), 9, 11
Clawson, Nicole, 110
Coaching Team, UW, 127
Collaborative for Academic, Social, and Emotional Learning (CASEL), 155
Community Catalyst Initiative (IMLS), 43
compensation for internships: Auburn Public Library, Georgia, 87–88; Chicago Public Library, Illinois, 118; laws and regulations concerning, 23; options and considerations, 38–40; Rancho Cucamonga Public Library, California, 108; Redefining Internships for Student Empowerment (RISE), 32; Waltham Public Library, Massachusetts, 128–29. *See also* funding
competencies from internships, 30
conclusion process. *See* evaluations and feedback
connected learning (CL), 9, 11
Connected Learning Lab, 140
Connected Learning Research Network, 11
connections, building, 15
contact information, 76–77
cooperative education, 17–18
coronavirus. *See* pandemic effects
Cosgrove, Rachel, 133, *134, 148*
Couch, Nena, 120

COVID-19. *See* pandemic effects
COVID slide. *See* learning slide/summer slide
Crain, Andrew, 164–65
Culbertson, Alaina, 110
culminating presentations and showcases, 147–48
curiosity engagement, 16
CyberTeen interns, Chicago, 118

de Leon, Jennifer, *134*
Delgado, Zayda, 122–23
developing internships, 53–82; applications, 55–59; contact information, 76–77; evaluations and feedback, 74–75; general information and FAQs, 75; history and mission statement of library, 69; interviews, 63–66; job descriptions, 53–55, 71–72; library policies and procedures, 72–73; library term glossary, 75–76; library tools and equipment, 73–74; orientation, 69–71; permission forms, 67–68; publicity for internships, 59–63; timeline overview, 78–81; unhired candidates, 66–67. *See also* Internship Plan Handbook
DeWeese, Kathy, 122
dismissal or resignation of interns, 152–54
District of Columbia (D.C.) Library website, 36
diversified education, 17–18
diversity in intern participation, 42–43
documenting and honoring interns, 146–47
Dollar General Literacy Foundation, 44
Dollar General Teen Library Internship Grants: Auburn Public Library, Georgia, 85; Charlotte Mecklenburg Library System, Charlotte Mecklenburg Counties, North Carolina, 93; Gadsden Public Library, Alabama, 94; Hussey-Mayfield Memorial Public Library, Zionsville, Indiana, 96; Indian Prairie Public Library, Darien, Illinois, 100; North Shelby Library, Birmingham, Alabama, 103, 105; overview, 44–46

ESRI StoryMaps, 127
evaluations and feedback, 139–54; attendance and performance requirements, 149–52; blogging and responding to prompts, 108, 141; culminating presentations and showcases, 147–48; dismissal or resignation of interns, 152–54; documenting and honoring interns, 146–47; exit interviews, 145–46; final performance reviews, 142–43; intern feedback form, 173–75; in Internship Plan Handbook, 74–75; midpoint evaluations, 140–42; North

Shelby Library, Birmingham, Alabama, 104; outcome considerations, 139–40; PLA survey responses, 86, 88; problems during internships, 148–49; reasons for, 140–41; self-evaluations, 143; Sonoma County Library, Santa Rosa, California, 123–24; supervisor, advisor, and mentor evaluations, 143–45
EVF Career Institute, Columbus, Ohio, 120
exit interviews, 145–46
Expanding Vision Foundation (EVF), Columbus, Ohio, 120–21
experiential learning, 5–8, 23–26, *24*
externships. *See* job shadowing
Ezra Jack Keats Foundation Mini-Grants, 47

Fair Labor Standards Act (FLSA), 23
final performance reviews, 142–43
Fisher, Joy, 115
flexible sponsorship, 14
Flynn, Kian, 126–28
FOL (Friends of the Library) groups, 40, 103
For Freedoms Fifty State Initiative, 130, 163
The Forum for Youth Investment, 157–58
Freire, Paulo, 127
Friends of the Library (FOL) groups, 40, 103
Friends of the San Francisco Public Library, 39
funding, 2, 9, 39–40, 46–48, 117. *See also* compensation for internships. *See also* Dollar General Teen Library Internship Grants. *See also* Young Adult Library Services Association (YALSA) grants
Future Ready Schools, 22

Gadsden Public Library, Alabama, 94–95, 149
Gala Philanthropic Auction, 92
Garcia, Brittany, 105–6, *105*
Garrett, Nancy, 127
general information and FAQs, 75
Graphic Design program (Career Academies), 119
Gray Foundation, 9
Greenburgh Public Library, Elmsford, New York, 161–62
Guilty Pleasures Night, 80
Gwinnett County Bicentennial Torch, 85

Hamm, Sereena, 134–36
handbooks. *See* Internship Plan Handbook; Real Talk Handbook
Harry S. Truman Library and Museum, Independence, Missouri, 124

Health, Matthew, 98
Helping Hawks and Reading Hawks, 164
Herring, Deidra, 120
high schools and internships, 21–22
Hillsborough County Schools, Florida, 32
hiring tips, 65–66
Hirsh, Mary, 43, *45*
history and mission statement of library, 69
Hussey-Mayfield Memorial Public Library, Zionsville, Indiana: intern duties, 10; intern report, 71; interns, *73*; internship program overview, 95–100; librarian support for interns, 25–26; midpoint evaluations, 142; self-evaluations, 143; Teen Volunteer Corps, 66; topics addressed in handbook, 75

Inclusive Internship Initiatives (III; PLA):
III meetings, *33*, *34*, *41*, *45*, 85, 88, 102, *144*, *147*, 148; Alameda County Library, Newark Branch, California, *34*, *45*, 83; Auburn Public Library, Georgia, 85; Baltimore County Public Library, *33*, 89, 90; Cabell County Public Library, Huntington, West Virginia, 93; Laredo Public Libraries, Laredo, Texas, 101; policies, 42–44, 86; purpose, 41–44; Sonoma County Library, Santa Rosa, California, 61–63, 123
Indian Prairie Public Library, Darien, Illinois, 100–101
individual development plans (IDPs), 140
Inspire Career Fair (Junior Achievement), 36
Institute of Museum and Library Services, 39, 41, 42, 47, 92
interest, defined, 15–16
intern advisory groups, 49–50
intern feedback form, 173–75
internship experiences, unique. *See* unique experiences
internship management during closures, 158–59
Internship Plan Handbook, 68–77; contact information, 76–77; evaluations and feedback, 74–75; general information and FAQs, 75; history and mission statement of library, 69; job descriptions, 71–72; library policies and procedures, 72–73; library term glossary, 75–76; library tools and equipment, 73–74; orientation, 69–71
internships: benefits, 6–7, 104; data on teen internships, 6; defined and described, 5–6, 25; resources, 7–8; scope and purpose, 16. *See also* compensation for internships

internships, developing. *See* developing internships
internships, reasons for, 29–51; career planning workshops, 36–38; Dollar General Teen Library Internship Grants, 44–46; funding for, 40, 46–48; Inclusive Internship Initiatives (PLA), 41–44; intern advisory groups, 49–50; job fairs, 36–38; library approval, obtaining, 48–49; library careers, promoting, 31–35; partnership cultivation, 31; positive youth development, settings for, 29–30; soft skills development, 35–36; website links, 36–38; YALSA grants, 44–46
Internships.com, 6
internship types, 53
intern timesheet and task record, 177–78
interviews, 63–66

Jacobs High School, Algonquin, Indiana, 115
Jean-Baptiste, Annie, *129*
Jefferson County Library, Port Hadlock, Washington, 54–55
job descriptions, 53–55, 71–72
job fairs, 36–38
job-readiness, 35
job shadowing, 18–21, 24
job skills, 5–28; application advice, 58–59; apprenticeships, 17–18; career clusters, 16–17; connected learning, 9, 11; cooperative education, 17–18; diversified education, 17–18; experiential learning, 5–8, 23–26, *24*; Future Ready Schools, 22; high schools and internships, 21–22; job shadowing, 18–21; legal considerations, 22–23; mentors/mentorships, 13–14, *13*; opportunities, 14–15; social-emotional learning, 9–11; supportive relationships, 11–12, *12*; teen brain, hardwiring, 8–10; teen interest, 15–16
Jones, Cheyenne, *24*, *87*, 88, *144*
Junior Achievement, 36
Junior CyberNavigators, 118–19

Kenneth S. and Faye G. Allen Library Endowment, 126
King County, Washington State, 39
Kirkland, Luke, 129–30, 133
Kolosov, Joanna, 122–23

Lakeman, Maddy, 115–16, 165
Laredo Public Libraries, Texas, *41*, 101–3
Laura Bush Twenty-First-Century Library Program Grants, 41, 42
La Vista Public Library, Nebraska, 78–81, 115
learning slide/summer slide, 44, 156–58
Lee, Morea, *12*, *46*, 107
legal considerations, 22–23
Librarians for Tomorrow Teen Internship Program, 92–93
librarian vantage point: Anna White, 90; Bel Outwater, 88–89, 145; Elliott Stevens, 126–27; Kian Flynn, 126–27; Lindsey Tomsu, 116; Luke Kirkland, 133; Patricia VanArsdale, 25–26
libraries' role combatting summer slide, 157
library approval, obtaining, 48–49
library careers, promoting, 31–35
library closures and interns, 155–66; internship management during closures, 158–59; learning slide/summer slide, 156–58; social-emotional development in teens, 155–56; successful ideas, 161–65; teen engagement in tough times, 159; virtual/remote internships, 159–61
Library Initiative for Teens and Tweens, 129
library policies and procedures, 72–73
Library Services and Technology Act, 47
library term glossary, 75–76
library tools and equipment, 73–74
Library Virtual Volunteer Program, 162

MacArthur Foundation, 39
MacLaury, Kerri, 163
makerspaces, 39, 100, 117
Marquand Library of Art and Archeology, 121
master class presentations (III), 43
Mayor Marion S. Barry's Summer Youth Employment Program, 36
McCaffrey, Angela, 111
mentors/mentorships: awareness of mentee needs, 16; Boulder Public Library, Colorado, 117; evaluations and feedback, 143–45; high schools and internships, 21–22; positives from, 11–12; qualities of, 13–14, *13*; responsibilities, 88; scheduling, 7; skills, 14; time and leadership expectations, 84
Metro Community College, La Vista, Nebraska, 80
The Metropolitan Museum of Art, 9
Michael Gendreau Community Services Scholarship, 83
micro-internships, 53

midpoint evaluations, 140–42
Millennial Branding, 6
Miller, Christina, *87*, 88–89
Millhill Child and Family Development Center, 121
mini internships. *See* job shadowing
Minor, Cortunay, 123
The Mix, 36, 39
Monterrosa, Janet, 105–6, *105*
Moulton, Amy, 111
Multicultural Mondays program, 93
My City, My Place internship, 35–36

National Parks and Recreation Association, 9
National Science Foundation, 117
Nebraska Library Commission, 47–48
new librarian vantage point, 20–21
New Orleans Public Library, Louisiana, 37
New Providence Memorial Library, New Jersey, 162
North Shelby Library, Birmingham, Alabama, 103–4

Oakland Has Jobs Instagram page, 37
Oakland Public Library, California, 37
Office of Community and Regional Affairs, Princeton, New Jersey, 121–22
Ohio Stadium, 120
Ohio State University Libraries, Columbus, Ohio, 120–21
Ohio State University Planetarium, 120
One Summer Chicago (OSC) initiative partnership, 118–19
opportunities for internships, 14–15
Opportunities for Teens page, 36
orientation, 69–71
outcome considerations, 139–40
Outwater, Bel, 85, 88–89, 145
Owings Mills Branch, Baltimore County Library, 32

pandemic effects: on internships, 3–4, 7, 83, 96, 122, 124–25; on job fairs, 37; learning slide/summer slide, 156–57; mask-making project, 117; online reading, 164; options, 162–63; PLA webinar, 42; supporting teens, 156; teen social-emotional development during, 155–56; TIPS adaptations, 50, 158–59; virtual internships, 53, 119, 130, 133–34, 159, 161, 162. *See also* library closures and interns

Pandy, Sierra, 21
Partner4Work, 7–8
partnership cultivation, 31
Paul A Biane Library, Rancho Cucamonga, California, 106
Pearson, Glenda, 126
peer teamwork, 11–12
Perez-Gomez, Analiza, 101, *102*
Period Action Drive (III), 43
period poverty, 91–92, *91*
permission forms, 67–68
photography at job fair events, 38
photos/videos for documentation, 140
Pima County Library, Tucson, Arizona, 162
Pima Love Notes Project, 162
PLA. *See* Public Library Association (PLA)
positive youth development, 9, 29–30
Poudre River Public Library District, 161
Princeton Regional Chamber of Commerce, 121
Princeton University Library, Princeton, New Jersey, 121–22
probationary form content, 150–52
problems during internships, 148–49
professional speakers at job fairs, 37–38
project-based/capstone learning, 24
projects and project plans: Algonquin Area Public Library District, Algonquin, Indiana, 115–16; Braille game, 117; "Build a Better Book," 117; "By Our Own Hand," 123; Camp Happiness, 111; children's activities, 100–101; connected learning (CL) projects, 85–86, 90; culminating presentations and showcases, 147–49; ESL activities, 84; Multicultural Mondays program, 93; oral history project, 85; period poverty, *91*; photography work, 99; Princeton University Library, Princeton, New Jersey, 121; proposal considerations, 48–49; Rancho Cucamonga Public Library, California, 107–8; Real Talk Conversation Forum leaders, 128–34; river landscape board game, 117; robotics, 103–4; University Libraries, University of Washington, Seattle, Washington, 127
Prologue, Inc., 92
Providence Public Library, Rhode Island, 35–36
publicity for internships, 59–63
publicity for job fair events, 38
Public Library Association (PLA): closing event, *147*; connected learning (CL) requirement, 11, 90, 101; internship grants, *13*, *24*; surveys, 88;

Vivanco on, 103; webinar during pandemic, 42. *See also* Inclusive Internship Initiatives
public library internships, 83–113; Alameda County Library, Newark Public Library Branch, California, 83–85; Auburn Public Library, Georgia, 85–89; Baltimore County Public Library, Owings Mills Library Branch, Owings Mills, Maryland, 89–92; Brooklyn Public Library, New York, 92–93; Cabell County Public Library, Huntington, West Virginia, 93; Charlotte Mecklenburg Library System, Charlotte Mecklenburg Counties, North Carolina, 93–94; Gadsden Public Library, Alabama, 94–95; Hussey-Mayfield Memorial Public Library, Zionsville, Indiana, 95–100; Indian Prairie Public Library, Darien, Illinois, 100–101; Laredo Public Libraries, Texas, 101–3; North Shelby Library, Birmingham, Alabama, 103–4; Rancho Cucamonga Public Library, California, 104–9; St. Louis County Library, St. Louis, Missouri, 110; West Custer County Library, Westcliffe, Colorado, 110–12

Rancho Cucamonga Public Library, California, 104–9: Adult 101 Life Skills for Teens Time and Stress Management program, *12*; blogging and responding to prompts, 141; exit interviews, 145–46; information and application form, 167–70; internship recruitment flyer, *109*
Reading Hawks and Helping Hawks, 164
Real Talk Conversation Forum leaders, 128–34, *148*, 164
Real Talk Handbook, 130, 132–33
real-world opportunities, 14
Redefining Internships for Student Empowerment (RISE), 32–33
Registered Apprenticeships, 17–18
Reiff, Makynna, 111
rejection letters, 67
remote internships. *See* virtual/remote internships
resignation of interns, 152–54
resources, 7–8
Resume Generator, 58–59
Rhyme and Reason Fund, Boston Foundation, 129
Robert Wood Johnson Foundation, 11
Rude, Zach, *73*

sample curriculum, 78–81
San Francisco Public Library, California, 36, 39
San Francisco YouthWorks, 36
scheduling, 7
School Library Journal sample curriculum, 78–81
schools and school district partnerships, 31
science of teen interest, 15–16
The Search Institute, 10
seasonal internships, 53
Seattle Public Library, Washington, 126–27
SEL (social-emotional learning), 9–11
self-evaluations, 143
Seminole Heights Branch Library, Hillsborough County, Florida, 33
Senior Toast, 128–30
service learning, 24
shared practices and purposes, 14
Shor, Ira, 128
Sidney Johnson Summer Internship, St. Louis County Library, 110
Siegel, Daniel, 155
Simmons University, Boston, Massachusetts, 163
Sivakumar, Jaishna, 142
social-emotional development in teens, pandemic effects on, 155–56
social-emotional learning (SEL), 9–11
soft skills, 10–11, 35–36
soft skills development, internships, reasons for, 35–36
Sonoma County History and Genealogy Library (SCH&G), 123
Sonoma County Library, Santa Rosa, California: III application, 171–72; III at, 59–63; publicity for internships, 61–63, *64*; unique experiences, 122–24
STEAM (science, technology, engineering, arts, and math) programs, 40, 103–4
STEM (science, technology, engineering, and math) programs, 40
Stevens, Elliott, 126–28
St. Louis County Library, St. Louis, Missouri, *64*, 110
St. Louis County Library Foundation, 110
Stucky, Sam, 98
Student Conservation Association, Pittsburgh, 7–8
student employee, defined and described, 25
The Studio Museum in Harlem, 9
successful ideas during closures, 161–65
Sugar Creek Library, 93–94
Summer Internship and Job Fair, 37
Summer Learning Interns, 118
Summer Learning Resource Grants, 44

Summer of Learning, 126
summer slide. *See* learning slide/summer slide
Summer Youth Employment Program, Princeton, New Jersey, 121, 122
Sump Memorial Library, Papillion, Nebraska, 80
supervisor, advisor, and mentor evaluations, 143–45
supporting teens in pandemic, 156
supportive relationships, 11–12, *12*
Suzzallo and Allen Libraries, University of Washington, 125

talkback boards, 140
technology availability, 160
Teen Advisory Board (TAB), 78–81
teen brain, development and hardwiring, 8–10
teen engagement in tough times, 159
teen interest, 15–16
Teen Mentors, 39
Teens in Public Service (TIPS), 39, 49–50, 1 58–59
Teens in Public Service internships, 39
teens of color, 9–10
Teen Squad, 35–36
Teens Take the Met night, 9
Teen Storytime Program, 80
Teen Summer Intern Program Grants, 44
teen vantage point: Aaron Vivanco, 103; Alia Touadjine, 131; Bethany Worrell, 10, 39, 98; Iris Alvarenga, 131–32; Jaishna Sivakumar, 142; Kathleen C., 71; Maddy Lakeman, 165; Makynna Reiff, 112; Morea Lee, 107; Nayana Thompson, 146; Sade Wilkins El, 32, 91–92; Ty Allen, 99; Yasmeen Chavez, 34
Teen Volunteer Corps, 10, 66, 96, *97*
termination notice content, 153
Thompson, Nayana, *12*, *46*, 107, 146
timeline overview, 78–81
Tims, Victoria, 32–33
Tomsu, Lindsey, 78–81, 115–16, 165
Touadjine, Alia, 131, *134*, 148
Truman Library and Museum, 124
Tudor, Nicole, 95

unhired candidates, 66–67
unique experiences, 115–37; Algonquin Area Public Library District, Algonquin, Indiana, 115–16, 119; Boulder Public Library, Colorado, 117–18; Chicago Public Library, Illinois, 118–19; Harry S. Truman Library and Museum, Independence, Missouri, 124; Ohio State University Libraries, Columbus, Ohio, 120–21; Princeton University Library, Princeton, New Jersey, 121–22; Sonoma County Library, Santa Rosa, California, 122–24; University Libraries, University of Washington, Seattle, Washington, 125–28; University of Virginia Library, Charlottesville, Virginia, 125; Waltham Public Library, Waltham, Massachusetts, 128–34; Washington Latin Public Charter School Library, Washington, D.C, 134–36
University Archives, Ohio State University, 120
University Libraries, University of Washington, Seattle, Washington, 50, 125–28, 126
University of Colorado, Boulder, 117
University of Virginia Library, Charlottesville, Virginia, 125, 141
USA Grant Watch, 47
US Department of Education Career Clusters, 7
US Department of Labor, 17, 23, 38
UW Career Center, 126
UW Dream Project, 126

VanArsdale, Patricia: intern experiences, 35; internship program overview, 95–100; intern support, 25–26; Kathleen C. on, 71; midpoint evaluations, 142; rejection letter, 67; welcome letter, 77
Vedantham, Anuradha, 121–22
Victoria Gardens Lifestyle Center, 106
Village of Arlington Heights, Illinois, 37
violence and teens, 9–10
virtual/remote internships, 53, 156, 159–61
Virtual VolunTeens, 161–62
visual impairment projects, 117
Vivanco, Aaron, *41*, 101–2, *102*, 103
volunteers, defined and described, 24

Wage and Hour Division, Dept. of Labor, 38
Wakefield High School, Raleigh, North Carolina, 40
Waltham High School (WHS), Massachusetts, 130
Waltham Public Library, Waltham, Massachusetts: For Freedoms Fifty State Initiative, 130; Kirkland on, 129–30; librarian vantage point, 133; Library Initiative for Teens and Tweens, 129; pandemic challenges, 130, 163–64; Real Talk Conversation Forum, 128–30, *129*, 132–33; Real Talk Handbook, 132–33; Real Talk teen leaders, *134*; Rhyme and Reason

Fund, Boston Foundation, 129; Senior Toast, 129; teen vantage points, 131–32
Ward, Matthew, 164
Washington Latin Public Charter School Library, Washington, D.C, 134–36
Wave Hill Cultural and Garden Center, Riverdale, 9
website links, 36–38
Weisler, Emma, *73*
welcome letter, 77
West Custer County Library, Westcliffe, Colorado, 110–12, 179–80
#WeWereHere Project, 162
White, Anna, 89, 90
Wilkens El, Sade, *13*, 32, *33*, 89–92, *91*
Williams, Natalie, 100
Willowbrook Corner, Illinois, 100
work-based learning, 22
Worrell, Bethany, 10, 39, 98

year-round internships, 53
Young Adult Library Services Association (ALA), 29
Young Adult Library Services Association (YALSA) grants: Auburn Public Library, Georgia, 85–86; Charlotte Mecklenburg Library System, Charlotte Mecklenburg Counties, North Carolina, 93; Gadsden Public Library, Gadsden, Alabama, 94; Hussey-Mayfield Memorial Public Library, Zionsville, Indiana, 96; Indian Prairie Public Library, Darien, Illinois, 100; North Shelby Library, Birmingham, Alabama, 103, 105; overview, 44–46
Youth Advisory Committee, TIPS, 49–50, 158
Youth Job and Paid Internship Fair, 37
"Youth Rules!" (Dept. of Labor), 23
Youth Today (publication), 47
Youyoute, Stevenson, *134*, *148*

About the Author

A former English teacher and high school drama director and coach, **Diane P. Tuccillo** earned her MLS degree from Rutgers University in 1980. After serving as a young adult librarian at the Rutherford (NJ) Public Library and the Reading (MA) Public Library, she became the longtime young adult coordinator at the City of Mesa Library in Arizona, where she led a dynamic, nationally known library teen advisory group for twenty-seven years. From 2007 until 2017, she was a teen services librarian at the Poudre River Public Library District in Fort Collins, Colorado, where she co-led a vibrant Interesting Reader Society teen advisory group.

Tuccillo has been actively involved in and has received awards from several professional organizations, including the Young Adult Library Services Association, the Assembly on Literature for Adolescents of the National Council of Teachers of English, and the Arizona Library Association. She has been a book reviewer and article contributor for professional journals such as *School Library Journal* and *Voice of Youth Advocates (VOYA)* magazine; has contributed to books such as Nilsen and Donelson's classic *Literature for Today's Young Adults*; and has been a regular and an emeritus member of the *VOYA* advisory board. Her second book, *Teen-Centered Library Service: Putting Youth Participation into Practice*, was published in 2010; her third book, the completely revised and updated second edition of *Library Teen Advisory Groups* (the first edition published in 2005), was published by Rowman & Littlefield in 2018; and her fourth book, *Totally Tweens & Teens: Youth-Created and Youth-Led Library Programs*, was published by Rowman & Littlefield in 2020.

Through the years of her professional involvement, Tuccillo has taught in-person and online college and university classes in library science; she has presented at many local, state, and national conferences; and she has offered workshops, programs, and webinars related to teen library participation and YA literature.

Tuccillo lives with her husband, Mick, in Fort Collins, Colorado, where she serves as a library volunteer and on the Board of Directors of the Poudre River Friends of the Library.

www.ingramcontent.com/pod-product-compliance
Lightning Source LLC
Chambersburg PA
CBHW060343010526
44117CB00017B/2952